Frommer's®

FIRST EDITION
WASHINGTON, DC
Free &
dirt cheap

by Tom Price & Susan Crites Price

WILEY
Wiley Publishing, Inc.

Published by:

Wiley Publishing, Inc.
111 River St.
Hoboken, NJ 07030-5774

ISBN: 978-0-470-58253-4 (paper); 978-0-470-87284-0 (ebk)

Editor: Kathleen Warnock
Production Editor: Jonathan Scott
Cartographer: Elizabeth Puhl
Production by Wiley Indianapolis Composition Services
Interior design by Melissa Auciello-Brogan
Photos by Tom Price

For information on our other products and services or to obtain technical
support, please contact our Customer Care Department within the U.S. at
877/762-2974, outside the U.S. at 317/572-3993 or fax 317/572-4002.

Wiley also publishes its books in a variety of electronic formats. Some content that appears in print may not be available in electronic formats.

Manufactured in the United States of America

5   4   3   2   1

CONTENTS

LIST OF MAPS

About the Authors

Tom and **Susan Crites Price** have lived in and written about Washington for more than two decades, Tom focusing on government, politics, business, technology, and education, and Susan on philanthropy and topics of importance to women and families. They coauthored the award-winning *Working Parents Help Book: Practical Advice for Dealing with the Day-to-Day Challenges of Kids and Careers*, which was featured by "Today," "Oprah," and in other broadcast and print media. They coauthored Frommer's *Irreverent Guide to Washington, D.C.*, and Tom wrote *Washington, D.C., For Dummies*. Tom also wrote, with former U.S. House representative and ambassador Tony Hall, *Changing the Face of Hunger: How Liberals, Conservatives, Democrats, Republicans and People of Faith Are Joining Forces to Help the Hungry, the Poor and the Oppressed*. Susan is author of *The Giving Family: Raising Our Children to Help Others*. Before becoming a full-time freelancer, Tom was a correspondent at the Cox Newspapers Washington Bureau. Susan still holds a day job, as vice president of the National Center for Family Philanthropy.

Acknowledgments

Our first thanks always go to Elise Ford, an accomplished travel writer who brought us to Frommer's in the first place, and to Kathleen Warnock, Tom's first editor at Frommer's and, to our great happiness, the editor of this first edition of *Washington, DC Free & Dirt Cheap*. We're also indebted to Henry and Lynne Heilbrunn—friends, neighbors, veteran world travelers, and experts at ferreting out what's free in DC—who shared their hard-earned knowledge with us. Fellow travel writer Kathy McKay provided great shopping tips. Our daughter Julie has contributed immensely to all our Washington guidebooks. From the time she was born, she helped us explore Washington as a family. Now grown and married to the estimable Rick Gruntz, she shares her independent DC discoveries with us as well. Finally, our perpetual tip of the hat to all the chefs, innkeepers, shopkeepers, waiters, bartenders, tour guides, artists, curators, park rangers, security guards, cops, historians, government officials, taxi and bus and Metrorail drivers, and all those other Washingtonians who, through their day-to-day work, make DC such a wonderful place for living and visiting.

—*Tom & Susan Crites Price*

How to Contact Us

In researching this book, we discovered many wonderful places—hotels, restaurants, shops, and more. We're sure you'll find others. Please tell us about them, so we can share the information with your fellow travelers in upcoming editions. If you were disappointed with a recommendation, we'd love to know that, too. Please write to:

Frommer's Washington, DC Free & Dirt Cheap, 1st Edition
Wiley Publishing, Inc. ● 111 River St. ● Hoboken, NJ 07030-5774

An Additional Note

Please be advised that travel information is subject to change at any time—and this is especially true of prices. We therefore suggest that you write or call ahead for confirmation when making your travel plans. The authors, editors, and publisher cannot be held responsible for the experiences of readers while traveling. Your safety is important to us, however, so we encourage you to stay alert and be aware of your surroundings. Keep a close eye on cameras, purses, and wallets, all favorite targets of thieves and pickpockets.

Free & Dirt Cheap Icons & Abbreviations

We also use **three feature icons** that point you to the *really* free stuff, the details that you need to keep in mind for a free or cheap deal, and the stuff that's particularly outstanding. Throughout the book, look for:

FREE Events, attractions, or experiences that cost no more than your time and maybe a trip on public transit.

FINE PRINT The unspoken conditions or necessary preparations to experience certain free and dirt cheap events.

★ The best free and dirt cheap events, dining, shopping, living, and exploring in the city.

Travel Resources at Frommers.com

Frommer's travel resources don't end with this guide. Frommer's website, **www.frommers.com**, has travel information on more than 4,000 destinations. We update features regularly, giving you access to the most current trip-planning information and the best airfare, lodging, and car-rental bargains. You can also listen to podcasts, connect with other Frommers.com members through our active-reader forums, share your travel photos, read blogs from guidebook editors and fellow travelers, and much more.

Welcome to the capital of the free (and dirt cheap) world.

LAND OF THE FREE (AND DIRT CHEAP)

Washington, DC deserves to be called the Capital of the Free World for at least two reasons: It's the capital city of the most powerful democracy on earth. And in no other place in the world will you find more terrific things to see and do for free.

Visit the great museums and historical buildings of many American cities, and you might pay $20 or more for the privilege (unless you go on one of the occasional "free days"). In DC, all but a tiny handful are free, all the time. It doesn't cost anything to tour government buildings or to watch Congress, or the Supreme Court, in session. (If you live in the United States, your taxes already have paid for them!)

Unless you have friends or relatives who can put you up—or have a house or apartment to trade—you won't sleep or eat for free in Washington. But we've worn out a lot of shoe leather, poked around hotel rooms, bed-and-breakfasts, and universities; studied menus and put our taste buds to work to find ways you can eat and sleep on a budget while enjoying free Washington in your waking hours. We eat at the restaurants we recommend, tarry at the bars, and go to the museums, theaters, and parks.

We've been able to do this partly because we've lived here for more than 25 years, raised a child from birth to adulthood, and conducted tours for countless visiting friends and relatives. One of the "us" we'll be referring to, Tom, also spent all that time covering all aspects of the federal government as a journalist. As a result, we really know our way around. So we can give you true insiders' advice on navigating everything from the streets of Adams Morgan to the halls of Congress.

We've also survived most of this time on earnings from newspaper reporting and freelance writing—neither of which will stir envy in the pocketbooks of Wall Street bankers. "Free and dirt cheap" for us is more than a book assignment: It's a way of life. But cheap, to us, doesn't mean dirty, uncomfortable, or unsafe. What you'll find in these pages are great things to do, good places to eat, and clean and comfortable places to stay.

This book is for visitors who don't want to spend much but want to be able to enjoy a trip to the nation's capital; it's for potential residents who wonder if and how they can afford to live here, and for residents—new or longtime—who, like us, are always looking for a bargain and a new way to enjoy Washington without breaking the bank.

DC is definitely a company town, and its business is government. That means there's a steady flow of intelligent, educated, ambitious people coming into the city, not just from all over the country, but all over the world.

They work hard, and party hard, and many of them get by on a student allowance, the lower end of the government pay scale, or an intern's stipend, so they desire, create, and partake in a diverse, lively, and affordable scene in their city. When you swing by, you can dine in eateries with world-spanning menus, enjoy an eclectic performing arts scene, from storefront rep companies and comedy clubs to world-class music, theater, and dance. In the bars and bookstores and lecture halls, you'll find constant social debate left, right, and center. Outdoors, in a climate where spring comes early and (well, until recently) winters are relatively temperate, you can stroll or exercise in beautiful public spaces and parks, and, of course, one of these years, the Nationals will win a pennant. We're just not going to predict when.

We love DC, with all its challenges, surprises, and hidden gems. We're proud to say that we live In the District of Columbia. We look forward to sharing our town with you, no matter how short—or long—your stay.

In DC, admission to most of the monuments, including the one named for the first president, is free.

THE BEST OF FREE & DIRT CHEAP DC

Washington is full of things you can do without spending a penny. With a little research and ingenuity, you can also find ways to hold down your spending on eating and sleeping here. When we're getting ready to play for a weekend, or when we're planning a night out, our biggest challenge is choosing from all our options. Our to-do list is enormous, and it's growing all the time. Here are our favorite things to see and do (and eat!) in Washington—many of them "only-in-DC" experiences.

1 Best Free Only–in–DC Experiences

● **Touring the Capitol.** Washington was created to be the capital of the United States, and the Capitol building housed two of the three branches of government until 1935, when the Supreme Court got its own building. You'll be amazed at the opulent decor within this temple of democracy. You're likely to bump into some members of Congress hurrying from one meeting to the next, but you probably won't recognize them. You can watch them in action in the House or Senate chamber—or inaction, as the case may be. See p. 97.

● **Visiting the Lincoln or Jefferson Memorials after Dark.** Many people—powerful and powerless, famous and obscure—have drawn inspiration from spending some quiet time with these two presidents. It's quiet at night, and the crowds are sparse. The memorials to Lincoln (p. 101) and Jefferson (p. 101) glow. And, from their steps, you can look out at other illuminated landmarks. At such a moment, Washington truly is an alabaster city gleaming.

● **Walking the Mall.** Climb the steps of the Lincoln Memorial and look to the east. The greatest sights of the National Mall stretch before you: the World War II Memorial, the Washington Monument, and the Capitol. Stroll more than 2 miles along what has been called "America's front yard," and you'll also catch glimpses of the White House, the Tidal Basin, and the Smithsonian museums before you arrive at the base of Capitol Hill. While these are sights for the millions of visitors who come to town each year, they're also well-loved parts of the neighborhood for residents.

● **Attending a Marine Corps Parade.** Friday evenings in summer, the Marine Corps Band, Silent Drill Team, and Drum-and-Bugle Corps parade on the grounds of the Marine Barracks on Capitol Hill. Marines conduct ceremonies all over the world. But only this one occurs at the oldest active Marine post in the world, opened in 1801 on the site picked personally by President Thomas Jefferson. See p. 157.

● **Visiting the Declaration of Independence.** The original Declaration, that is, which is displayed on the Mall in the National Archives, along with the Constitution, the Bill of Rights, and other historic documents. The Archives—formally titled the National Archives and Records Administration—is responsible for *billions* of documents. It gave its display areas a major modernization recently, which makes it easier for visitors to understand the historic materials they're looking at. See p. 120.

- **Ascending the Washington Monument.** You take an elevator to the top, rather than climbing all those stairs, which makes the trek to the obelisk's 555-foot peak a bit easier. The view of Washington is spectacular. And inside you get to see commemorative stones that were donated by states, Indian tribes, foreign governments, and private organizations. See p. 113.

- **Attending a Capitol Holiday Concert.** The National Symphony—accompanied by celebrities and guest musicians—celebrate Memorial Day, Independence Day, and Labor Day on the Capitol's West Lawn each year. On July 4, the concert ends as the fireworks begin to launch from near the Washington Monument. Especially on July 4, people arrive hours ahead of time to get a decent place to sit. You've probably seen it on PBS; it's all the more thrilling when you're there in person. It's less crowded at the dress rehearsal the day before. See p. 155.

- **Take Me Out to the Opera (at the Ball Park).** The Washington Nationals baseball team may not be very good, but they've found a way to put their ballpark to good use when they're out of town: Turn it over to the Washington National Opera. Early each autumn, the opera simulcasts a performance on the ballpark's enormous scoreboard video screen. See p. 161.

- **Celebrating Christmas at the Willard.** The historic, luxurious, and expensive Willard Intercontinental Hotel is the place for cheapskates to hang out in December. The Willard decorates its opulent lobby, books a bunch of musicians, and invites the riff-raff in for free holiday concerts almost every night. See p. 162.

2 Best Dirt-Cheap Only-in-DC Experiences

- **Visit Arlington National Cemetery.** Get an idea of the sheer numbers of America's military men and women who have died in their country's service as you contemplate the 300,000 grave markers here. There's no admission charge to the cemetery, but most people take

WASHINGTON, DC AT A GLANCE

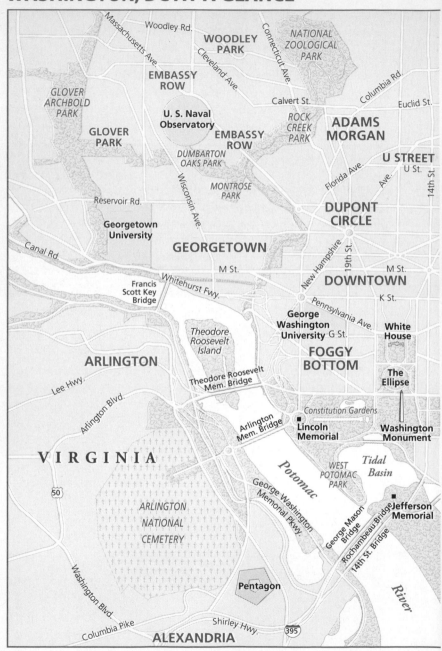

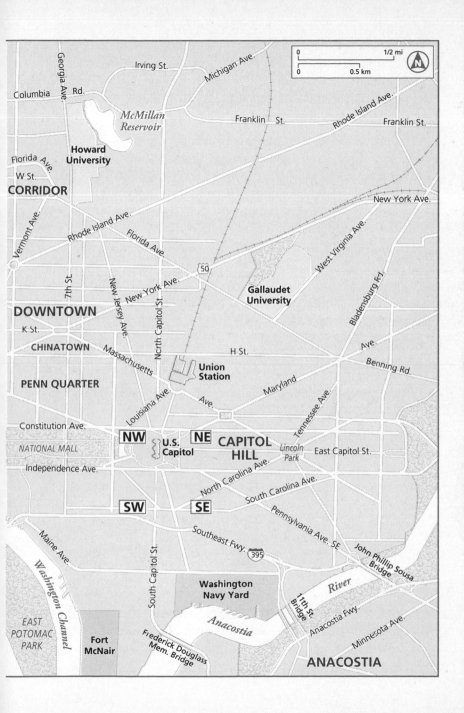

the Tourmobile (which requires a ticket to ride) through the large and hilly cemetery. You also should visit the nearby Marine Corps War Memorial—you'll recognize the famous sculpture of Marines raising the U.S. flag on Iwo Jima during World War II—and the memorial to women in the military. See p. 99.

● **Explore Washington National Cathedral.** There's an enormous amount to see and do in this Episcopal cathedral that often serves as the nation's place of worship. Inaugural prayer services and presidential funerals have been conducted here. The stained glass windows include a Space Window with a moon rock. Darth Vader is one of the gargoyles. Its towers are the tallest points in Washington and offer great views of the city and land beyond. (While there's no official charge to enter the cathedral, you're asked to make a donation when you visit). See p. 126.

● **Have Lunch at the White House . . .** Well, not exactly *at* the White House. Grab a sandwich and a beverage at a nearby food spot, then park yourself on a bench in Lafayette Square. Washingtonians who work in the neighborhood do this all the time. The White House stands across Pennsylvania Avenue. Historic 18th-century homes line the west side of the square. And there's almost always a collection of demonstrators waving their signs at the president's front door. See p. 129.

● **Dine with the Denizens of Capitol Hill.** You can buy cheap eats for breakfast, lunch, or dinner at the **Union Station Food Court** (p. 67) or at other eateries scattered around the station's main floor. Or grab a couple of tacos at **Taqueria Nacional** (p. 65). Then carry your goodies to one of the benches scattered about under the trees in the parkland between Union Station and the Capitol. Watch for senators grabbing some fresh air between smoke-filled-room meetings. (Well, they're not so smoke filled anymore.) Check out Senate staffers grabbing the same cheap, quick meal you are.

3 Best Low-Cost Lodging in DC

● **Best Location: The Inn at Dupont Circle South** (p. 44) is just where it says it is: in the heart of the Dupont Circle action and a block south of the Dupont Circle Metrorail station, which is your gateway to everyplace else in Washington.

- **Best Deal for Families or Groups:** Rooms and suites at the **Downtown Hotel Harrington** (p. 43) vary greatly in size—from some that can sleep only one to others that can accommodate up to seven. The largest are furnished with three full-size beds, several chairs, a compact refrigerator, and room to squeeze in rollaway. The next-largest have two queen beds, one twin bed, and a fridge. The location's not bad either: 1 block from Pennsylvania Avenue and 2 blocks from the Metro Center Metrorail Station.

- **Best Activities for Guests:** Travelers who stay at the **Hostelling International Washington, DC** property (p. 42) can choose from many activities available to guests. Free tours include the monuments, Georgetown, Kennedy Center, and a historic tour of DC that's led by a professional guide who volunteers at the nonprofit hostel. Evening tours of Georgetown and Adams Morgan end in pub crawls through these nightlife neighborhoods. For the more fine-arts oriented, two poets lead regular poetry readings and workshops.

- **Best Cheap Luxury:** The trick at Logan Circle's **Aaron Shipman House** (p. 47) is to grab the cheapest room and enjoy all the amenities of this beautifully restored 1887 town house that's become a marvelous bed-and-breakfast. The room is small but comfortable. Its bath is off the hall but is not shared. When the weather's nice, there are several attractive and comfortable places to lounge outside. In the off season, you can get this room for as little as $95 a night.

4 Best Cheap Eats in DC

- **Break Bread with the Insiders (National Edition):** Members of Congress, Supreme Court justices, and their staffs have to eat, too, you know! And most of their cafeterias and restaurants are open to the public. You can chow down in the court, the Library of Congress, or the congressional office buildings. It's not gourmet food, but it's okay and it's reasonably priced. See p. 62.

- **Break Bread with the Insiders (Local Edition):** Ben's Chili Bowl (p. 88), opened on U Street by Ben and Virginia Ali in 1958, became a Washington institution long before Ben died in 2009. Their children now run the place and still serve Ben's half-smoke sausage with chili—a spicy sandwich that some label Washington's official city food. This is a must-stop for local politicians. National figures (Bill Cosby, Barack Obama) also have been known to come in.

- **Best House Hangout:** Because it's so close to the House of Representatives office buildings on Capitol Hill, **Bullfeathers** (p. 60) is a popular lunch and after-work spot for congressional staffers and journalists who cover the House. Save money by coming for the discounted food and drink during Bullfeathers' happy hours, including 5-buck burgers all day Saturday.

- **Best Cheap Place to See the Rich and Powerful:** You get extremely good food at **C.F. Folks** (p. 72). You may also get to see some famous Washingtonians—if you eat at an outdoor table, that is. That's because this little Dupont Circle lunch spot is next door to the Palm, the quintessential Washington steakhouse for a power lunch. Hang out with the Folks, and you can spot the likes of James Carville heading in for his much-more-expensive lunch.

- **Best Food on the National Mall:** Since the National Museum of the American Indian opened in 2004, its **Mitsitam Café** (p. 81) has outdone the other Mall eateries with interesting and tasty meals. Each of the five stations in this cafeteria serves food that represents a different region of the Americas. The dishes are either Native American or Native American inspired.

- **Best Combination of Ethnic Cuisines:** The founders of **Amsterdam Falafel Shop** (p. 56) in Adams Morgan had reason to give it this apparently silly name. It actually describes the little restaurant's Dutch and Middle Eastern specialties. For your main course, pick a falafel— middle-eastern croquets stuffed in pita bread. For your side, you'll want twice-cooked Dutch-style fried potatoes.

- **Best Burger Born in the DC (well, a DC suburb):** In Arlington, VA, in 1986, the original **Five Guys** location opened, and it's since grown into a national chain. Fortunately for Washington burger lovers, it's stayed true to its local beginnings, using fresh ground beef and grilling the plump and juicy burgers to order. See the review on p. 68 for the Downtown location. There are also locations in Dupont Circle, Georgetown, Penn Quarter, and Union Station.

- **DC's Best Pizza:** Authentic Neapolitan pizza comes out of the wood-fired oven at **2 Amys** (p. 87) in Upper Northwest—so authentic that it carries the official "Denominazione di Origine Controllata" (DOC) certification from the Italian government. Real Italian pizzas are weighed down with fewer toppings than many Americans like, so 2 Amys lets you add extra ingredients if you wish.

- **Best Texas-Style Barbecue:** Nick Fontana moved to Washington from Texas to set up **Capital Q** (p. 82), in a remnant of Chinatown. Testimony to its authenticity is that Fontana was asked to cater a Republican National Convention party for Texan Dick Armey, who then was House majority leader.

- **Best Grilled Cheese:** For 4 decades, **Stoney's** (p. 80)—now in Logan Circle—has been best known for two things: cheap beer and grilled cheese. The Super Grilled Cheese comes with tomato, bacon, onions, and a side of fries. You can order it without the extras if you prefer.

- **Best Enormous Burrito:** If you're incredibly, stupendously, ridiculously hungry—or just plain gluttonous—you can buy a very good, 2-pound burrito from **Burrito Brothers** (p. 60) for just $6.50. Most folks would be more than satisfied by the 1-pound burrito, and your doctor would probably steer you to the 8-ounce version. Other Tex-Mex dishes—plus vegetarian and vegan offerings—also are available.

- **Best Place for Food with Your Beer:** The first time we visited the **Brickskeller** (p. 72), we were pleasantly surprised by the quality of the food. This Dupont Circle saloon, after all, is best known for its claim to have 1,000 kinds of beer in stock. The fish and chips are quite good, as are the juicy burgers and the crispy onion rings.

- **Best College Pub:** Georgetown University students and faculty—as well as Georgetown residents and workers—find unusually good food at **The Tombs** (p. 80) at the edge of campus. That's because of the influence of fine-dining **1789 Restaurant,** which shares a building and management with the pub.

- **Best Place to Arrive Very Early:** Washingtonians in the know stand in line for a stool at the communal table at **Market Lunch** (p. 64) in Capitol Hill's Eastern Market. Buckwheat-blueberry pancakes are popular at breakfast, deep-fried crab cakes at lunch.

- **Best for Carnivore-Vegetarian Détente:** Vegetarians aren't relegated to a couple dishes at **Harmony Café** (p. 78) in Georgetown. Almost all of this Asian restaurant's meat-based dishes can be ordered in a veggie version. Harmony is so accommodating, one of the "Chef's Specialties" is "Your Favorite Dish (ask for it)."

● **Best for Hip Intellectuals:** You can get good food and drink at **Busboys and Poets** (p. 87); it is, after all, a restaurant. But it's also a bookstore, lecture hall, and performance space. Actually, it's two of all those things: at the original B&P in the U Street Corridor and the more recently opened spot near Mt. Vernon Square. The menu runs from sandwiches and pizza to full meals with vegetarian and vegan options.

● **Best Splurge:** The pre/post theater menu at **Marcel's** (p. 76), one of Washington's finest and most-expensive restaurants, is a super deal, though not cheap. For $52, this West End French-Belgian place gives you appetizer and main course, then limo rides to and from Kennedy center, then dessert.

● **Best Cheap Splurge:** This is a tough call, because there are so many superb DC restaurants that offer excellent small plates at reasonable prices. We've settled on **Rasika** (p. 85), in Penn Quarter, because its Modern Indian menu includes an incredible salad called *palak chaat:* crispy, deep-fried baby spinach, served with sweet yogurt and tamarind date chutney. So good!

5 Best DC Shopping Bargains

● **Best Souvenir:** Congressional staffers run flags up and down Capitol flagpoles so you can buy a "Flag Flown Over the Capitol" (p. 220) for $13 plus shipping and handling.

● **Best Handmade Gifts:** Go to Downtown DC to buy the folks back home some high-quality handicrafts made by artisans in developing countries. **Pangea Market** (p. 238) sells, at reasonable prices, unique bags, jewelry, toys, baskets, scarves, and more.

● **Best Flea Market:** Every Sunday, more than 100 vendors hawk their wares to decorators, collectors, tourists, Washington bargain-hunters, and the occasional celebrity shopper at the **Georgetown Flea Market** (p. 226). You'll find furniture, china, silver, antiques, garden accessories, art, books, chandeliers, jewelry, clothing, posters, tools, lamps, linens, and political memorabilia.

- **Best Farmer's Market:** You'll be shopping at one of the best farmers markets on the East Coast when you peruse the produce at the **Dupont Circle Fresh Farm Market** (p. 235). A mark of its quality: DC chefs come here to stock their restaurants.

- **Best Used Furniture:** If you're planning on settling into DC, Thursday usually is the day when **Miss Pixie's Furnishings and Whatnot** (p. 230) puts out its latest acquisitions. Beyond furniture, Miss Pixie's also carries artwork, photographs, books, quilts, and more.

- **Best Home Furnishings:** The wide price-range for unique items from around the world for yourself or for gifts means even cheapskates can find attractive and affordable furnishings at **Go Mama Go!** (p. 238) in the U Street Corridor. Among the offerings: Asian ceramics, Murano glassware, and woven placemats.

- **Best Used Bookstore:** Many used books in good condition is the hallmark of **Second Story Books** (p. 232), a longtime Dupont Circle establishment.

- **Best Vintage & New Clothing:** "Eclectic" is the word for **Junction** (p. 233), on U Street, where men's and women's clothes—vintage and new—are sold at reasonable prices.

- **Best Shoe Bargains:** Look for great deals on designer and brand-name shoes at **Shoes by Lara** (p. 240), a small local chain of discount stores. On any given day you might encounter half-price sales on Versani and Zanotti or deep discounts on Naturalizer and Rockport.

6 Best Free & Dirt Cheap DC Entertainment

- **Best Daily Free Show:** Every single day of the year—yes, including Christmas—an artist or group performs on **Kennedy Center's Millennium Stage** (p. 159): all music genres, dancers, comedians, puppets . . . You name it.

- **Best Free Films:** The Library of Congress mines its immense film and video collection for screenings in its **Mary Pickford Theater** (p. 155). Offerings range from classic movie features to documentaries. The library's Music Division sponsors its own screenings with musical themes.

- **Best Free Theater:** The highly regarded **Shakespeare Theatre Company** (p. 152) offers multiple free performances of one play each year in Penn Quarter. FINE PRINT This deal is so popular, you might have to stand in line for a few hours to get a ticket.

- **Best Cheap Jazz:** The nonprofit Center for the Preservation of Jazz & Blues charges an $8 cover for 4-hour jam sessions at its club, **HR-57** (p. 172), near Logan Circle. BYOB and pay a $3 per person corkage fee.

- **Best Dirt Cheap Sports:** They're as far up and away from the field as you can get, but sit in these seats and you can watch the **Washington Nationals** (p. 164) play Major League Baseball for $5. Bring your binoculars.

- **Best Entertainment Splurge:** The best comedy in Washington is performed by a troupe of former congressional staffers who call themselves **The Capitol Steps** (p. 184). Talented singers, satirists, and parodists, they write hilarious new lyrics to well-known tunes to skewer the politicians they used to work for. From a recent show: "Barackin' Around the Christmas Tree." From an older show: "Dutch, the Magic Reagan." Way-too-long-current sample: "Papa's Got a Brand New Baghdad."

CALENDAR OF EVENTS

Special events mark the Washington calendar all year long. DC takes its national holidays personally. You can't beat the Independence Day fireworks on the National Mall with the Washington Monument as a backdrop, for instance, or the reading of the Declaration of Independence at the National Archives. Where better to commemorate Martin Luther King's birthday than at the Lincoln Memorial where the great Civil Rights leader delivered his famed "I have a dream" speech? The famous cherry blossoms bloom spectacularly in the spring, so we celebrate with a festival. We don't light just one gigantic Christmas tree, but two—one at the Capitol and one the White House. (The Capitol's is better.) And we celebrate the December holidays with a Pageant of Peace. As with so many things to see or do in Washington, most of the events in this calendar are free. Remember that dates and details can change from year to year, so check the listed websites or phone ahead.

JANUARY

Martin Luther King Jr.'s Birthday FREE   The civil rights leader's life and legacy are commemorated in music in the Interior Department Auditorium. A wreath is placed on the steps of the Lincoln Memorial, where King delivered his "I have a dream" speech. Music and recitation of the speech accompany the wreath-laying. Interior Department, 18th and C streets NW. ☎ **202/426-6841.** Metro: Farragut West. 3rd Mon in Jan, 11am. Also at the Lincoln Memorial, West end of the National Mall at 23rd St. (btw. Constitution and Independence aves.). ☎ **202/426-6841.** www.nps.gov/linc. Metro: Foggy Bottom. Bus 13A, 13B, 13G, or 13F. 3rd Mon of Jan, 1pm.

Inauguration Day FREE   The President is sworn in every 4 years at noon on the West Steps of the Capitol, but inauguration festivities begin before that date and culminate with inaugural balls on inauguration evening. To get good tickets for the ceremonies—or an invitation to a ball (which is not free)—you need to have been active in the president-elect's campaign or know someone important in his political party. Otherwise, you can go stand in the crowd for the inauguration and/or try to grab a spot to stand along the parade route, which runs up Pennsylvania Avenue from the Capitol to the White House. And if you're marking your calendar that far ahead, the next inauguration will be on January 20, 2013. FINE PRINT January is Washington's coldest month, so the inauguration can be a bone-chilling event. Dress for the weather. **Democratic National Committee:** 430 S. Capitol St. SE, Washington, DC 20003. ☎ **202/863-8000.** www.democrats.org. **Republican National Committee:** 1st St. SE, Washington, DC 20003. ☎ **202/863-8500.** www.gop.com. January 20, after presidential elections. Inauguration ceremony begins 11am, parade around 2:30pm.

FEBRUARY

Black History Month Activities   African Americans' struggles and achievements are commemorated throughout the city. Museums, libraries, and other sites offer readings, speeches, musical performances, and other events. Check with some of the following organizations for details: **National Park Service:** 900 Ohio Dr. SW, Washington, DC 20024. ☎ **202/426-6841.** www.nps.gov/ncro/PublicAffairs/Calendar.htm. **Smithsonian Institution:** SI Building,

Room 153, MRC 010, Washington, DC 20013. ℂ **202/633-1000.** www.si.edu/events. **Destination DC:** 901 7th St. NW, 4th Floor, Washington, DC 20001. ℂ **202/789-7000.** www.washington.org/calendar.

Abraham Lincoln's Birthday `FREE` Where better to celebrate Lincoln's birthday than at the Lincoln Memorial? The ceremonies include a wreath-laying, band music, and a reading of the Gettysburg Address. West end of the National Mall at 23rd St. (btw. Constitution and Independence aves). ℂ **202/426-6841.** www.nps.gov/linc. Metro: Foggy Bottom. Bus 13A, 13B, 13G or 13F. February 12, noon.

MARCH

Women's History Month As with Black History Month, many Washington institutions commemorate the achievements of women during Women's History Month. For details on some of the events, check the following websites. **National Park Service:** 900 Ohio Dr. SW, Washington, DC 20024. ℂ **202/426-6841.** www.nps.gov/ncro/PublicAffairs/Calendar.htm. **Smithsonian Institution:** SI Building, Room 153, MRC 010, Washington, DC 20013. ℂ **202/633-1000.** www.si.edu/events. **Destination DC:** 901 7th St. NW, 4th Floor, Washington, DC 20001. ℂ **202/789-7000.** www.washington.org/calendar.

Smithsonian Kite Festival `FREE` When folks at the Smithsonian tell you to go fly a kite, they really mean it! Go on . . . head out and have some fun on Washington Monument grounds. You can enter the handmade kite competition, watch the experts fly their kites, or just find a place to fly your own. In addition to the kite flying, organizations pitch kid-oriented activity tents. The Smithsonian Associates and the National Air and Space Museum sponsor the event, usually on a Saturday in late March or early April. Washington Monument Grounds, between Constitution Avenue NW, Independence Avenue SW, and 15th and 17th streets. ℂ **202/633-1000.** www.tsa.si.edu. Metro: Smithsonian.

National Cherry Blossom Festival `FREE` Activities bloom all over town during the Cherry Blossom fest, which runs for about 2 weeks in late March and early April of each year. The official highlight is the **parade,** which runs along Constitution Avenue NW from 7th to 17th streets, beginning at 10am on the Saturday before the festival ends. The real stars, of course, are the **cherry blossoms,** especially those around the Tidal Basin, and they make their appearances whenever they darn well please. Click "Bloom Watch" at the festival's website for projected peak blooming dates. The blooms provide a great backdrop and canopy for a picnic at the Tidal Basin or on the Washington Monument Grounds. FINE PRINT Most events are free, but you can buy grandstand seating on the parade route for $17 per person. ✆ **877/442-5666.** www.nationalcherryblossom festival.org.

Easter Egg Roll FREE Since 1870, presidents have invited children to roll eggs on the White House lawn the Monday after Easter. We took our daughter Julie during the Clinton and Bush I administrations and have the wooden eggs with the mass-produced presidential signatures to prove it! Modern presidents have added entertainment—inside and outside the White House grounds—to occupy the youngsters during the inevitable waits in line. President Obama implemented a wonderful innovation in 2009: making tickets available on the Internet. Previously, you had to stand in a gargantuan line to get tickets, then in another line to get onto the White House lawn. Phone or start checking the White House website about a month before Easter. The event is open to children 10 and younger and their families. Participants enter from the Ellipse, south of the White House. FINE PRINT Rules for Egg Roll admission (ages of children admitted, how many relatives they can bring with them, and so on) have changed over the years, so be sure to check before your visit. Remember that outdoor events can be affected by bad weather. The Ellipse, between the White House and Constitution Avenue. ✆ **202/456-7041.** www.whitehouse.gov/eastereggroll. Mon after Easter, 8am–5pm. Metro: Federal Triangle.

APRIL

Filmfest DC For a quarter century, Filmfest DC has brought the world of film to Washington. For 11 days, over 100 movies of all genres are screened in theaters around town. Directors and actors participate in workshops, Q&A sessions, and other programs. Among past Filmfest participants are Cicely Tyson, Morgan Freeman, Sigourney Weaver, Peter Bogdanovich, John Malkovich, and Sydney Pollack. Check the website for screening schedule. Some of the programs are free, but a ticket to a film will only set you back about $10, and multi-show passes are available for purchase. Mid-to late April. © **202/274-5782.** Tickets © **800/955-5566.** www. filmfestdc.org or www.tickets.com.

Smithsonian Craft Show   For 4 days in late April, more than 100 artisans from around the country—selected from more than 1,000 entrants—display their expertise at basketry, ceramics, decorative fiber, furniture, glass, jewelry, leather, metal, mixed media, paper, wearable art, and wood. The Smithsonian has described the show as "the nation's most prestigious juried exhibition and sale of con-temporary American crafts." Daily admission is $15, with a $3 discount for seniors, students, members of the military, and Smith-sonian associates. Children 12 and younger are free, but strollers are not permitted. If you come with nine friends, you can purchase 10 tickets in advance for $100. National Building Museum, 401 F St. NW (btw. 4th and 5th sts.). © **888/832-9554** or 202/633-5006. www.smithsoniancraftshow.org. Metro: Judiciary Square.

May

Memorial Day Concert FREE   The National Symphony Orchestra performs on the West Lawn of the Capitol the Sunday before Memorial Day. This event is eclectic—with classical, popular, and patriotic music performed by the orchestra and guest stars—and it draws a big crowd. You can catch the dress rehearsal at 3:30pm the day before. West Lawn of Capitol. © **800/444-1324** or 202/467-4600.   www.kennedy-center.org/nso/programs/summer.   Metro: Union Station or Capitol South. Memorial Day, 8pm.

Memorial Day Wreath Laying   One of the most moving Memorial Day ceremonies is the wreath laying at the Tomb of the Unknowns in **Arlington National Cemetery,** where members of the Army's 3rd Infantry—the Old Guard—place flags at more than 260,000 graves just prior to the weekend. Usually, the president or another high-ranking government official participates. FINE PRINT While you don't have to pay to enter the cemetery, you might want to ride the Tour-mobile rather than hiking to the tomb from the Metrorail station or parking lot. Tourmobile costs $6.50 for those 65 and older, $3.75 for those 3 to 11, free for those younger, and $7.50 for everyone else. Parking is $1.75 an hour for the first 3 hours, $2 for each addi-tional hour. In Arlington, VA, across Memorial Bridge from the

Lincoln Memorial. ② **703/607-8000.** www.arlingtoncemetery.org. Metro: Arlington Cemetery. Memorial Day, 11am.

JUNE

Capital Pride FREE LGBT Washingtonians and their families, friends, and supporters gather for the weeklong Capital Pride celebration in early to mid-June each year. The festivities begin with five days of educational programs, performances, poetry readings, films, concerts and other activities around town. The culminating weekend features a parade and festival along Pennsylvania Avenue. More than 150 units usually march in the parade—from an AARP contingent to the popular DC Different Drummers marching band. Festival offerings include refreshments, musical performances, and a family section with activities for children. Parade/festival Pennsylvania Ave. btw 3rd and 7th sts. **www.capitalpride.org**. Metro: Archives.

Smithsonian Festival of American Folklife FREE Hordes descend on the National Mall in late June and early July for this annual celebration and demonstration of traditional music, crafts, and ethnic foods from the United States and around the world. One of Washington's premier outdoor events, the festival typically features several states and foreign countries. The concerts and displays are free. You can buy food and drink. On the National Mall. ② **202/663-6440.** www.folklife.si.edu/center/festival.html. Metro: Smithsonian.

JULY

Independence Day Parade FREE Bands, fife-and-drum corps, drill teams, military units, horseback riders, floats, big balloons, and assorted VIPs and celebrities march down Constitution Avenue NW from 7th to 17th streets to celebrate the Fourth of July. ② **800/215-6405.** www.july4thparade.com/index.html. July 4, 11:45am.

Independence Day Concert FREE The National Symphony Orchestra (with big-name guests) performs on the Capitol's West Lawn. The program is hosted by a big-name celebrity and draws some Washington VIPs as well as a large crowd of just plain folks (and is often broadcast nationally). It ends with the 1812 Overture—complete with cannons—as the fireworks begin. To beat the crowds, attend the dress rehearsal here at 3:30pm July 3. FINE PRINT This program draws an *enormous* crowd. Get there early if you expect to find a decent place to spread your blanket. West Lawn of

Capitol. ℭ **800/444-1324** or 202/467-4600. www.kennedy-center.org/nso/programs/summer. Metro: Union Station or Capitol South. July 4, 8pm.

Independence Day Fireworks FREE   About the time the cannons are booming the Independence Day Concert to a conclusion, the fireworks begin to shoot into the air from near the Lincoln Memorial Reflecting Pool. People pack the Mall to watch and listen to the bright, colorful, and loud show in the sky. But there are other fine spots for viewing, most of which require early arrival: the Jefferson Memorial, the Ellipse, the Francis Scott Key Bridge (an appropriate place to see *the rockets' red glare/the bombs bursting in air*), the Marine Corps War Memorial, and areas along the Virginia side of the Potomac River that can be reached from George Washington Memorial Parkway parking lots. FINE PRINT You will have to pass through at least one security checkpoint. You can't bring alcoholic beverages, glass bottles, fireworks, or grills to the Mall or surrounding federal land, including the banks of the Potomac and Anacostia rivers. Jefferson Memorial: East Basin Drive SW on southeast side of the Tidal Basin. ℭ **202/426-6841.** www.nps.gov/thje. Metro: Smithsonian. Bus 13A, 13B, 13G, 13F, or 11Y. Ellipse: Between the White House and Constitution Ave. Metro: Federal Triangle. Francis Scott Key Bridge: M St. NW (at 35th St.). Metro: Georgetown, or Connection bus from Dupont Circle or Rosslyn Metro. Bus D5 or 38B. Marine Corps War Memorial: Walk a fifth of a mile from Arlington Cemetery Metro Station. July 4, 9pm.

Capital Fringe Festival   Washington's theater festival for independent artists began in 2006, and has rapidly become a local theatrical institution. During the festival, more than 100 productions are presented in a dozen venues over about 15 days. Genres include cabaret, comedy, dance, drama, experimental, and musical theater. Tickets usually run from $10 to $15, and if you're a real theater fanatic, there are also discounted passes to see multiple shows. Call ℭ **202/737-7230.** www.capfringe.org. July 8–25, 2010.

SEPTEMBER

Kennedy Center Open House FREE   Washington's premier performing arts venue marks the opening of the traditional new season with a festival of performances in music, theater, and dance, along with special activities for kids. This Saturday event in September is popular, so be prepared to stand in line. Phone or check the Kennedy Center website for details. 2700 F St. NW (at New Hampshire Ave.). ℭ **800/444-1324** or 202/467-4600. www.kennedy-center. org. Parking $18. Free shuttle bus from Foggy Bottom Metro Station. Bus 80.

Black Family Reunion Thousands of parents, grandparents, and children flock to the National Mall for the 2-day Black Family Reunion each September. Sponsored by the National Council of Negro Women, this weekend celebration of African-American heritage features music, food, arts, crafts, and pavilions dedicated to such subjects as health, sports, and education. National Mall. ℭ **301/390-8408.** www.ncnw.org/events/reunion.htm. Metro: Smithsonian.

National Book Festival `FREE` The National Mall transforms into a gigantic library/bookstore for one Saturday each September. Sponsored by the Library of Congress, the festival features book-signings, talks by authors, and other book-related activities, many especially for children. National Mall between 7th and 14th streets. www.loc.gov/bookfest. ℭ **202/707-1550** or 202/707-8000. Metro: Smithsonian. 10am–5:30pm.

OCTOBER

Marine Corps Marathon `FREE` It's free to watch "The People's Marathon," which is so popular that registration for the 30,000(!) runners' slots fills up in a few days. The Marines proudly call this the "Marathon of the People" because it's open to all who register online before the slots fill up. It's also nicknamed the "Marathon of the Monuments" because it runs by the Jefferson Memorial, Lincoln Memorial, Franklin Roosevelt Memorial, Korean War Memorial, Vietnam Veterans Memorial, Marine Corps War Memorial, Washington Monument, the Capitol, the Pentagon, and Arlington National Cemetery, among other landmarks. You don't have to be a world-class runner to participate. But you do have to maintain a 14-minute-per-mile pace for the first 20 miles or you won't be able to complete the run. That's because the 14th Street Bridge reopens to motor vehicle traffic at 1:15pm and runners are barred from the bridge from that point on. Runners must also be at least 14 years old. Online registration opens around the beginning of April. Check the website for the specific date. If you plan to watch the race, check the website for an online map of the course. Metrorail opens at 5am on race day. FINE PRINT If you'd like to participate, rather than cheer the runners on, there's an $88 registration fee (if you manage to get one of the coveted spots). Starting Line: Jefferson Davis Highway (near Arlington Memorial Bridge and Arlington National Cemetery Entrance). ℂ **800/7868762.** www.marinemarathon.com. Metro: Arlington Cemetery. Last Sun in Oct, 7:50am.

DC Drag Queen Race FREE   A shorter and very different kind of race draws crowds to Dupont Circle at about the same time as the Marine Corps Marathon each year. About 9pm on the Tuesday before Halloween, well-dressed drag queens run along 17th Street in the vicinity of Q Street. This is not an officially organized event, but it comes off every year thanks to the efforts of local business owners and volunteers. Thousands of spectators begin to gather between P and S streets as early as 6pm, contestants show off their outfits before the race begins, and people keep partying afterward. Prime viewing space is in sidewalk cafes along 17th Street, although spectators standing on the sidewalk can block the view. Dupont Circle Metrorail station. Metro: Dupont Circle.

November

Veterans Day Ceremony FREE   The armistice that stopped the fighting of World War I went into effect at the 11th hour of the 11th day of the 11th month of 1918. President Woodrow Wilson thus proclaimed November 11 "Armistice Day," to celebrate the end of what then was called the "War to End All Wars." Unfortunately for humankind, the War to End All Wars was followed by World War II, then the Korean War. So, in 1954, Congress renamed the holiday "Veterans Day." In Washington, Veterans Day is marked by an 11am ceremony at the Tomb of the Unknowns in Arlington National Cemetery. Military bands perform, flags are presented by a color guard composed of members from each military service, and a wreath is laid by the president or some other high-ranking government official. FINE PRINT While you don't have to pay to enter the cemetery, you might want to ride the Tourmobile rather than hike to the tomb from the Metrorail station or parking lot. The Tourmobile costs $6.50 for those 65 and older, $3.75 for those 3 to 11, free for those younger, and $7.50 for everyone else. Parking is $1.75 an hour for the first 3 hours, $2 for each additional hour. In

Arlington, VA, across Memorial Bridge from the Lincoln Memorial. ℂ **703/607-8000.** www.arlingtoncemetery.org. Metro: Arlington Cemetery. November 11, 11am.

DECEMBER

White House Tree Lighting FREE   Near the beginning of December, a member of the First Family throws a switch to light the large Christmas tree on the Ellipse. But that's just a part of the annual tree-lighting ceremony. A military band and nationally known entertainers perform. The eclectic 2009 lineup included rock/pop singer Sheryl Crow, hip-hop artist Common, folk singer Ray LaMontagne, American Idol Jordin Sparks, jazz saxophonist Joshua Redman, jazz pianist Brad Mehldau, and the Irish music ensemble Celtic Woman. Tickets to get close to the celebration are available through an online lottery in early November. Start checking the website in October for specific information. The Ellipse, between the White House and Constitution Avenue NW. ℂ **202/426-6841.** www.nps.gov or www.thenationaltree.org. Metro: Federal Triangle.

Pageant of Peace FREE   The lighting of the White House Christmas Tree kicks off a month of holiday activities on the Ellipse. Surrounding the White House tree are 56 smaller trees that represent the states, territories, and the District of Columbia. Residents of each state make the ornaments that decorate the trees. The trees line the Christmas Pathway of Peace. Musical groups perform each evening. A large Yule Log burns. A large-scale model train runs around the tree (although in 2009 the train didn't start running until Dec 15). The 2009 pageant included a Santa's Workshop and times children could visit Saint Nick. FINE PRINT Washington weather is unpredictable, and it can get quite cold in December. If you're not bundled up good when it does, you might end up spending all your time at the pageant huddled by the Yule Log. The program can change from year to year, so make sure you check the White House website for details. The Ellipse, between the White House and Constitution Avenue. ℂ **202/208-1631.** www.nps.gov/whho/national_christmas_tree_program.htm. Metro: Federal Triangle. Early Dec–Jan 1. Music Mon–Fri 6–8:30pm, Sat–Sun 4–8:30pm. Lights on dusk–11pm. Train runs 11am–11pm.

That's hostel, not hustle; but they do have a pool table (and free Wi-Fi) at DC's Hostelling International residence (p. 42).

CHEAP SLEEPS

As we were planning this book, we told our editor that finding "free" in DC would be a snap. Cheap, not so much. That's especially true when it comes to lodging. On average, Washington has the fourth-highest hotel rates in the United States, trailing only New York, Boston, and Chicago. Because it's substantially smaller than New York and Chicago, Washington has fewer hotels in all categories, including cheap ones.

We also set ourselves a substantial challenge when we launched our journey to find cheap sleeps: We wanted to keep you within the city, so you can spend your time exploring the many wonderful things you can do here for free rather than commuting from the suburbs. (Should you decide to go for a budget lodging in a DC suburb, we've addressed that, as well.) We wanted to put you in safe neighborhoods with easy access to mass transit. We wanted to put you in clean, comfortable quarters. And we wanted to find rooms for two that can be had for as much under $150 a night as we could find, and preferably under $100 (at least in the off season).

We met those criteria, for the most part, with bed-and-breakfasts, small hotels, and hostels. B&Bs can be especially attractive for the cheapskate traveler who doesn't mind a whiff of comfort and luxury. A luxurious inn with gourmet breakfast and afternoon hors d'oeuvres may have a couple of small rooms that share a bath. Book one of these at a bargain rate, and you can enjoy the rest of the inn's wonderful amenities on the cheap. The downside: You rarely have access to an elevator.

What we've tried to do is give you a range of lodging choices: if you just need a place to leave your things, and don't mind sharing a room or a bathroom; if you can live with something simple (but want your own room); if you've budgeted a little extra for a nice room with some amenities.

SHOPPING TIPS FOR CHEAP LODGING

If saving money is your primary goal in planning a DC trip, come from November through February. Washington has high and low seasons, and you can get the bargains if you know when to hit town. It's cheapest when Congress is not in session and tourists are not traipsing its streets. The city is most expensive in the spring, when pleasant weather and cherry blossoms lure visitors, especially school field trips, and Congress usually is at work.

Both visitors and Congress—and the hordes who try to influence Congress—tend to stay away in November and December. You won't find a lot of tourists here in January or February, either. If you come in the dead of winter, you'll miss our pleasant spring and fall weather and our glorious flowering landscape. Much of that time, you won't be able to watch Congress in session. But every place you want to visit—including the Capitol—will be open. Washington can be gorgeous after a snowfall. (And yes, it snows sometimes in DC. It snowed a *lot* in DC the winter of 2009–10. You may remember a little something called "Snowmageddon.") But back to the upside: There are many holiday events (lots of them free). The U.S. Botanic Garden puts on a Christmas poinsettia display, and you can check out the Capitol and White House Christmas trees. (The Capitol's is better.)

Congress often leaves town in July and August as well, which drives down rates then. But that's a time you'll often see lots of families with children visiting during school vacations, so prices generally don't drop as much as in winter. Because many hotel guests come here on business, and don't tarry after Friday afternoon, you can often save money on weekends, too. Pick a weekend in December, and you can stay in some of the best hotels in town for less than $100. Really.

Another key to getting the best rates is to do a lot of comparison shopping. Check several online travel sites (**expedia.com** or **hotels. com**, or other favorites of yours, or aggregators like Kayak). Check AAA (**www.aaa.com**); the auto association often has great deals, even for nonmembers.

Check the hotel/motel chains' websites. See if the individual hotel has a website. Call the chain's toll-free number. Call the hotel directly. There's a good chance one of these options will offer lower rates than the others. Online, look for packages. When you call, ask if there are cheaper rates than what you were quoted. Then ask again. Mention affiliations that might earn you discounts—auto club membership, hotel frequent-sleeper membership, your status as an employee of the government or of a corporation that might have negotiated discounts.

If you reserve well in advance, check back periodically. If a hotel has many vacancies near the date you want to visit, it may lower its rates.

Don't automatically reject places that say they require a longer stay than you want. An inn facing vacancies may be willing to negotiate. Don't hesitate to try to negotiate the rate, either, especially when making a last-minute reservation.

The prices we list in the reviews are the ranges from the cheapest double during the off season to the most expensive double in season, unless otherwise noted.

HOSTEL? THEY WERE VERY NICE TO ME

You'll find hostels and hostel-like facilities listed in this chapter, because they tend to be cheap and tend to offer some nice extras, such as companionable fellow guests, activities, and knowledgeable

CHEAP SLEEPS IN DC

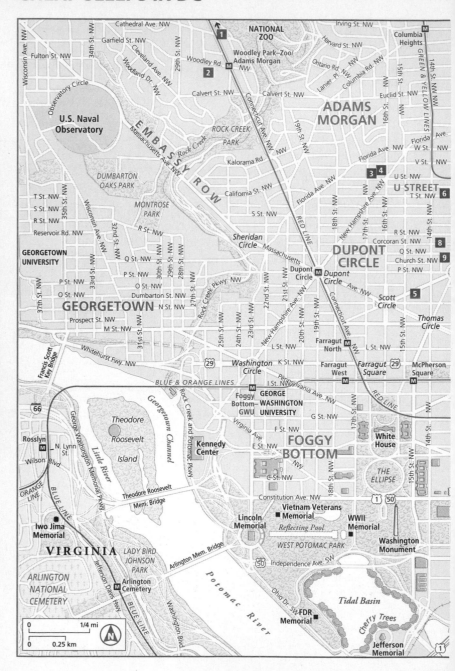

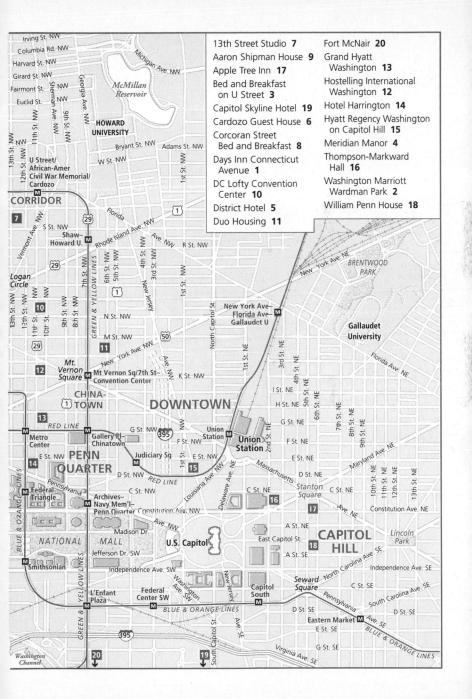

13th Street Studio **7**
Aaron Shipman House **9**
Apple Tree Inn **17**
Bed and Breakfast
on U Street **3**
Capitol Skyline Hotel **19**
Cardozo Guest House **6**
Corcoran Street
Bed and Breakfast **8**
Days Inn Connecticut
Avenue **1**
DC Lofty Convention
Center **10**
District Hotel **5**
Duo Housing **11**

Fort McNair **20**
Grand Hyatt
Washington **13**
Hostelling International
Washington **12**
Hotel Harrington **14**
Hyatt Regency Washington
on Capitol Hill **15**
Meridian Manor **4**
Thompson-Markward
Hall **16**
Washington Marriott
Wardman Park **2**
William Penn House **18**

Staying Safe in DC

Two questions we routinely put to innkeepers are: What do you tell your guests about safety in this neighborhood? And: Do you feel comfortable walking between here and the nearest Metrorail station late at night?

Inevitably, they say the neighborhood is safe. Usually they say they're comfortable walking around late at night.

After decades of gentrification, one Capitol Hill innkeeper pointed out, blocks that once were ravaged by crime have been transformed into affluent neighborhoods. The hookers and drug dealers have been replaced by families who renovated old houses and now park baby strollers on their porches. An Adams Morgan innkeeper added important advice to this analysis: "Use your urban street smarts." After 9pm or so, she recommends that her guests use cabs when getting to her inn.

Here's what all this means: With the caveat that crime happens everywhere in America, every place we recommend is in a neighborhood that is safe during daylight hours. The main commercial blocks of these neighborhoods are safe after dark when lots of folks are wandering the sidewalks. Exercise your urban street smarts by not walking alone on deserted streets after dark and not exploring dark alleys. If you feel uncomfortable, hail a cab or, if your hotel offers shuttle service, use it.

staff with good tips about what to do in DC. If you did the backpack/ Eurail Pass thing at some point, you know about hostels. You don't have to be a youth to stay at a hostel. Most are not called "youth hostels" anymore. Other misconceptions we can correct: You don't need to bring your own bedding, and most hostels no longer have a daytime "lockout" period, but are accessible 24/7. You should bring a lock, since most hostels provide lockers or other storage space you have to secure.

There are several recommendable (and *non*-recommendable) places in Washington, including (recommendable!) the official Hostelling International hostel (see review p. 42), and private hostels. You can count on clean, safe, and well-managed properties with a Hostelling International hostel, all of which are part of an international nonprofit

Staying in a Hotel/Motel Chain in the Suburbs

Except for the Days Inn Connecticut Avenue, we haven't been able to find cheap prices in chain hotels in decent locations in DC unless they're offering specials. The suburbs, however, are another matter. The farther you get away from town, the better chance you have of finding cheap rates. (Or, if you have enough points/miles for a free stay, the only DC-area branch of the chain might be in a Maryland or Virginia suburb.) What you need to do if you're going the 'burb lodging route is to make sure you choose a place that's either within walking distance of a Metro station, or one that offers free shuttle service to a station, or is a short bus ride from one. The most remote Metrorail station is 35 minutes from Metro Center when the trains are running on time. Do phone the property you're considering to confirm if it really has easy Metrorail access (despite what it may say on the corporate website). If you're willing to put up with significant commuting hassles, you often can find *really* cheap deals near Dulles Airport. Look for places with a free airport shuttle (see p. 280 for ways to get yourself from the airport to central DC). Sometimes you also can find good deals near National Airport, where a shuttle to the aiport would put you near an 18-minute Metrorail ride to Metro Center. You'll need to calculate costs if you find a great rate in a distant suburb—Rockville or Gaithersburg, MD, for example. If the hotel doesn't offer free transportation to a Metrorail station, is it still a good deal when you factor in the costs of driving and parking at the station or taking a cab or bus? All-day parking at a Metrorail station costs $4.75. Most short-term meters at Metrorail lots charge a buck an hour. Get detailed informartion at **www.wmata.com/rail/parking**.

that "promote[s] international understanding of the world and its people through hostelling." You don't have to be a member of HI to stay, but you do get a slight discount if you are a member.

For information on how to join **Hostelling International USA** (which also gives you membership in all international HI hostels), visit **www.hiusa.org**. Membership is free if you're under 18, $28 annually for people 18 to 54. As a member, you can make pre-paid reservations at HI hostels, and are eligible for a lot of discounts, from long-distance calling to bus travel to organized tours.

If you haven't stayed at a hostel, here's what you can expect: Most offer shared rooms (either same sex or mixed), with shared bathrooms, usually for less than (sometimes a *lot* less than) $50 a night; prices can vary by season. Some hostels offer private rooms for one, two, or three people, or en suite bathrooms, with the price going up accordingly, though the top end for private rooms is still usually well under $100. Most hostels have a communal kitchen/dining area, free Wi-Fi, a lounge, lockers or other locked storage, and free or low-cost organized activities, ranging from local tours, movies, and pub crawls, to day or overnight trips. The staff members are usually pretty good at helping you plan individual activities based on your interests.

You'll find a comprehensive listing of hostels (as well as budget hotels and guesthouses) at **www.hostelworld.com** and **www. hostels.com**. Hostels.com claims to list "every hostel, everywhere." Both publish reader reviews and a numerical average reader rating for each property. At hostelworld. com, you can sort the hostels by their average rating. This kind of system can be a bit of a crap-shoot. But the more readers who rate a property, the more likely you are to get a reasonably good idea of its quality. You can make reservations through these websites, or you can go to the hostel's site.

Another comprehensive source of cheap DC housing, both short

More Sources for B&Bs

As you peruse our reviews of bed-and-breakfasts, you may notice that several have the same telephone number. That's because they're represented by the same booking firm, **Bed and Breakfast Accommodations** (© **877/893-3233** or 202/328-3510; www.bedandbreakfastdc.com). If none of our B&B recommendations appeals to you—or if you can't get rooms in these inns— you can check what else Bed and Breakfast Accommodations might offer you. It's a well-respected organization that sets standards and holds its innkeepers to them. Its staff inspects the inns at least twice a year and updates photos on its website at least every 18 months. The ones that we visited in preparing this book were unfailingly comfortable, clean, and well maintained.

and longer-term, is **www.dchousing.net**. Created for low-paid interns and activists, the website is open to anyone who wants to use it.

In addition to the hostels we review in this chapter, here are some other top-rated hostels in Washington:

- **Hilltop Hostel** (300 Carroll St. NW; ✆ **202/291-9591;** www.hosteldc. com) is far from the main tourist attractions in DC's Tacoma Park neighborhood, but it is close to the Tacoma Metrorail Station. Beds are $22 to $24 a night.

- **Washington International Student Center** (2451 18th St. NW; ✆ **800/ 567-4150** or 202/667-7681; www.dchostel.com) sits in the heart of the Adams Morgan nightlife district. To get to other DC attractions, you can catch Metrobus 96 to the Woodley Park Metro Station or the Circulator bus to the Woodley Park Metro Station or downtown. Beds cost $23 a night.

- One of **Duo Housing**'s (1112 6th St. NW; ✆ **202/640-3755;** www. duohousing.com/locations/washington-dc) unusual amenities is free use of a bicycle. We're not sure how much you'd ride, however, since this place is in the center of the city, less than 2 blocks from the Mount Vernon Square Metro Station. Rates start at $25 per bed.

1 Adams Morgan

Adams Inn   The three adjacent town houses that comprise this comfortable B&B stand across the street from a fire station that shares a wall with the town house next door to it. The innkeeper assures us that "the firemen take pains to be quiet." The location is a half block from buses that go downtown or to the Woodley Park Metrorail Station. Also nearby: the heart of Adams Morgan's dining and nightlife. Breakfast is served at three tables spread over two rooms. Guests can relax in the back garden with fountain and attractive landscaping as well as in the century-old town houses' several sitting rooms. The rooms are clean, neat, and well maintained. The cheapest rooms have shared baths. Check the website for specials. We've been able to turn up deals where rooms with private baths were going for $99 if rented within 48 hours of arrival ($89 for shared bath). There's no smoking inside.

1746 Lanier Place NW (btw. Adams Mill and Ontario roads), Washington, DC 20009. ✆ **800/578-6807** or 202/745-3600. Fax 202/319-7958. www.adamsinn.com. 26 units, 12 with private bath. $119–$169 double. Rates include continental breakfast.

Luxury for Less Than $100 a Night?

Even cheapskates can sleep in luxury if their timing's right. When Congress is not in session and tourism traffic is low (think Nov–Feb most years), some expensive hotels drop rates to around $100 for a double—or even lower. Here are some nice hotels where we found such rates during winter 2009 to 2010:

Hyatt Regency Washington on Capitol Hill, 400 New Jersey Ave. NW (at D St.), Washington, DC 20001; ℂ **888/591-1234** or 202/737-1234; fax 202/7375773; www.washingtonregency.hyatt.com; $93 double. Metro: Union Station.

One Washington Circle Hotel, 1 Washington Circle NW (at New Hampshire Ave.), Washington, DC 20037; ℂ **800/424-9671** or 202/872-1680; www.thecirclehotel.com; $98 double for room with queen bed, sofa bed, and full kitchen. Metro: Foggy Bottom/George Washington University.

Washington Marriott Wardman Park, 2660 Woodley Rd. NW (btw. Connecticut Ave. and 27th St.), Washington, DC 20008; ℂ **888/236-2427** or 202/328-2000, fax 202/234-0015; www.marriott.com; $99 double. Metro: Woodley Park—National Zoo.

AE, DC, DISC, MC, V. Limited covered parking $10. Circulator, Metrobus 96 from Woodley Park Metrorail Station, or Metrobus L2 from Downtown. **Amenities:** Computer w/Internet access; cooking facilities; fridge; pay phone; TV; VCR. *In room:* Window A/C, Wi-Fi. *Available by request:* Hair dryer. TV in 2 rooms.

Gallery Inn   At the southern edge of Adams Morgan, the Gallery Inn stands as an interesting combination of hostel and traditional hotel. The comfortable, well-maintained inn has six private rooms as well as 12 beds in dormitory rooms. All the rooms have private baths, phones, and flatscreen TVs. The inn serves a continental breakfast each morning. Staying here puts you a few blocks away from three major dining and nightlife neighborhoods: Dupont Circle and the U Street Corridor as well as Adams Morgan. Smoking is not allowed inside.

1850 Florida Ave. NW (btw. 18th and 19th sts.), Washington, DC 20009. ℂ **202/234-8788.** www.hostelworld.com/availability.php/Gallery-Inn-Hotel/Washington-DC/21986. 6 private rooms, 12 dormitory beds. Private rooms $120–$220. Dorm beds $30–$50.

⭐ **Grand Hyatt Washington,** 1000 H St. NW (at 10th St.), Washington, DC 20001; ✆ **888/591-1234** or 202/582-1234, fax 202/637-4781; www.grandwashington.hyatt.com; $99 double. Metro: Metro Center.

Here's a true story our fellow bargain-hunters can aspire to emulate: We stayed at the Grand Hyatt during what Washingtonians dubbed "Snowmageddon" in February 2010. We had tickets to a Washington Capitals hockey game, and the forecasters were predicting a blizzard with deep snowfall, destructive winds, and uncertain mass transit availability, so we came up with a plan to make sure we wouldn't miss the game. We looked for packages at hotels near the venue, and found a $99 "Romance Package" at the Grand Hyatt, which has indoor access to Metrorail and is but 5 blocks from Verizon Center, where the Caps play.

After checking into our king bedroom, we grabbed an inexpensive Asian dinner on the way to Verizon Center, enjoyed the Caps' 13th straight win, then returned to the Hyatt for the complimentary full bottle of champagne (which, alas, we couldn't finish) and chocolate-covered strawberries. After grazing among the offerings at the next morning's breakfast buffet (also included), we headed home, contemplating our enormously enjoyable (and cheap) mini-vacation.

Rates include continental breakfast. AE, DC, MC, V. Limited parking $10. Metro: Dupont Circle or Metrobus L2. **Amenities:** Internet cable; microwave; computer w/ Internet access 8am–midnight. *In room:* Window A/C, TV, Wi-Fi.

2 Capitol Hill

Apple Tree Inn Staying in this Victorian town house really is like staying with folks you know, because there's just one guest room and the owners often become friends with their repeat visitors. Guests have access to the living room, dining room, and English (finished) basement—all with working fireplaces—as well as the lovely garden in back. Oriental rugs cover the hardwood floors in this immaculately maintained property. Built in 1881, it was renovated in the 1990s. The second-floor guest room has a queen bed, 35-inch flatscreen HD TV, wingback chair, and window that looks out through the maple tree in the front yard to a quiet section of Constitution Avenue. The guests' private bath with tub and shower is off the hall. A full breakfast is served in the basement dining area or, if you like, in the garden. Teddy the Spanish waterdog and Freddy the cat are permanent residents. The inn is about 7 blocks from Union Station and the Capitol grounds, which is a bit of a hike but also quite well situated if you're willing to do the walking. You can wander all over Capitol Hill from here, and get to the rest of Washington from the Union Station Metrorail Station. The rates qualify as cheap only in the off season. No smoking inside.

Constitution Ave. NE and 5th St., Washington, DC 20002. ℂ **877/893-3233** or 202/328-3510. Fax 413/582-9669. www.AppleTreeInnDC.com. 1 unit. $110–$205 double. Rates include full breakfast. AE, DISC, MC, V. Covered parking for small car $15. Metrobus X8 or D6, or walk from Union Station Metrorail Station. **Amenities:** Central A/C; fridge; wet bar. *In room:* TV, Wi-Fi.

Capitol Skyline Hotel   Some day, this will be a hot neighborhood, and the Capitol Skyline's rates will go up—when the recession is fading into memory and the Nationals start winning baseball games. As it is, to get to anything but nearby Nationals Park (out-of-town teams and fans stay at the Skyline), you have to take a long 4-block walk that includes trekking under the Southeast Freeway. So, off season, we've found double rooms for as low as $89 here. To address its location's shortcomings, the Skyline offers free transportation to Metrorail, the Capitol, and the Mall. Among the hotel's many amenities are popular summer parties by its large outdoor pool. Every Sunday, star chef Spike Mendelsohn (see review of his **Good Stuff Eatery,** p. 63) grills burgers poolside. A jazz band plays from 7 to 10pm Friday in the hotel's lounge. Standard rooms have two double beds, two easy chairs, a desk, a TV, and a bath with shower and tub. Major renovation was completed in late 2008, and additional improvements are continuing.

10 I St. SW (at S. Capitol St.), Washington, DC 20024. ℂ **800/458-7500** or 202/488-7500. Fax 202/488-0790. www.capitolskyline.com. 203 units. $89–$329 double, children 17 and younger free in parent's room. AE, DISC, MC, V. Covered parking $20. Hotel shuttle from Capitol South Metrorail Station. **Amenities:** Central A/C; restaurant; lounge; 24-hr. fitness center; gift shop; accessible rooms; free newspapers in lobby; ATM. *In room:* TV, Wi-Fi and wired Internet access, phone (local calls $1.05), hair dryer.

Thompson-Markward Hall: The Young Women's Christian Home   If you're a young woman, coming to Washington for at least 2 weeks, and are willing to abide by the rules, this might be the spot for you. The Young Women's Christian Home was chartered by Congress in

House Swapping

The cheapest way to sleep in Washington is to have friends who live here who will put you up during your visit. They may even feed you for free, too. (In that case, you really ought to say thanks by taking them out to dinner at least once, perhaps to one of the restaurants we recommend in the "Cheap Eats" chapter!) If you don't have friends here, you might be able to stay with strangers.

Craig's List (www.craigslist.org) has a category called "housing swap." Click on "Wash DC," then on "housing swap," and look for DC-area residents offering their homes. Some want to trade with someone in a specific location. Others are willing to consider vacationing anywhere. You also can check on your community's Craig's List site to see if anyone from DC is looking for a place to stay in your town, and is willing to trade.

If you're willing to spend an amount that's about the equivalent of 1 night's stay in an inexpensive hotel, you can join a **home swapping service.** We have friends who belong to **HomeLink International** (www.homelink.org), and they highly recommend the service. They've told us of friends who use **Home Exchange** (www.homeexchange.com). HomeLink charges $115 a year or $181 for 2 years. A 1-year membership in Home Exchange is $100.

In its 14 years of operation, Home Exchange says it's never had a report of a theft, malicious vandalism, or "a case of someone getting to their exchange home and finding a vacant lot." The organization encourages its members to communicate with each other, exchange photos, and request referrals before agreeing to a swap.

The most common swap is simultaneous: You and the people you're swapping with live in each others' home at the same time. A variation is the "hospitality exchange," in which they stay with you as your guests and you do the same in their home.

1887 to provide housing for 18- to 34-year-old women who were new to the capital. The current facility, spectacularly located on the Senate side of the Hill, was built in 1931. Many residents staying here are congressional interns or graduate students from around the world.

If You're Active or Retired Military . . .

. . . you can stay at **Fort Myer** or **Fort McNair** for no charge, but the pickings can be slim and checking in can be complicated. If you're not on official business, you must call to confirm availability on the day you want to stay. Check-in is at Fort Myer in northern Virginia, even if you're staying at Fort McNair. You can walk to Fort McNair from the Waterfront Metrorail Station, but you'll still need to drive or take a taxi to Fort Myer to check in. If you do score a room, you'll be happy with the facilities, which are kept inspection ready for the active-duty officers who usually use them. In addition to rooms, there are suites with sitting room and sleeper sofa. Some have kitchens. Guests can use post amenities, which include dining facilities, tennis courts, swimming pools, and fitness centers. Fort McNair has a golf course. Check-in is at Wainwright Hall, Building 50, 318 Jackson Ave., on Fort Myer. If you drive, enter the post through the Hatfield Gate from Washington Boulevard (Virginia Rte. 27). If you're not driving, the cheapest route would be a cab from the Rosslyn or Arlington Cemetery Metrorail station. After you've checked in, if you're staying at Fort McNair, take a cab and Metrorail to the Waterfront station and walk 3 blocks south on 4th Street to the P Street gate. Rates range from $69 double for a room with shared bath at Fort Myer to $150 for a Fort McNair suite (© **703/ 696-3576;** fax 703/696-3490; www.fmmc.army.mil/sites/newcomers/ lodge.asp and www.fmmcmwr.com/lodging.htm).

Because Thompson-Markward doesn't cater to overnight guests, you need to bring some things most hotels provide: bedroom and bathroom linens and a small rug for the bedrooms' chilly tile floors. If you want a clock, TV, or radio in your room, bring them, too. The home prohibits smoking and alcoholic beverages. Men cannot go beyond the lobby. Among the amenities: a living room with fireplace, a library, a garden, and a sun deck. Residents get breakfast and dinner Monday through Saturday and brunch on Sunday. All but three of the rooms are singles.

235 2nd St. NE (south of C St.), Washington, DC 20002. © **202/546-3255.** www.ywch. org. 117 rooms. $40 a day to maximum $900 a month. 2-week minimum stay. Rates include breakfast and dinner Mon–Sat, brunch Sun. No credit cards. Metro: Union

Back to School: University Housing

Several DC universities make campus housing available to a wider public when their own students aren't filling the rooms, usually during summer terms, which run from May into August.

Most of these schools require residents to be in Washington for an internship or educational activities, but **American University** (☎ 202/885-3370; www.american.edu/ocl/housing/intern-housing.cfm) throws open its doors to anyone who is at least 18 years old. AU housing is in dormitories on the university's Tenley Campus, on Nebraska Avenue NW, just west of Wisconsin Avenue and a block south of the Tenleytown Metro Station in Upper Northwest. Weekly rates range from $235 per person in a triple room to $330 for a single. You must stay at least 4 weeks.

Catholic University of America (☎ 202/319-5291; http://conferences.cua.edu/summer) offers housing to anyone in DC for educational purposes. That includes interns and scholars conducting research as well as students enrolled in classes. The university is off the beaten path in Northeast Washington, but it does have the Brookland Metrorail Station at the edge of campus. Rates range from $27 per person per night in a double room to $30 in a single. You must stay at least 2 weeks.

Staying at **George Washington University** (☎ 202/994-6883; www.summerhousing.gwu.edu) puts you in one of the best locations in DC—near the Foggy Bottom Metrorail Station and not far from Georgetown, Downtown, the Kennedy Center, and the Mall. GW's housing is open to interns who are at least 18 years old. Weekly rates range from $231 per person in a four-bed room to $343 for a single with private bath. The lower rates require a stay of at least 9 weeks. The shortest stay allowed is 5 weeks. There's also a one-time $150 "administrative fee."

Station. **Amenitites:** Central and window A/C, cable TV in common area, VCR, DVD, fridge, microwave, 3 free computers w/Internet access. *In room:* Phone, Wi-Fi one-time $50 fee.

William Penn House   This hostel-like facility in a 1917 town house is a Quaker lodging and program center. Guests can participate in silent worship from 7:30 to 8am each day, as well as weekly yoga sessions, twice-monthly potluck meals with program, and various dialogues and workshops. "All are welcome," William Penn House proclaims, "especially activists and do-gooders." The place is well located, about 5 blocks from the Supreme Court, the Library of Congress buildings, and the Capitol grounds. Rooms range in size from 2 to 10 beds. Smoking and alcoholic beverages are prohibited.

515 E. Capitol St. SE (btw. 5th and 6th sts.), Washington, DC 20003. ✆ **202/543-5560.** Fax 202/543-3814. www.williampennhouse.org. 30 beds in 5 rooms, all with shared bath. $40–$50 per person; $125 for family of 4 plus $25 for each additional family member. Rates include continental breakfast. No credit cards. Metro: Capitol South, or Metrobus 96 or 97 to Union Station. **Amenities:** Central A/C; phone; Internet access $5 for 24 hr.; fridge; microwave; teapot. *Available by request:* Hair dryer.

3 Downtown

SUPER-CHEAP SLEEPS

★ **Hostelling International Washington, DC**   You get a lot with your clean, basic, Ikea bed at this hostel. The bulletin board that greets you in the lobby tells of myriad activities—tours, pub crawls, movies on the hostel's 60-inch TV, and the like. The lobby area sports sofas, easy chairs, a pool table, a piano, eight computers, Wi-Fi, lots of maps, and other DC information. Out back, there's a patio with tables, chairs, a smoking area, and 15 bike racks. The full kitchen facilities include utensils and tableware. The TV room has 20 leather lounge chairs. A theater with projector, screen, and stadium seating should have been built by the time you get hold of this book. Rooms hold from 4 to 10 single and bunk beds. There are two two-bed suites with kitchen and private bath. There are male, female, and co-ed rooms. Each floor has a men's and women's bathroom with showers, soap, shampoo, hair dryers, and accessible facilities. The entire hostel was painted and all carpeting was replaced in 2009. New beds are being placed in every room. Bring a lock for your locker or buy one here. Most hostel clients are 18 to 30 years old, according to general manager Mark Schneider. The recession of 2008 (and onward . . .) brought an increase in older guests and some families, he added. FINE PRINT If you want to book a suite or turn a four-bedder into a private room, Mark suggests reserving 1 to 2 months ahead. No smoking or alcoholic beverages are permitted inside the building.

1009 11th St. NW (at K St.), Washington, DC 20001. © **888/464-4872** or 202/737-2333. Fax 202/737-1508. www.hiwashingtondc.org. 250 beds, 246 without private bath. Dorm rooms $25–$45 per person; private rooms $79–$109 double; suites $89–$129 double. Add $3 per person if you're not a member of Hostelling International USA. Rates include continental breakfast. MC, V. Metro: Metro Center. **Amenities:** Central A/C; elevator; pay phones; TV; VCR; DVD; Wi-Fi; wired Internet access; computers w/Internet $4/hr.; hair dryers in bathrooms; coffee and tea all day; fridges, cooking, and eating facilities.

★ **Hotel Harrington**   There are reasons the Harrington has been popular with budget-minded travelers for nearly a century. It stands 1 block from Pennsylvania Avenue—an easy walk to the White House, the Mall, and other attractions. It's 2 blocks from the Metro Center Metrorail Station, which provides easy access to the rest of Washington. It's clean and comfortable and well maintained. And it's a good buy. You can get a double room with a queen bed for $135 in high season, for below $100 when discounted. If you're traveling with your family or a group of friends, this place can really be a bargain: Two-room suites that can sleep up to six can be had for as little as $155. Two-room suites with two baths cost $159 to $189. Most rooms have mini-fridges, and king rooms have microwaves as well. The Harrington has been owned by the same two families since it opened in 1914. Although the hotel has an ongoing renovation process, which spruces up some rooms each winter when occupancy is lower, historical touches remain—old-fashioned lights on the hall walls, baths with old-fashioned black-and-white tiles, a mail-drop system installed in 1918. *Trivia note:* In 1938, the Harrington became the first hotel in Washington to air-condition all of its rooms. There's one floor where smoking is permitted in the rooms.

436 11th St. NW (at E St.). © **800/424-8532** or 202/628-8140. Hotel fax 202/347-3924. Fax for guests 202/393-2311. www.hotel-harrington.com. 240 units, including 60 suites. $99–$179 double. AE, DISC, MC, V. Parking off site $15. Metro: Metro Center. **Amenities:** Central A/C; 3 restaurants; lounge; gift shop. *In room:* Phone (local calls 25¢), TV, Wi-Fi, microwave in king rooms, fridge in most rooms. *Available by request:* Hair dryer, iron, ironing board.

4 Dupont Circle

Embassy Inn   The family that purchased this century-old hotel in early 2009 has been hard at work on renovations. Before the end of that year, the Embassy had new paint, new furniture (including beds), and new bedding. By the time you read this, the carpeting should have been replaced, the bathrooms redone, and an elevator installed. The Embassy also is in the process of shifting from window A/C units to central air-conditioning. The result is a more comfortable, homey atmosphere than you find in larger hotels with higher prices. Also unlike most larger hotels, the Embassy serves a complimentary full breakfast in the morning and sherry and hors d'oeuvres in the lobby from 5 to 8 each evening. Guests have access to a shared microwave, fridge, and coffee and tea dispensers.

1627 16th St. NW (btw. Corcoran and R sts.), Washington, DC 20009. ℂ **877/968-9111** or 202/234-7800. Fax 202/234-3309. www.embassy-inn.com. 39 units. $89–$189 double. Rates include full breakfast. AE, DISC, MC, V. Metro: Dupont Circle, or Metrobus S1, S2, S4, or S9. **Amenities:** Coffee and tea dispensers; fridge; microwave; pass to nearby fitness center ($12). *In room:* Window A/C, TV, Wi-Fi, phone (free local calls), hair dryer. *Available by request:* Iron, ironing board.

Inn at Dupont Circle South   You can't beat this inn's location—just south of Dupont Circle—especially at these prices. Each room is different, and a few are quite large. If you wandered through all the rooms you'd notice hardwood floors, Oriental rugs, a crystal chandelier(!), antique (and simply old) furniture, and some homey touches. Shelves in one room hold a silver service. Another has dolls on the shelves and books on the mantle. Several rooms contain twin beds that can be pushed together to form a king. Most have gas fireplaces. One room, called The Nook, is barely big enough for its one single bed and TV. It's the only room without phone and coffeemaker. But, if you're traveling alone, it's a neat and clean room in the heart of Dupont Circle for less than $100. The inn cooks a full breakfast in the morning, serves desserts and nonalcoholic beverages between 4 and 5 in the afternoon, and allows guests to graze on coffee, tea, lemonade, and snacks all evening. ***Trivia note:*** Astrologer Jeanne Dixon once lived here.

1312 19th St. NW (south of Dupont Circle), Washington, DC 20036. ℂ **866/467-2100** or 202/467-6777. Fax 202/529-5585. www.thedupontcollection.com/dupontsouth.html. 8 units, 3 with shared bath. $110–$140 double. Rates include full breakfast. AE, MC, V. Parking within 1 block $25. Metro: Dupont Circle. **Amenities:** Laundry service. *In room:* Window A/C, TV, fridge, hair dryer, Wi-Fi, phone (free local calls). Smoking not allowed inside.

CHEAP SLEEPS IN ADAMS MORGAN, DUPONT CIRCLE, AND FOGGY BOTTOM

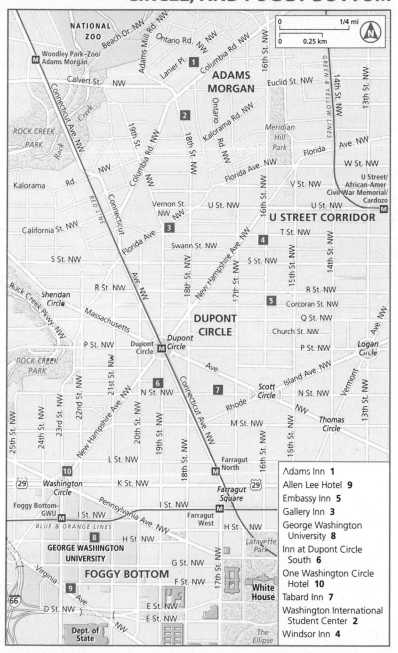

Adams Inn 1
Allen Lee Hotel 9
Embassy Inn 5
Gallery Inn 3
George Washington
   University 8
Inn at Dupont Circle
   South 6
One Washington Circle
   Hotel 10
Tabard Inn 7
Washington International
   Student Center 2
Windsor Inn 4

SPLURGE

★ **Tabard Inn**   If you've traveled in Europe under Frommer's tute-
lage, the Tabard will remind you of all those inexpensive but marvelous inns that have been cobbled together from adjacent buildings that
measure their age in centuries. The Tabard isn't that old, but it was
created from three adjacent Victorian town houses on a tree-lined
street. Each room is unique, and they're furnished with a combination
of antiques and—uh, well—pre-owned items. The Tabard is an eclectic and eccentric—and, yes, charming—place. All rooms come with
free admission to the Tabard's fabulously equipped health club: the
Capital YMCA around the corner. The Tabard's lounge is the prover-
bial comfortable old shoe, a well-worn place for luxuriating by the
fire. Jazz bands perform from 7:30 to 10pm Sunday. No smoking
allowed.

1739 N St. NW (btw. 17th and 18th sts.), Washington, DC 20036. ℂ **202/785-1277.**
Fax 202/785-6173. www.tabardinn.com. 40 units, 9 with shared bath. $128–$213
double. Rates include continental breakfast. AE, DC, DISC, MC, V. Valet parking $30.
Metro: Dupont Circle. **Amenities:** Restaurant; lounge; pass to YMCA; computer
w/printer and Internet. *In room:* Window A/C, Wi-Fi, phone (local calls 50¢). *Available
by request:* Hair dryer, a few TVs without cable, iron, ironing board.

Windsor Inn   Mona the cat is likely to greet you when you arrive at
the Windsor. Maybe she'll be sitting on the sofa or on one of the easy
chairs in the lobby. She's part of the homey greeting you get here. The
lobby also offers books, board games, several newspapers and magazines, and a fridge and microwave for guests' use. Sherry and hors
d'oeuvres are served from 5 to 8 each evening. The least expensive
rooms here are way more than adequate for the cheapskate's tastes—
private baths, king or queen beds, all of the hotel's standard amenities. Some of the more expensive rooms have mini-fridges and/or
kitchenettes. The Windsor, built in 1913, underwent major renovations that should be completed by the time you read this. The one
disappointment when Tom visited: that hotel disinfectant smell in the
hallways. Maybe it will disappear with the completion of the renovations. As with the Inn at Dupont Circle North, the Windsor is closer to
the U Street Metrorail Station than to Dupont. Smoking is not allowed.

1842 16th St. NW (btw. T and Swann sts.), Washington, DC 20009. ℂ **800/423-9111**
or 202/667-0300. Fax 202/667-4503. www.windsor-inn-dc.com. 44 units. $89–$189
double. Rates include full breakfast. AE, DISC, MC, V. Limited parking $15. Metro: U
St., or Metrobus S1, S2, S4, or S9. **Amenities:** Fridge; microwave; pass to nearby

fitness center ($12). *In room:* Window or central A/C, TV, hair dryer, phone (local calls free), Wi-Fi. *Available by request:* Iron, ironing board.

5 Foggy Bottom

Allen Lee Hotel   The peeling white paint on this four-story brick hotel matches the worn carpeting in the halls. But the Allen Lee is clean and offers basic accommodations at good rates. It's 4 blocks from the Lincoln Memorial and 3 blocks from the Foggy Bottom Metro Station, with easy access to the rest of Washington. You wouldn't notice at first glance, but new owners have made some improvements to this place, which was built in 1918 and owned by the same family until a few years ago. They went to Ikea to replace all the beds and linens. They're also in the process of repainting and recarpeting. Some rooms have fridges. Smoking is not allowed.

2224 F St. NW (btw. 22nd and 23rd sts.), Washington, DC 20037. ⓒ **800/462-0186** or 202/331-1224. Fax 202/296-3518. www.theallenleehotel.com. 85 units, 40 with shared bath. $79–$119 double. Rates include continental breakfast. AE, DISC, MC, V. Metro: Foggy Bottom. **Amenities:** Elevator; Wi-Fi; computer w/Internet; complimentary coffee and tea in lobby. *In room:* Window A/C, TV, phone (local calls 25¢). *Available by request:* Hair dryer, iron, ironing board, DVD player, laundry service.

6 Logan Circle

★ **Aaron Shipman House**   If you can score the cheapest room here, you'll enjoy luxurious surroundings while paying as little as $95 a night. This room is small, but light and airy and comfortable. It has a double bed, a nightstand, one chair, and almost all the in-room amenities of the more expensive rooms. The bathroom with shower is off the hall, but it's yours alone. Best of all, you enjoy all the public amenities in this exquisitely restored 1887 town house. There's a piano in the bay window of the living room, stained glass windows in the dining room, oriental rugs on the hardwood floors, and fireplaces that the innkeepers sometimes light on cold evenings. The outdoor space might be even better. On the attractive side porch, you can lounge on wicker furniture with comfortable cushions. In the enclosed side and back yards are a garden and a patio with fountains and more seating. These are great places to bring carryout food for a cheapskate's meal in deluxe surroundings. If you're traveling with kids or a group of friends, consider the basement apartment, which rents for as little as $110 double in low season and $140 for a group of four. It's got a bedroom with a queen bed, a large living room with a queen sofa bed, a full kitchen (you don't get the free breakfast), a dining nook, a TV with VCR, and a collection of children's movies. Smoking is not allowed inside.

Q and 13th sts. NW, Washington, DC 20009. ✆ **877/893-3233** or 202/328-3510. Fax 413/582-9669. www.aaronshipmanhouse.com. 7 units. $95–$250 double. Rates include full breakfast. AE, DISC, MC, V. Limited parking $15. Metro: U St., or Metrobus 52, 53, or 54. *In room:* A/C, TV, phone (local calls free), hair dryer, Wi-Fi.

Corcoran St. B&B   Modern accommodations greet you at this 1873 Victorian row house, which was renovated in 1998. The second floor guest room has a double bed, bath with tub and shower, and windows and decor that make the space light and airy. Down a tight spiral staircase from the first floor is a basement room which also has a private outside entrance. Here you have a queen sofa bed, a rocker, two easy chairs, desk, and a bath with tub and shower. Smoking is not allowed inside. Children are not allowed.

Corcoran and 13th sts. NW, Washington, DC 20009. ✆ **877/893-3233** or 202/328-3510. Fax 413/582-9669. www.bedandbreakfastdc.com/index.php?id=54. 2 units. $100–$185 double. 2- or 3-night reservations sometimes required. Rates include full breakfast. AE, DISC, MC, V. Free parking available for stays longer than 2 nights. Metro: U St. or Metrobus 52, 53, or 54. *In room:* A/C, TV, phone.

★ **DC Lofty Convention Center**   This hostel may exaggerate a bit when describing itself as "affordable *luxury* lodging." But the all-new facilities make it an unusally nice place to stay if you're okay with dormitory facilities. How clean is it? You're asked to remove your shoes when you enter! Sleeping accommodations range from four- to eight-bed rooms, some all-male, some female, some co-ed. Two have their own bath. Among the amenities: satellite and cable television on flatscreen HDTVs; free detergent, softener, and dryer sheets in the free laundry; modern kitchen with cookware and dinnerware; and a staff that's full of suggestions for how you can best spend your time in DC. You must make advance arrangements to arrive before 10am or after 10pm. Earliest check-in is 9am, latest 11pm. There's a $10 charge for checking in after 10pm. Smoking is not allowed inside.

1333 11th St. NW (btw. N and O sts.), Washington, DC 20001. ✆ **202/506-7106.** www.dclofty.com. 32 beds, 2 rooms with private bath. $28–$48/bed. DISC, MC, V.

Metro: Mount Vernon Square or Metrobus 64. **Amenities:** Free domestic long-distance; central AC; HDTV; DVD; VCR; Wi-Fi; computers w/Internet; kitchen; outdoor barbecue; free washer, dryer, detergent, softener, and dryer sheets. *In room:* Wi-Fi. *Available by request:* Hair dryer, iron, ironing board.

District Hotel   Guests' satisfaction with accommodations at the District Hotel depends a great deal on the attitude they take through the front door. If you remember that you chose this place because it's inexpensive, you'll probably be happy. Some rooms are quite small. Others can be noisy. But you get the basic amenities, including in-room phone, TV, Wi-Fi, hair dryer, and bath. Smoking is not allowed inside.

1440 Rhode Island Ave. NW (btw. 14th and 15th sts.), Washington, DC 20005. © **800/ 350-5759** or 202/232-7800. Fax 202/265-3725. www.districthotel.com. 58 units. $79–$179. Rates include continental breakfast. AE, DC, MC, V. Limited parking $20. Metro: Dupont Circle, or Metrobus 52, 53, or 54. *In room:* Window A/C, phone, TV, hair dryer, Wi-Fi. *Available by request:* Iron, ironing board.

7 Upper Northwest

Days Inn Connecticut Avenue   Chain hotels within Washington tend to price themselves out of cheapskate territory, but this Days Inn close to a Metro Station often has rooms below $100. There's nothing special here. It's a Days Inn. But it can be cheap, and it's a 10-minute Metro ride to Metro Center. This hotel is especially good for families with kids, because children younger than 18 stay with their parents for free. Smoking is not allowed.

4400 Connecticut Ave. NW (btw. Van Ness and Windom sts.), Washington, DC 20008. © **800/952-3060** or 202/244-5600. Fax 202/244-6794. www.dcdaysinn.com. 155 units. $69–$169 double. AE, DC, DISC, MC, V. Parking $22. Metro: Van Ness. **Amenities:** Restaurant; lounge; accessible and nonsmoking rooms available. *In room:* Central A/C, TV, phone, hair dryer, room service, Wi-Fi.

International Guest House   This hostel-like accommodation in a residential neighborhood is close to Carter Barron Amphitheater's free concerts, but not to much else. You'll need to walk half a block to 16th Street to catch a 20-minute bus ride Downtown, traffic permitting. Beds are just $35 each, however, and there's a good chance you'll meet some interesting young international travelers. There are two or three single beds in each of five rooms on the third floor. The men's bathroom is off the hall; women have to walk down to the second floor. In addition to the morning continental breakfast, you can take evening tea with cookies at 9pm. The guest house is a mission of the Mennonites of the Allegheny Conference, and that affects some of the rules. You can't consume alcohol on the property, and smoking isn't allowed inside. A bell rings at 7:20am to waken you for the 8am continental breakfast. From 10am to noon each day, rooms and bathrooms have to be vacated so they can be cleaned. You have to vacate the premises between 9am and 3pm Sunday so the staff can go to church. You have to be back inside by 11 each night.

1441 Kennedy St. NW (btw. 14th and 16th sts.), Washington, DC 20011. ✆ **202/726-5808.** Fax 202/882-2228. http://mysite.verizon.net/igh_dc. 12 beds, all with shared bath. $35 per person; children 6–12 half price; younger children $5. Rates include continental breakfast. V, MC. 3 free parking spaces. Metrobus S1, S2, S4, or S9. **Amenities:** Central A/C; TV; DVD; hair dryers in bathrooms; kitchenette; Wi-Fi.

8 U Street Corridor

Bed and Breakfast on U Street One innkeeper is Russian; the other has lived in Russia. So they've scattered Russian art around this town house on the edge of the U Street dining and nightlife district. The cheapest rooms here share a bath. Both have queen beds. One has an easy chair, the other a sofa. The rooms with private baths also have queen beds and start at $125 off season. One has an adjoining sitting room with a sofa bed. Smoking is not allowed inside.

U and 17th sts. NW, Washington, DC 20009. ✆ **877/893-3233** or 202/328-3510. Fax 413/582-9669. www.bedandbreakfastonustreet.com. 4 units, 2 with shared bath. $100–$225 double. 2- or 3-night stay usually required. Rates include continental breakfast. AE, DISC, MC, V. Limited parking $15. Metro: U St. or Metrobus S1, S2, S4, or S9. *In room:* Window A/C, TV, fridge, hair dryer, microwave, Wi-Fi.

Cardozo Guest House The innkeeper here has taken several steps to hold down his costs and therefore his prices, too. So what you'll find here is a clean and comfortable—as well as quite inexpensive—place to stay, just south of the U Street Metrorail Station. The inn is "self-hosted," which means the innkeeper drops by from time to time. You don't get breakfast or daily housekeeping. All but one of the rooms have a mini-fridge and coffeemaker, and there's a microwave for guest use. The least expensive room, which starts at $65, has a full-size four-poster bed. The bath, shared by three rooms, has a tub and shower. The other shared-bath units start at $75 and $85 and top out at $125. For $125 during the off season, you can rent a large room with king bed, TV, and an enormous private bath with Jacuzzi, walk-in shower, and twin sinks. In the basement apartment, you find a king brass bed, sofa, desk, dining table and chairs, kitchen, washer and dryer—for $100 off season, $195 tops. Children younger than 18 are not allowed. Smoking is not allowed.

T and 13th sts. NW, Washington, DC 20009. ℭ **877/893-3233** or 202/328-3510. Fax 413/582-9669. www.CardozoGuesthouse.com. 5 units, 3 with shared bath. $65–$195 double. 2- or 3-night stay usually required. AE, DISC, MC, V. Parking $15. Metro: U St. *In room:* A/C, TV, mini-fridge.

Meridian Manor   The cheapest rooms in this recently renovated 1885 brownstone have something the more expensive rooms don't: a view of the Capitol dome from their fourth floor windows. These rooms share a bath—with tub and shower—and a large common area with two sofa beds, tables, and chairs. When the innkeepers complete their planned rooftop deck, residents in these rooms will have the easiest access. The entire floor can be reserved as a suite that can sleep up to six guests. All rooms have queen beds; some have full sofa beds to accommodate additional guests. Meridian Manor also has a basement apartment with private entrance that includes a queen bed in the bedroom, a full-size sofa bed in the living/dining room, full kitchen, full bath, washer and dryer. You don't get daily housekeeping in the apartment, and you have to pay extra if you want breakfast. The apartment and the rooms with private baths cost as little as $125 off season. Smoking is not allowed inside.

16th and U sts. NW, Washington, DC 20009. ℭ **877/893-3233** or 202/328-3510. Fax 413/582-9669. www.MeridianManorDC.com. 7 units, 2 with shared bath. $100–$225 double. 2- or 3-night stay usually required. Rates include continental breakfast. AE, DISC, MC, V. Limited parking $15. Metro: U St., or Metrobus S1, S2, S4, or S9. **Amenities:** Central A/C. *In room:* TV, hair dryer, Wi-Fi.

13th Street Studio   This basement apartment, a block and a half south of the U Street Metrorail Station, is an incredible value in low season, with rates starting at $100. It was renovated in 2007, and has a queen bed, private bath with Jacuzzi and shower, kitchen, and a small table with two chairs. Guests also have access to a washer and dryer. Housekeeping is provided only between guests. The cleaning crew had just left when Tom visited, and the air smelled of too much Pine Sol. The apartment has a private entrance. Smoking is not allowed.

13th and T sts. NW, Washington, DC 20009. Ⓒ **877/893-3233** or 202/328-3510. Fax 413/582-9669. www.bedandbreakfastdc.com/index.php?id=26. 1 unit. $100–$195 double. 3-night stay usually required. Weekly and monthly rates available. Metro: U St. AE, DISC, MC, V. **Amenities:** A/C; TV; hair dryer; phone (local calls free); washer and dryer.

Ben's Chili Bowl: a historic (and delicious!) DC institution. See p. 88.

CHEAP EATS

S ay "Washington dining" to many people and they'll con-
jure images of fat-cat lobbyists savoring cigars after a three-
martini lunch of steak, lobster, and caviar. In reality, Washington is
full of modestly paid worker bees—congressional staffers, political
activists, clerks, bureaucrats, journalists—who seek out cheap restaurants when they aren't brown-bagging it. As a result, the city is full of
reasonably priced coffee shops, sandwich places, burger joints, pizza
parlors, carryouts, government cafeterias, and other cheap eateries.
As the Capital, Washington attracts residents from every state and
nation, and they bring a lot of cheap cuisine with them—whether it's
Texas barbecue or Asian noodles.

Smoker, Get Thee to a Hookah Bar!

By law, Washington's restaurants and bars now are smoke free, except for cigar and hookah bars. The ban also covers offices and the lobbies of hotels and apartment buildings. Many hotels designate nonsmoking rooms, as well.

We've surveyed the scene and what follows is a bouquet of restaurants where you can purchase main courses, including sandwiches, for less than 10 bucks. And you'll find them all over town. What you won't find in this book are Mickey D, cute l'il Wendy, or the slightly grotesque Burger King, although you can find plenty of those joints on your own should you want to.

We've also identified a handful of splurges, and what we call "cheap splurges," where it's worthwhile to bust the cheapskate budget we usually adhere to.

Prices listed at the end of the reviews are for dinner main courses, including sandwiches, unless the restaurant is not open for dinner.

1 Adams Morgan

Amsterdam Falafelshop *MIDDLE EASTERN/DUTCH* This place specializes in the delicious Middle Eastern croquettes in pita bread and twice-cooked Dutch-style fried potatoes. You place your order, then watch the balls of mashed chickpeas fry up crunchy on the outside and fluffy on the inside. You can choose white or whole wheat pita and select from 21 salad fixings, sauces, and pickles to top the sandwich. To spice the fries, you can have Dutch mayonnaise, peanut sauce, malt vinegar, Old Bay seasoning (a regional favorite), or ketchup.

2425 18th St. NW (btw. Belmont and Columbia roads). ☎ **202/234-1969.** www. falafelshop.com. Falafels $4–$5.70. Fries $2.75–$3.85. No credit cards. Sun–Mon 11am–midnight; Tues–Wed 11am–2:30am; Thurs 11am–3am; Fri 11am–4am. Circulator or Metrobus 96 from Woodley Park Metro.

Himalayan Heritage *NEPALESE/INDIAN* You've probably eaten Indian cuisine, but have you ever had Nepalese? The styles are similar, but the latter uses more preserved foods. Yak butter is another staple of the Nepalese diet, but it's easier to get olive oil in Washington, so that's what the Nepalese who run this attractive, comfortable place use. Main courses run up to $18 here, but the menu also offers

CHEAP EATS AROUND ADAMS MORGAN & DUPONT CIRCLE

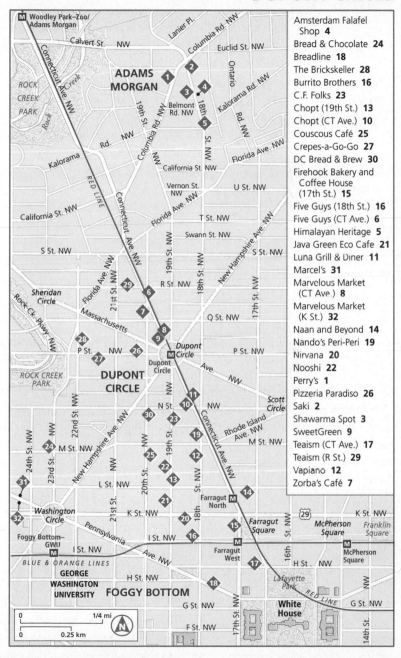

Amsterdam Falafel Shop **4**
Bread & Chocolate **24**
Breadline **18**
The Brickskeller **28**
Burrito Brothers **16**
C.F. Folks **23**
Chopt (19th St.) **13**
Chopt (CT Ave.) **10**
Couscous Café **25**
Crepes-a-Go-Go **27**
DC Bread & Brew **30**
Firehook Bakery and Coffee House (17th St.) **15**
Five Guys (18th St.) **16**
Five Guys (CT Ave.) **6**
Himalayan Heritage **5**
Java Green Eco Cafe **21**
Luna Grill & Diner **11**
Marcel's **31**
Marvelous Market (CT Ave.) **8**
Marvelous Market (K St.) **32**
Naan and Beyond **14**
Nando's Peri-Peri **19**
Nirvana **20**
Nooshi **22**
Perry's **1**
Pizzeria Paradiso **26**
Saki **2**
Shawarma Spot **3**
SweetGreen **9**
Teaism (CT Ave.) **17**
Teaism (R St.) **29**
Vapiano **12**
Zorba's Café **7**

lots of dishes for less than $10. Try the *momo*—dumplings stuffed with spiced chicken or vegetables, which cost $9 to $10. Also excellent is the $7.50 Gobi Manchurian—cauliflower in corn flour batter that's fried then dipped in a hot and sweet sauce. Fried vegetable samosa pastries go for $3.25 each.

2305 18th St. NW (at Kalorama Rd.) ℂ **202/483-9300.** www.himalayanheritageDC. com. $9–$18. MC, V. Sun–Thurs 11:30am–3pm and 5:30–11pm; Fri–Sat 11:30am– 3pm and 5:30–11:30pm. Circulator or Metrobus 96 from Woodley Park Metro.

Perry's *TAPAS/SUSHI* An Adams Morgan institution, Perry's has long been famous for its Sunday **brunch with drag queens** ($23; 10:30am–2:30pm). Recently it added tapas to its menu, which gives you lots of under-$10 small plates to choose from. Chef Jose Picazo previously cooked at Jaleo—the superb tapas restaurant run by superstar chef Jose Andres—so you know he's good. Among Picazo's best offerings: roasted sweet *piquillo* peppers stuffed with goat cheese and mushrooms, chorizo sausage with garlic mashed potatoes, and chicken croquettes. Perry's offers several seating options as well, among them a sushi bar, couches, and rooftop dining.

1811 Columbia Rd. NW (at Biltmore St.). ℂ **202/234-6218.** www.perrysadamsmorgan. com. Small plates $4–$14. AE, DC, DISC, MC, V. Sun–Thurs 5:30–10:30pm; Fri–Sat 5:30–11:30pm (brunch Sat 11am–3pm; Sun 10:30am–2:30pm). Circulator or Metrobus 96 from Woodley Park Metro.

Saki *SUSHI* The enormous menu in this small restaurant offers some cooked Japanese dishes as well as many sushi selections. You'll probably be more comfortable at the sushi bar than at the small and crowded tables. Prices for the rolls start at $4, and some prices are slashed in half between 5 and 7:30pm each day. Cooked offerings include a deep-friend tuna roll, tempura shrimp and lobster, and a deep-fried vegetable roll.

2477 18th St. NW (btw. Columbia and Belmont roads). ℂ **202/518-9820.** www. sakiasiangrille.com. Small plates $4–$12. AE, DISC, MC, V. Mon–Wed 5pm–midnight; Thurs 5pm–5am; Fri–Sat 5pm–3am. Circulator or Metrobus 96 from Woodley Park Metro.

Shawarma Spot *MIDDLE EASTERN* A shawarma sandwich is usually made with spiced, marinated lamb, but the Shawarma Spot substitutes beef or chicken in an attempt to appeal to the American palate. The meat is cooked on a vertical rotisserie, shaved into thin slices, and placed in a Middle Eastern bun. You then pick from a dozen toppings, such as hummus, grilled onions, and *baba ghanouj* (roasted eggplant, sesame seeds, lemon, and garlic). There's also a vegetarian version made with hummus, eggplant, and tomato. If you feel like a pizza, try *manakeesh*—thin crust topped with combinations of feta cheese, olive oil, tomato, ground beef, and other ingredients. For dessert, there's baklava or rice pudding. With one exception, even the platters cost less than $10.

2418 18th St. NW (btw. Columbia and Belmont roads). ✆ **202/332-3797.** www. shawarmaspot.com. $4–$13. AE, DISC, MC, V. Sun–Wed 11am–11pm; Thurs 11am–2am; Fri-Sat 11am-4am. Circulator or Metrobus 96 from Woodley Park Metro.

2 Capitol Hill

★ **Bagels and Baguettes** *AMERICAN*   The menu is large (eight kinds of egg sandwiches, for instance), and the prices are small at this crowded (because it's good) breakfast and lunch place. A plain bagel will set you back 90¢. Make that $2.05 with cream cheese. The plain egg sandwich is $2.75. Lunch items start at $3.20 for a baguette sandwich of avocado, sprouts, cream cheese, and tomato—one of Tom's favorite combinations. It's among a half-dozen veggie sandwiches offered, along with combinations of turkey, chicken, ham, bacon, tuna, corned beef, pastrami, and other meats and cheeses. Or you can opt for a salad. For dessert, how about an apple turnover for $1.70?

236 Massachusetts Ave. NE (btw. 2nd and 3rd sts.). ✆ **202/544-1141.** www.bagels andbaguettes.net. $2.75–$7. No credit cards. Mon–Fri 7am–4pm; Sat–Sun 8am–3pm. Metro: Union Station.

Billy Goat Tavern *AMERICAN*   This small, sleek, modern coffee shop and bar has none of the original's atmosphere and tradition (located underneath the Chicago streets, inspiration for the Saturday Night Live "cheezeborger cheezeborger" sketches, home of the goat that cursed the Cubs to perpetual futility). But two eggs, hash browns, and toast, served on paper plates with plastic flatware, set you back just $2.95. And you can add meat for a buck. At lunch, dinner, and late-night, most sandwiches go for less than $5. True to its Chicago roots, the Billy Goat stays open late when da Bears play on Sunday.

500 New Jersey Ave. NW (btw. E and F sts.). ✆ **202/783-2123.** www.billygoattavern. com. $2.95–$6.25. AE, DC, DISC, MC, V. Mon–Sat 7am–2am; Sun 7am–4pm. Metro: Union Station.

Bullfeathers *AMERICAN*   Because it stands a stone's throw from the House office buildings, Bullfeathers is a magnet for congressional staffers and the journalists who cover them, and that makes it an interesting spot for visitors to check out. Bar munchies—wings, quesadillas, spinach-and-artichoke dip, and so forth—cost $4 or less from 3:30 to 6:30pm, Monday through Saturday. From 4 to 8pm those days, various beers go for from $2.25 to $3.50, some wines and mixed drinks from $3 to $3.50, depending on the day. All day Saturday, all burgers are $5, Bloody Marys $3.50, and some beers cost $2.50 to $3.25. The restaurant says its name comes from Teddy Roosevelt's favorite euphemism, which is hurled about quite a bit around these parts.

410 1st St. SE (btw. D and E sts.). ℭ **202/543-5005.** www.bullfeatherscapitolhill.com. Salads and sandwiches $6–$13, full dinners $11–$25. AE, DC, DISC, MC, V. Mon–Sat 11:15am–midnight; Sun closed. Metro: Capitol South.

★ **Burrito Brothers** *TEX-MEX*   Enormous servings of very good Tex-Mex food at rock-bottom prices puts Burrito Brothers high on the list for hungry cheapskates. The smallest burrito—called the Little Brother—weighs in at 8 ounces. The Regular weighs a full pound and is more than enough to satisfy most normal appetites. For the seriously famished, the Big Daddy is 24 ounces of 14-inch rolled tortilla plus whatever you want to stuff into it. Despite their name, the Brothers also serve up tacos, quesadillas, fajitas, salads, combination platters, nachos, and a Tex-Mex breakfast. There's lots of meat on this menu, but also vegetarian and vegan options. The Little Brother goes for as little as $2.75, the Big Daddy for no more than $6.50. Tacos start at 2 bucks. For $3.25, you get two tacos with your choice of fillings, including beans, meat, cheese, and spinach.

205 Pennsylvania Ave. SE (btw. 2nd and 3rd sts.). ℭ **202/543-6835.** www.ourburrito brothers.com. $3.25–$9.50. AE, MC, V. Mon–Fri 10:30am–9pm; Sat 10:30am–8pm; Sun 10:30am–7pm. Metro: Capitol South. Also Downtown: 1825 I St. NW (downstairs in food court at 18th St.). ℭ **202/887-8266.** Mon–Fri 7am–5:30pm; Sat–Sun closed. Metro: Farragut West.

Firehook Bakery and Coffee House *AMERICAN*   One of seven Firehooks in the city (plus four more in Northern Virginia), this bakery features fresh-baked breads, cakes, and pastries, as well as locally roasted Quartermaine coffee (Tom's favorite). (According to ancient Egyptian hieroglyphics, the company's founders say, the baker was known as the "Fire Hook." The name came from the tool used to pull

CHEAP EATS ON CAPITOL HILL

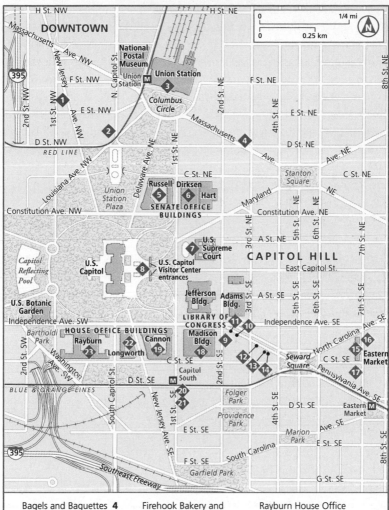

Bagels and Baguettes **4**
Billy Goat Tavern **1**
Bullfeathers **21**
Burrito Brothers **11**
Cannon House Office
  Building Cafeteria **19**
Capitol Visitor Center
  Restaurant **8**
Dirksen Senate Office
  Building Cafeteria **6**

Firehook Bakery and
  Coffee House **10**
Good Stuff Eatery **12**
Hawk 'n' Dove **13**
Library of Congress
  Cafeteria **18**
Longworth House Office
  Building Cafeteria **22**
Market Lunch **15**
Marvelous Market **17**
Pete's Diner **9**

Rayburn House Office
  Building **23**
Russell Senate Office
  Building Cafeteria **5**
Supreme Court Cafeteria **7**
Taqueria Nacional **2**
Tortilla Café **16**
Tortilla Coast **20**
Tune Inn **14**
Union Station Food Court **3**

Eating with the Insiders

Cynics may find this hard to believe, but members of Congress and their aides tend to work pretty hard. More often than not, they grab lunch in a hurry in the building in which they work. You'll find that Capitol Hill is full of government cafeterias, most of which are open to the public. This is not gourmet dining, but the government restaurants tend to offer pretty good prices for pretty decent food. Here's where you can eat, if you'd like.

The **Capitol Visitor Center Restaurant** is the one congressional eatery that's designed specifically for the public. It's open Monday through Saturday from 8:30am till 4pm in the lower level of the center. Breakfast fare includes pastries, cereal, fruit, eggs, and breakfast meats and costs from $1.25 to $3.75. The large lunch menu includes burgers, hot dogs, sandwiches, barbecue, pasta, pizza, and salads that cost from $3.50 (a hot dog) to $11 (shrimp Cobb salad). You enter the visitor center from the Capitol plaza near 1st and East Capitol streets.

You might run into a justice if you eat at the **Supreme Court Cafeteria** (1 1st St. NE at Maryland Ave.), which is open Monday through Friday from 7:30 till 10:30am and 11:30am till 2pm. The court also has a **snack bar** that's open Monday through Friday from 10:30am to 3:30pm.

The **cafeteria** in the **Rayburn House Office Building** (entrances near the intersection of South Capitol St. and Independence Ave.) is

the pots filled with baked breads out of the oven.) The breads can be stuffed with various ingredients to become good, fat sandwiches.

215 Pennsylvania SE (btw. 2nd and 3rd sts.). ✆ **202/544-7003.** www.firehook.com. Most sandwiches about $6; salads $3–$7. AE, MC, V. Mon–Fri 6:30am–7pm; Sat–Sun 7am–5pm. Metro: Capitol South. Downtown: 555 13th St. NW (btw. E and F sts.). ✆ **202/393-0952.** Mon–Fri 6:30am–6:30pm; Sat–Sun closed. Metro: Metro Center. Downtown: 912 17th St. NW (btw. I and K sts.). ✆ **202/429-2253.** Mon–Fri 6:30am–7pm; Sat–Sun closed. Metro: Farragut North. Judiciary Square: 441 4th St. NW (btw. D and E sts.). ✆ **202/347-1760.** Mon–Fri 6:30am–6pm; Sat–Sun closed. Metro: Judiciary Square. Judiciary Square: 401 F St. NW (btw. 4th and 5th sts., in the National Bldg. Museum). ✆ **202/628-0906.** Mon–Fri 8:30am–4:30pm; Sat 10am–4:30pm; Sun 11am–4:30pm. Metro: Judiciary Square.

open Monday through Friday from 7:30am to 2:30pm. The Rayburn **Pizza Plus** is open those days 11am to 7pm.

You can eat in the **cafeteria** at the **Longworth House Office Building** (at New Jersey and Independence aves. SE) Monday through Friday 7:30am to 2:30pm, and get food at the **Longworth Carryout** Monday through Friday 7:30am to 4pm.

The **Cannon House Office Building** (across New Jersey Ave. from Longworth) has a **carryout** that's open Monday to Friday 8am to 4pm, and a **Pizza Plus** open those days 11am to 7pm.

On the Senate side of the Hill, the **Dirksen Office Building** (entrances on 1st St. NE at C St. and Constitution Ave.) has a **dining room** open Monday through Friday from 7:30am till 3:30pm, and a **buffet** open Monday through Friday 11:30am to 2:30pm.

The **coffee shop** in the **Senate Russell Office Building** (across 1st St. from Dirksen) is open Monday through Friday 7:30am to 4pm.

The **Library of Congress Cafeteria** is in the Madison Building on Independence Avenue SE, between 1st and 2nd streets. It's open Monday through Friday 12:30 to 2pm.

FINE PRINT Be warned that federal workers get first crack at federal food. Outsiders may be turned away if a dining spot gets especially crowded between 11:45am and 1:15pm.

★ **Good Stuff Eatery** *AMERICAN*   The pedigree of this burger joint is spectacular. On one hand, it's a mom-and-pop eatery run by Mom and Pop Mendelsohn and others of their family. On the other, their son Spike—the owner and chef—has the credentials to be fronting a multi-star, expensive, white-tablecloth spot. Spike graduated from the Culinary Institute of America, apprenticed with well-regarded chefs in France, California, and New York, spent some time learning Vietnamese cuisine in Vietnam, was a "Top Chef" contestant, has his own Food Network 2 show, and in 2009 buried the competition at the South Beach (Florida) Food & Wine Festival Burger Bash. Michelle Obama brought Malia and Sasha to taste Spike's burgers, fries, and shakes. And, oh, the chef is just approaching his 30th birthday. You'll probably want to try the Colletti's Smokehouse burger, which won the South Beach competition. It's topped with applewood bacon, sharp cheddar cheese, fried Vidalia onion rings, and chipotle barbecue sauce for $6.70. The Blazin' Barn is the Vietnamese-inspired offering. Our daughter, Julie, a vegetarian, loves the portobello mushroom burger stuffed with cheese. You also can get wedge salads of iceberg lettuce and various toppings and good shakes and floats. Yuengling and Blue Moon are on tap for $3.50 and $4.50, Sam Adams and Red Stripe in bottles for $4. FINE PRINT This popular place can be a zoo at mealtime. You order at the counter, then find a table, which can be a challenge when the line at the counter is long and all the tables are occupied.

303 Pennsylvania Ave. SE (at 3rd St.). ℂ **202/543-8222.** www.goodstuffeatery.com. $5.50–$7.70. AE, DC, MC, V. Mon–Sat 11:30am–11pm. Sun closed. Metro: Capitol South.

Hawk 'n' Dove *AMERICAN*   Hawks and doves, and Republicans and Democrats, are supposed to be able to eat and drink together—or at least in the same building—at this longtime hangout for Hill workers and residents. Historical political figures hang from the walls—or at least their portraits do. The decor includes old church pews and stained glass windows. During nice weather, you can eat at the sidewalk cafe. Late risers can get full breakfast from 10 to 11:30am for less than $7. Breakfast for night owls is served after 9pm. Most soups, salads, and sandwiches cost less than $10. A veggie sandwich goes for $5.95. Full dinners run from $10 to $20. There's a Sunday brunch from 10:30am to 3:30pm. You can buy some beers and rail drinks for 2 bucks from 4 to 7pm Monday through Friday, and there are other drink and food specials every day.

329 Pennsylvania Ave. SE (btw. 3rd and 4th sts.). ℂ **202/543-3300.** www.hawkand doveonline.com. $5.50–$20. AE, DC, DISC, MC, V. Sun–Thurs 10am–2am; Fri–Sat 10am–3am. Metro: Capitol South.

Market Lunch *AMERICAN*   Washington almost lost this beloved institution when fire gutted Eastern Market in 2007. But the market's rebuilt, Market Lunch is reopened, and all's well on Capitol Hill. Be warned that this is a *very* popular place, and you'll probably have to stand in line for a stool at the communal table around mealtimes. In the morning, regulars probably are waiting for the buckwheat-blueberry pancakes

($5.45) or The Brick ($4.25), a big sandwich of egg, potato, cheese, and bacon. Later, they may have their eyes on the deep-fried crab cakes, the only thing on the menu that costs more than $10.

225 7th St. SE (btw. North Carolina Ave. and C St.). ℂ **202/544-0083.** $3–$11. AE, DC, MC, V. Wed–Fri 7:30am–2:30pm; Sat 8am–3pm; Sun 9am–3pm. Metro: Eastern Market.

★ **Marvelous Market** *AMERICAN*   If the weather's nice, the best thing to do here is to grab a sandwich and beverage and head for the shady sidewalk cafe. Marvelous Market started as a high-quality bakery, and the bread contributes more than its share of tastiness to the good sandwiches. They start at about six bucks. For $9, you get a sandwich, chips, and beverage. Also available: soup, salad, cookies, croissants, and cheese. Everything is made fresh that day (well, not the cheese), and what isn't sold is donated to food banks, shelters, and other charities.

303 7th St. SE (at C St.). ℂ **202/544-7127.** www.marvelousmarket.com. $6–$9. AE, MC, V. Mon–Sat 7am–9pm; Sun 8am–7pm. Metro: Eastern Market. Dupont Circle: 1511 Connecticut Ave. NW (btw. Massachusetts Ave. and Q St.) ℂ **202/332-3690.** Mon–Fri 8am–8:30pm; Sat 8:30am–8:30pm; Sun 8:30am–7pm. Metro: Dupont Circle. West End: 2424 Pennsylvania Ave. NW. ℂ **202/293-0049.** Daily 7am–9pm. Metro: Foggy Bottom. Georgetown: 3217 P St. NW (at Wisconsin Ave.). ℂ **202/333-2591.** Sun–Thurs 7am–8pm; Fri–Sat 7am–10pm. Circulator or Metrobus 31, 32, or 36.

Pete's Diner *AMERICAN*   This small, crowded, popular spot is short on decor but long on value. Its regulars include congressional staffers, Hill residents, blue-collar workers, and even the occasional member of Congress. They come for traditional diner fare at rock-bottom prices. Full breakfasts can be had for less than five bucks. Ditto the sandwiches. Even full meals—turkey, roast beef, or steak with mashed potatoes, vegetables, and bread—are just $7.95. In nice weather you can eat on the patio out front.

212 2nd St. SE (btw. Pennsylvania Ave. and C St.). ℂ **202/544-7335.** $2.50–$7.95. No credit cards. Mon–Fri 5am–3pm; Sat–Sun 6am–3pm. Metro: Capitol South.

Taqueria Nacional *MEXICAN*   Chef Ann Cashion's cooking has many influences. A Mississippi native, she worked in Italy, France, and California before settling into DC, where she rose to prominence at Cashion's Eat Place, an American restaurant with hints of the South. When she left Eat Place, her primary stage became Johnny's Half Shell, a seafood spot named for her partner John Fulchino. Neither of those restaurants makes a dirt-cheap list, but Cashion and Fulchino's latest endeavor, Taqueria Nacional, does. Small soft tacos—starting at $1.75—are the signature items at this carryout (plenty of park benches nearby). But there's also a daily *"Plato Tipico Americano"* special—cheeseburger or pot pie, for example. In the morning, you can get breakfast tacos (egg, cheese, bacon, sausage), scrambled eggs, or waffles. The tacos are small so you probably should order two.

400 N. Capitol St. NW (btw. Louisiana Ave. and E St.). ℭ **202/737-7070.** www.taqueria national.com. $1.75–$7.25. AE, MC, V. Mon–Fri 7–9am and 11am–3pm. Metro: Union Station.

Tortilla Cafe *MEXICAN/SALVADORAN*   *Pupusas*—handmade corn tortillas filled with pork and/or cheese—are the stars here. But the large menu is filled with other Latin American and U.S. dishes, most under $6. The tacos and tamales are especially worth tasting. You can also get a hamburger, cheeseburger, chicken wrap, Caesar salad—even a Philly cheese steak. Breakfast runs from a sausage burrito to omelets and pancakes.

210 7th St. SE (btw. Independence Ave. and C St.). ℭ **202/547-5700.** $1.65–$8.25. AE, MC, V. Mon–Fri 10am–7pm; Sat–Sun 7am–7pm. Metro: Eastern Market.

Tortilla Coast *TEX-MEX*   This is another hangout for congressional staffers (primarily Republicans), even closer to the House office buildings than Bullfeathers. The menu features typical, good Tex-Mex fare, many items under $10. Monday nights, enchiladas go for $8. Same for burritos on Tuesday nights. All day Saturday gets you all the chicken fajitas you can eat for $11.

400 1st St. SE (at D St.). ℭ **202/546-6768.** www.tortillacoast.com. $8–$15. AE, MC, V. Mon–Wed 11:30am–10pm; Thurs–Fri 11:30am–11pm; Sat 11:30am–10pm; Sun 11am–9pm. Metro: Capitol South.

Tune Inn *AMERICAN*   Somewhat inexplicably, this dive has attracted so many Hill denizens for so long that it's become an institution. They like the prices and they like the food, and even members of Congress make an occasional appearance. Try the Buffalo wings, omelets, burgers, or fries. Go with friends, buy a pitcher of beer, and feel you're part of the in-crowd.

331½ Pennsylvania Ave. SE (btw. 3rd and 4th sts.). ℭ **202/543-2725.** $3.50–$9.50. AE, DC, DISC, MC, V. Daily 8am–1am. Metro: Capitol South.

Food Court Grazing

The lower-level **food court at Union Station** isn't as big and diverse as it used to be, perhaps a victim of the Great Recession of 2008 and beyond. But it's still larger and more diverse than most. You'll see national chains, but also branches of local restaurants. The wide range of cuisines includes Greek, Indian, Italian, Asian, Cajun, sushi, and barbecue, as well as sandwiches, fries, ice cream, cookies, pasta, salads, donuts, and smoothies. If that doesn't satisfy you, you can take the escalator up to the next level, where other eateries—from fast-food stands to full-service restaurants—are scattered among the train gates and boutiques. They tend to be open Monday to Saturday from 10am to 9pm, and Sunday from noon to 6pm.

Diversity also is the hallmark of the food court in the lower level of **International Square** Downtown. Two of Washington's best, inexpensive fast-food operations are here: **Five Guys** hamburgers (p. 68) and the **Burrito Brothers** (p. 60). Among the cuisines at the other stands here are Greek, Italian, Cajun, Cuban, Chinese, and sushi. You'll also find a cafeteria with hot food in warming trays, and counters selling sandwiches and other standard lunch fare. The food stands tend to be open during standard office hours, some opening as early as 6:30am, some closing at 6pm. You can enter the food court at 18th and I streets or 19th and K streets NW.

3 Downtown

In addition to the restaurants reviewed below, you'll find two branches of eateries reviewed in other sections. Look for the downtown branches of **Burrito Brothers** (p. 60) and **Firehook Bakery** (p. 60).

Breadline *AMERICAN* Creative sandwiches and delicious soups lead large numbers of downtown office workers—including White House staffers—to get in the Breadline every day. If you've got a flexible schedule, come early or late to avoid the worst of the crowd. If you're adventurous, try the prosciutto, mascarpone, gorgonzola, and fig jam on walnut bread. If you're not, order the turkey sandwich, which is roasted fresh here every day. Breadline also bakes its own bread. Most sandwiches cost $7.55. Add a cuppa soup and you're out $10. You also can choose from pizzas and salads. Breadline serves up muffins, French toast, and more at breakfast.

1751 Pennsylvania Ave. NW (btw. 17th and 18th sts.). ℂ **202/822-8900.** www.the breadlineDCblogspot.com. $6.60–$8.40. AE, MC, V. Mon–Fri 7:30am–3:30pm; Sat–Sun closed. Metro: Farragut West.

Chopt *AMERICAN* The latest Washington dining trend seems to be restaurants devoted to salads. This one's an import from New York that has opened four DC branches, and promises more. You can order what co-owner Tony Shure calls "chef-designed" salads or "salad sandwiches"—the "kabob Cobb," for instance: grilled chicken, feta cheese, red onions, peppers, romaine lettuce, and pita chips. Or you can build your own from a lengthy list of ingredients. Start by choosing from five kinds of greens. Add from a list of about 60 "choppings"—meats, veggies, eggs, cheeses, croutons, and so on and on. Then pick from 30 dressings. Pricing is a bit complicated. The chef-designed salads and sandwiches cost between $5.50 and $9. The basic build-your-own version—greens plus four choppings—costs less than $6. The bill rises as you add more stuff.

1105½ 19th St. NW. (at L St.). ℂ **202/55-0665.** www.choptsalad.com. Most salads and sandwiches $5.50 and $9. AE, MC, V. Mon–Fri 10:30am–9pm; Sat 11am–5pm; Sun closed. Metro: Farragut North. Also: 618 12th St. NW (btw. F and G sts.). ℂ **202/ 783-0007.** Mon–Fri 10:30am–9pm; Sat 11am–6pm; Sun noon–5pm. Metro: Metro Center. Dupont Circle: 1300 Connecticut Ave. NW (at N St.). ℂ **202/327-2255.** Mon–Fri 10:30am–9pm; Sat 11am–7pm; Sun closed. Metro: Dupont Circle. Penn Quarter: 730 7th St. NW (btw. G and H sts.). ℂ **202/347-3225.** Mon–Thurs 10:30am–10pm; Fri 10:30am–11pm; Sat 11am–11pm; Sun 11am–9pm. Metro: Gallery Place.

★ **Five Guys** *AMERICAN* Already widely regarded as the Washington area's best hamburger joint, Five Guys got additional boosts when Barack and Michelle Obama paid visits to Five Guys early in his presidency. The president's excursion got extra attention because he's the president, of course, but also because he dragged NBC News anchor Brian Williams along while Williams was taping a "day-at-the-White-House" special. The burger run got prominent display when the program aired. You get lots of choices of toppings here, and the president chose cheese, jalapeños, tomatoes, and mustard. The burgers are juicy and tasty—made from fresh beef grilled to order—and well

CHEAP EATS ON U STREET, DOWNTOWN, PENN QUARTER & THE MALL

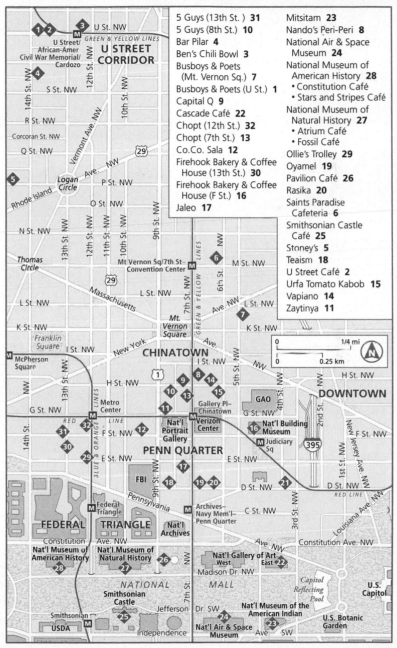

5 Guys (13th St.) **31**
5 Guys (8th St.) **10**
Bar Pilar **4**
Ben's Chili Bowl **3**
Busboys & Poets
  (Mt. Vernon Sq.) **7**
Busboys & Poets (U St.) **1**
Capital Q **9**
Cascade Café **22**
Chopt (12th St.) **32**
Chopt (7th St.) **13**
Co.Co. Sala **12**
Firehook Bakery & Coffee
  House (13th St.) **30**
Firehook Bakery & Coffee
  House (F St.) **16**
Jaleo **17**

Mitsitam **23**
Nando's Peri-Peri **8**
National Air & Space
  Museum **24**
National Museum of
  American History **28**
• Constitution Café
• Stars and Stripes Café
National Museum of
  Natural History **27**
• Atrium Café
• Fossil Café
Ollie's Trolley **29**
Oyamel **19**
Pavilion Café **26**
Rasika **20**
Saints Paradise
  Cafeteria **6**
Smithsonian Castle
  Café **25**
Stoney's **5**
Teaism **18**
U Street Café **2**
Urfa Tomato Kabob **15**
Vapiano **14**
Zaytinya **11**

priced. Founded in Arlington, VA, in 1986, Five Guys now counts more than 450 spots in more than 30 states.

1825 I St. NW (downstairs in food court at 18th St.). ℭ **202/223-2737.** www.fiveguys.com. $3.70–$6.40. AE, DC, MC, V. Mon–Fri 10am–5pm; Sat–Sun closed. Metro: Farragut West. Also at 13th and F sts. NW (in the Shops at National Place). ℭ **202/393-2135.** Mon–Sat 11am–6pm; Sun closed. Metro: Metro Center. Dupont Circle: 1645 Connecticut Ave. NW (btw. Q and R sts.). ℭ **202/328-3483.** Daily 11am–11pm. Metro: Dupont Circle. Georgetown: 1335 Wisconsin Ave. NW (at Dumbarton St.). ℭ **202/337-0400.** Sun–Thurs 11am–11pm; Fri–Sat 11am–4am. Circulator or Metrobus 31, 32, or 36. Penn Quarter: 808 H St. NW (btw. 8th and 9th sts.). Metro: Gallery Place.

Java Green Eco Cafe *VEGETARIAN/KOREAN*　Green doesn't refer to the color of the coffee served here but to this popular vegetarian restaurant's ecofriendliness and kindness toward animals. Many restaurants bask in praise from local food critics. This place boasts certification by People for the Ethical Treatment of Animals as the "Most Progressive Restaurant" of 2008. Its food is organic, vegetarian, and fair trade. It purchases wind power and uses biodegradable materials in takeout containers. Most sandwiches, salads and soups are $8 to $9. But you can get California *gimbob*—Korean sushi made of rice, soy chicken, avocado, asparagus and seaweed—for $5. It's best to come here early or late to avoid the big lunchtime crowds.

1020 19th St. NW (btw. K and L sts.). ℭ **202/775-8899.** www.javagreencafe.com. $5–$9. V, MC. Mon–Tues 9am–8:30pm; Wed–Fri 9am–9pm; Sat 10am–6pm. Sun closed. Metro: Farragut North or West.

Naan and Beyond *INDIAN*　Sandwiches on India's *naan* flatbread are what bring lots of downtown office workers to this carryout, but it offers a few dinnerlike entrees as well. Try the tandoori tikka sandwiches—chunks of chicken or lamb cooked in a clay tandoor oven—for less than $7. You can get half a tandoori chicken dinner with salad and naan for $7. A platter with one meat, one vegetable, rice, and naan costs $7.25. The restaurant also offers a few vegetarian items.

1710 L. St. NW (at 17th St.). ℭ **202/466-6404.** www.naan-and-beyond.com. $5–$12. AE, MC, V. Mon–Fri 11am–9pm; Sat 11am–5pm; Sun closed. Metro: Farragut North. 1331 Pennsylvania Ave. NW (btw. 13th and 14th sts.). ℭ **202/737-0890.** Mon–Fri 10:30am–7:30pm; Sat 10am–5pm; Sun closed. Metro: Metro Center.

Nirvana *INDIAN/VEGETARIAN*　The menu here is portrayed as the food equivalent of Buddhists' quest for Nirvana along the Eightfold Path. The steps along the Buddhist's path are described as right views, right intent, right speech, right conduct, and so forth. The restaurant's menu contains such headings as right nectars (beverages), right foundation (rice dishes), and blissful end (desserts). More important for the seeker of food, the cooking is quite good. And much of the menu can be had for less than $10.

1810 K St. NW (btw. 18th and 19th sts.). ℭ **202/223-5043.** www.dcnirvana.com. $8–$11. AE, MC, V. Mon–Thurs 11:30am–3:00pm and 5–9pm; Fri–Sat 11:30am–3pm and 5–10pm; Sun 5–9pm. Metro: Farragut West.

Nooshi *ASIAN*   The odd name here stems from the popular Oodles Noodles noodle house adding sushi to its menu. Specialties now are an interesting collection of Pan-Asian noodle dishes as well as an extensive and well-priced sushi selection. In addition, you can order traditional Asian appetizers (spring rolls, wontons), soups, salads, and grilled dishes. This is another place to hit early before nearby office workers grab all the tables at lunch.

1120 19th St. NW (btw. L and M sts.). ℭ **202/293-3138.** www.nooshidc.com. Sushi $2–$12; other dishes $6–$19. AE, MC, V. Mon–Sat 11:30am–11pm; Sun 5–10pm. Metro: Farragut North.

Ollie's Trolley *AMERICAN*   In the family- and budget-friendly Hotel Harrington, Ollie's Trolley offers traditional diner fare at bargain prices. Hamburgers start at $4.30. Platters with fries and beverage are less than $10. Milkshakes start at $2.75. At breakfast, two eggs, sausage or bacon, home fries and toast will set you back $5. You'll pay less for pancakes, French toast, or waffles with breakfast meat. In nice weather, you can sit at sidewalk tables.

425 12th St. NW (at E St.). ℭ **202/347-6119.** www.olliestrolleydc.com. $3.25–$10. AE, DISC, MC, V. Mon–Thurs 8am–9pm; Fri 8am–10pm; Sat 9am–10pm; Sun 10am–8pm; (winter hours sometimes shorter). Metro: Metro Center.

★ **Teaism** *ASIAN/AMERICAN*   Choices can drive you mad at this local chain of Asian teahouses with many twists. First there are the 30 or so teas. Then there are the breakfasts, which can range from a sourdough waffle with maple syrup for $5.75 to scrambled tofu with cilantro for $6. Bento boxes—the Japanese fast-food and carryout specialty—are featured at $8.75; try the teriyaki salmon with cucumber-ginger salad, edamame, and rice. Teaism also will sell you a buffalo burger on wheat focaccia with Asian slaw, or a turkey-and-brie sandwich with apple-cranberry chutney and mustard on French bread. Beyond tea, beverages include such creative offerings as ginger limeade and a chai shake with cinnamon gelato. Menus can vary from location to location. Only the Penn Quarter Teaism serves alcohol.

800 Connecticut Ave. NW (at H St.). 🕿 **202/835-2233.** www.teaism.com. $4.50–$9.50. DISC, MC, V. Mon–Fri 7:30am–5:30pm; Sat–Sun closed. Metro: Farragut West. Dupont Circle at 2009 R St. NW (west of Connecticut Ave.). 🕿 **202/667-3827.** Mon–Thurs 8am–10pm; Fri 8am–11pm; Sat 9am–11pm; Sun 9am–10pm. Metro: Dupont Circle. Penn Quarter at 400 8th St. NW (at D St.). 🕿 **202/638-6010.** Mon–Fri 7:30am–10pm; Sat–Sun 9:30am–9pm. Metro: Archives.

4 Dupont Circle

To find the restaurants reviewed below, see the map on p. 57.

Also in Dupont Circle, look for branches of the following places: **Chopt** (p. 68), **Five Guys** (p. 68), **Marvelous Market** (p. 65), and **Teaism** (p. 71).

The Brickskeller *AMERICAN*　The draw here is the beer. The Brickskeller claims to have more than 1,000 kinds here—from Abita Amber of Louisiana to Zywiec of Poland. But the food is surprisingly good and well priced. The fish and chips are crispy and tasty, come with coleslaw and cost $7.95. The juicy burgers with fries are excellent choices for less than $8. A half-dozen other sandwiches-plus-sides are similarly priced. You can get an enormous pile of onion rings for $4.75. The decor here is college pub—red brick walls, red-and-white checkered tablecloths, beer cans and bottles as a primary decorating motif.

1523 22nd St. NW (btw. P and Q sts.). 🕿 **202/293-1885.** www.lovethebeer.com/brickskeller.html. $7–$16. AE, MC, V. Sun 6pm–2am; Mon–Tues 5pm–2am; Wed–Thurs 11:30am–2am; Fri 11:30am–3am; Sat 6pm–3am. Metro: Dupont Circle.

★ **C.F. Folks** *AMERICAN*　This tiny restaurant and carryout is one of Susan's favorites. Partly it's the view: When you sit at one of the outside tables, you can watch the rich and powerful troop into the Palm steakhouse next door, where they will pay a great deal more for their lunch than you will. But mostly it's the excellent food. C.F. (the last initials of owners Art Carlson and Peggy Fredricksen) serves good sandwiches, soups, and salads for $6.25 to $8.25 every day. Chef George Vetsch worked at several DC restaurants before settling here, and his daily specials run a gamut of cuisines—red beans and rice one day, veal Marsala another, cabbage rolls yet another.

1225 19th St. NW (btw. M & N sts.). 🕿 **202/293-0162.** www.cffolksrestaurant.com. $6.25–$14. AE, DC, DISC, MC, V. Mon–Fri 11:30am–2:15pm. Sat–Sun closed. Metro: Dupont Circle.

Couscous Café *MIDDLE EASTERN/MOROCCAN*   The North African and Middle Eastern dishes found here—along with some American standards—let you eat cheap at breakfast lunch and dinner. Breakfast sandwiches run from $4 to $5. At lunch and dinner, soups, salads, and sandwiches—including platters—cost $3 to $7. Only one entrée tops $9. Among the best offerings are lamb cubes skewered and broiled with green peppers and tomatoes and served on rice; saffron chicken tajine with green olives served on basmati rice; and roasted spiced chicken rolled in phyllo with sweet almond paste. You also can get such American standbys as Caesar and tuna salads. Baklava for a buck makes for a sweet ending.

1195 20th St. NW (at M St.). ℂ **202/689-1233.** www.couscouscatering.com. $4–$11. AE, MC, V. Mon–Fri 8am–9pm. Metro: Dupont Circle.

★ **Crepes-a-Go-Go** *CREPES*   This small, modern cafe traces its origins to a Paris creperie "many years ago." Washington is its newest U.S. location, after spots in California and Maryland. The DC venue has eight small tables inside, a stand-up counter, and four tables outside. French music serenades you. One crepe with savory filling— avocado, tomatoes, and feta cheese, for instance, or chicken, bell pepper, tomatoes, garlic, and onions—will satisfy most appetites. Crepes-a-Go-Go lists 52 sweet and 22 savory crepes on its menu. The savory number really is higher, because you can choose among cheeses.

2122 P St. NW (btw. 21st and 22nd sts.). ℂ **202/955-5655.** www.crepes-a-gogo.com. $4–$8.50. DISC, MC, V. Mon–Thurs 8am–10pm; Fri–Sat 8am–midnight; Sun 8am–8pm. Metro: Dupont Circle.

DC Bread & Brew *AMERICAN*   Fresh and natural are the watchwords at this cafe and craft-beer bar. Dairy, meat, eggs, and vegetables come from nearby farms. Bread & Brew's cooks roast meats in-house each day, and make soups, prepare stocks, and bake pastries here. Takeout orders are served in biodegradable containers, with biodegradable plates, flatware, napkins, and cups. Vegetarians, vegans, and bargain-hunters will be happy here. The food is good and inexpensive. Most soups on the changing menu are $4, most quiches $7. A combination of soup and sandwich, sandwich and salad, or salad and soup goes for $7.50.

1247 20th St. NW (btw. M and N sts.). ℂ **202/466-2676.** www.breadandbrew.com. $7–$14. AE, MC, V. Mon–Fri 7am–midnight; Sat–Sun 9am–2am. Metro: Dupont Circle.

Luna Grill & Diner *AMERICAN*   One of Luna's distinguishing charac-
teristics is that its Blue Plate Special is accompanied by a Green Plate
Special for vegetarians. The Green Plate usually—and the Blue Plate
sometimes—costs less than $10. The Green Plate might be eggplant
parmigiana, wild mushroom ravioli, or a taco salad with vegetarian
chili. The Blue Plate is likely to be comfort food—fried chicken with
mashed potatoes and broccoli, for instance, or beef Stroganoff. Burgers
and other sandwiches come in under $10. Breakfast may be the best
time to eat here. You can get two eggs with home fries or grits for
$4.95. Pancakes, French toast, and waffles cost $5.95—with eggs
$7.95, with eggs and meat $9.95. The menus and the whimsical murals
are kid friendly. There's an easy-to-overlook outdoor dining area out
the back door. This is another place that fills up fast at lunchtime.

1301 Connecticut Ave. NW (at N St.). ℂ **202/835-2280.** www.lunagrillanddiner.com.
$6–$18. AE, DISC, MC, V. Sun–Thurs 8am–11pm; Fri–Sat 8am–midnight. Metro:
Dupont Circle.

Nando's Peri-Peri *PORTUGUESE*   According to Nando's, Africans
taught Portuguese explorers how to make this marinated and grilled
chicken dish, and the Europeans made it their own. The chicken is
marinated for 24 hours, and then cooked to order over an open flame.
You pick your level of spiciness—mild to extra hot, which the menu
warns is "highly combustible" and for "daredevils only." You can get
a quarter chicken for $4.95, a half for $7.95. Sides—fries, rice, coleslaw, corn, garlic bread, mashed potatoes—raise the price by $1.90
for one, $3.70 for two. The chicken also is available on sandwiches,
and Nando's offers salads as well.

1210 18th St. NW (btw. M St. and Jefferson Pl.). ℂ **202/621-8600.** www.nandosperi
peri.com. $4.95–$11. AE, DISC, MC, V. Sun–Thurs 11:30am–10pm; Fri–Sat 11:30am–
11pm. Metro: Dupont Circle. Penn Quarter at 819 7th St. NW (btw. H and I sts.). ℂ **202/
898-1225.** Sun–Thurs 11:30am–10pm; Fri–Sat 11:30am–11pm. Metro: Gallery Place.

★ **Pizzeria Paradiso** *PIZZA*   The wood-burning oven here turns out
excellent pizza prepared in the traditional Neapolitan manner. You
can top the light, thin crust—baked at 650°—with whatever you
want. For the taste of classic Neapolitan pizza, order the Margherita,
which comes with tomato, basil, and mozzarella cheese. The Atom-
ica is spicy, thanks to hot pepper flakes combined with the tomato,
salami, black olives, and mozzarella. Paradiso also serves sandwiches, salads, and desserts. Pizza prices range from $9.95 for the
8-inch Paradiso (tomato and mozzarella) to $19 for the 12-inch,

10-topping Siciliana. Salads and sandwiches cost $5.25 to $12. In the Georgetown Paradiso's basement, dubbed Birreria Paradiso, you can select among 80 bottled beers and 16 on tap.

2003 P St. NW (west of 20th St.). ✆ **202/223-1245.** www.eatyourpizza.com. $5.25–$19. DISC, MC, V. Mon–Thurs 11:30am–11pm. Fri–Sat 11:30am–midnight. Sun noon–10pm. Metro: Dupont Circle. Georgetown: 3282 M St. NW (btw. Potomac and 33rd sts.). ✆ **202/337-1245.** Metro: Georgetown. Connection bus from Dupont Circle or Rosslyn Metrorail station, or Metrobus D5 or 38B.

SweetGreen *AMERICAN*   Good for you and good for the environment is the message at this salads-wraps-and-yogurt spot. The menu features fresh, organic, and healthy ingredients. The walls, floor, and ceiling are built with reclaimed lumber from a Virginia barn. The lumber for the communal tables and stools comes from an old bowling alley. The food containers and utensils are made from recycled products and are recyclable themselves. You can order "chef-crafted" salads, or design your own mix. The chef-designed salads cost $8 to $9. The design-your-own start at $6 for greens, three add-on veggies, and one crunch item. Add more and you pay more.

1512 Connecticut Ave. NW (north of Dupont Circle). ✆ **202/387-9338.** www.sweet green.com. $6–$9. Daily 11am–10pm. Metro: Dupont Circle. Georgetown: 3333 M St. NW (btw. 34th St. and Bank Alley). ✆ **202/337-9338.** Mon–Fri 11am–10pm; Sat–Sun noon–10pm. Georgetown Metro Connection bus from Dupont Circle or Rosslyn Metrorail station, or Metrobus D5 or 38B.

Vapiano *ITALIAN*   Try to wrap your mind around this concept: an Italian restaurant created by a German McDonald's maven that offers traditional pizzas, pastas, and salads, along with a few creative concoctions such as pasta with chicken breast, bell peppers, orange-chili sauce, and bok choy. Oh, and the other Washington Vapiano is next to the Chinese arch in what's left of DC's Chinatown (or Chinablock, as some locals put it). The food here is good, though not the best pizza or pasta in town. The ordering, cooking, and consuming of it is unique. You place your order with your personal cook, then watch as he/she prepares it. In nice weather, you can eat outside. The pasta is made in-house. You can pick among many fresh ingredients. Pastas and pizzas cost from $9 to $11, salads big enough for a meal from $7 to $10.

1800 M St. NW (at 18th St.). ✆ **202/640-2127.** www.vapiano.com. $7–$11. AE, DC, DISC, MC, V. Daily 11am–11pm. Metro: Farragut North. Penn Quarter at 623–625 H St. NW (btw. 6th and 7th sts.). ✆ **202/621-7636.** Mon–Tues 11am–11pm; Wed–Thurs 11am–midnight; Fri–Sat 11am–1am; Sun noon–10pm. Metro: Gallery Place.

Zorba's Café *GREEK*   Family-owned Zorba's has been serving Washingtonians good Greek food at reasonable prices for a quarter century. The dining room is light, attractive and comfortable, with blue-and-white tablecloths, pictures of Greece on the walls, and Greek music. In nice weather, you can dine outside at small tables, some of which are shaded by umbrellas. The way to minimize your bill here is to order an $8 Greek sandwich—souvlaki, gyro, falafel. The souvlaki and gyro come with Zorba's tasty, tangy yogurt-cucumber dressing. Or you can ask for chicken salad, cheese steak, or an Italian sub. Pizza starts at $2.30 a slice.

1612 20th St. NW. ℭ **202/387-8555.** www.zorbascafe.com. $7.95–$14. AE, DISC, MC, V. Mon–Sat 11am–11:30pm; Sun 11am–10:30pm. Metro: Dupont Circle.

5 Foggy Bottom/West End

To find the restaurants reviewed below, see the map on p. 57. For a review of the West End *Marvelous Market* bakery and sandwich shop, see p. 65.

★ **Bread & Chocolate** *AMERICAN*   This bakery/cafe is one of our favorite places for light meals and sweets. Come here for breakfast and try the French toast (which is made with cinnamon challah bread) or the *pfannkuchen* (German crepes with apple compote and Bavarian cream)—$8 each. Later in the day, you can eat your fill of salads, sandwiches, quiche, pastries, and a couple of Greek entrees—almost nothing over $9.

2301 M St. NW (at 23rd St.). ℭ **202/833 8360.** www.breadandchocolate.net. $7–$12. AE, MC, V. Mon–Sat 7am–6pm; Sun 8am–6pm. Metro: Foggy Bottom.

SPLURGE

★ **Marcel's** *FRENCH/BELGIAN*   In the Washington world of fine dining, what we're about to recommend is actually far from a splurge. It is, in fact, a great way to enjoy the work of one of the city's best chefs—with some extras—for less than you normally would have to pay. Chef/owner Robert Wiedmaier normally charges $75 to $125 for his four-to-seven-course tasting menus. His pre/post-theater menu is $52, however, and here's what you get: any two courses from the dinner menu, a limousine ride to Kennedy Center for a show, followed by a limo ride back to Marcel's for dessert. (You are responsible for obtaining your theater tickets. See chapter 5 for how you can do so cheaply.) If your show ends after Marcel's closing time, you can have all three courses before you head to the theater. Wiedmaier describes his fare as "French cuisine with a Belgian flair." What might you find on the changing menu? Butter poached lobster with spinach risotto; crab cake in aged sherry shallot butter; roasted cod with pink grape-fruit and ginger; sautéed snails with garlic flan; lamb tenderloin wrapped in phyllo pastry with spinach and Madeira sauce; and Frangelico mousse for dessert. FINE PRINT Dress to impress. Men must wear jackets.

2401 Pennsylvania Ave, NW (at 21th St.). ① 202/296-1166. www.marcelsdc.com. $52–$125. AE, MC, V. Sun 5:30–9:30pm; Mon–Thurs 5:30-10pm; Fri–Sat 5:30–11pm. Metro: Foggy Bottom.

6 Georgetown

You'll find reviews of the Georgetown **Five Guys'** burgers on p. 68, **Marvelous Market**'s sandwiches on p. 65, **Pizzeria Paradiso**'s pizza on p. 75, and **SweetGreen**'s salads on p. 75.

Amma Indian Vegetarian Kitchen *INDIAN/VEGETARIAN* This quiet and unassuming Southern Indian restaurant offers numerous ways to sample Indian vegetarian cooking on the cheap. The best choices are the *uttappams* and *dosas*. Both are Indian pancakes or crepes with various toppings or fillings. The masala dosas, for instance, are wrapped around potatoes and onions. The uttappams are topped with various combinations of onion, chili, vegetables, and chutney. Amma also serves soups, salads, breads, desserts, Indian beverages, beer, and wine.

3291-A M St. NW (btw. 33rd and Potomac sts.). ① **202/625-6652.** $6.60–$9. DISC, MC, V. Mon–Fri 11:30am–2:30pm and 5:30–10pm; Sat 11:30am–3:30pm and 5:30-10:30pm; Sun noon–3:30pm and 5:30–10pm. Georgetown Metro Connection bus from Dupont Circle or Rosslyn Metrorail station, or Metrobus D5 or 38B.

Booeymonger *AMERICAN* The Price family has eaten many times at this bizarrely named deli. One branch is near our home, and the food is both good and inexpensive. Susan likes the Manhattan (roast beef, spinach, bacon, and cheddar cheese on a French baguette with house dressing) and the carrot cake. Tom bounces between the extremes—hot pastrami on rye with mustard one day, the veggie-and-cheese Pita Pan on the other. The menu offers lots of sandwiches, salads, sides, beer, and wine to choose from (some dishes, as you've noticed, with silly names). And you can get a full breakfast in the morning.

3265 Prospect St. NW (at Potomac St.). ℰ **202/333-4810.** www.booeymonger.com. $5.25–$8.25. AE, MC, V. Daily 8am–midnight. Georgetown Metro Connection bus from Dupont Circle or Rosslyn Metrorail station, or Metrobus 31, 32, 36, 38B, or D5. Upper Northwest at 5252 Wisconsin Ave. NW (at Jenifer St.). ℰ **202/686-5805.** Sun–Thurs 7:30am–midnight; Fri–Sat 7:30am–1am. Metro: Friendship Heights.

Café La Ruche *FRENCH* Susan and Julie like to eat in this little restaurant off Georgetown's beaten path because it reminds them of France. From the outside, you can imagine it as a house in the French countryside (if you ignore the surrounding big-city buildings). Inside, it's like a well-worn neighborhood hangout in Paris (though the TV at one end of the dining room intrudes upon the fantasy). The quiches and sandwiches cost about $9. If you feel like splurging, order the fruit tart for dessert and pretend it's health food. That's what Tom does. When the weather's nice, you can eat outside.

1039 31st St. NW (btw. M and K sts.). ℰ **202/965-2684.** www.cafelaruche.com. $9–$20. AE, DC, DISC, MC, V. Mon–Thurs 11:30am–midnight; Fri 11:30am–1am; Sat 10am–1am; Sun 10am–midnight. Circulator; Georgetown Metro Connection bus from Dupont Circle or Rosslyn Metrorail station; or Metrobus 31, 32, 36, 38B, or D5.

Garrett's *AMERICAN* Climb the stairs just east of the first-floor bar in this old-school saloon, and you'll discover a surprisingly pretty, bright, and airy dining room, with large windows and a glass roof, tucked into a corner of the second floor. Eating cheap here means focusing on the burgers, sandwiches, and salads, almost all of which cost less than $10. For $11 or $12 you can get fish and chips, jambalaya, or Tom's favorite—pulled chicken and roasted potatoes smothered in gravy and accompanied by fruit and coleslaw. A large bowl of chili is $5; add macaroni and it's $7.

3003 M St. NW (at 30th St.). ℰ **202/333-1033.** www.garrettsdc.com. $5–$17. AE, DC, DISC, MC, V. Mon–Thurs 1130am–1:30am; Fri 11:30am–2:30am; Sat noon–2:30am; Sun 6pm–1:30am. Circulator; Georgetown Metro Connection bus from Dupont Circle or Rosslyn Metrorail station; or Metrobus 31, 32, 36, 38B, or D5.

Harmony Café *ASIAN* Our vegetarian daughter likes this place—not because its strictly vegetarian, but because most of its meat-based dishes come with a veggie version. Here, the vegetarians aren't relegated to a small corner of the menu. Want Kung Pao chicken without the chicken? No problem, thanks to the ability of soy products to

CHEAP EATS IN GEORGETOWN

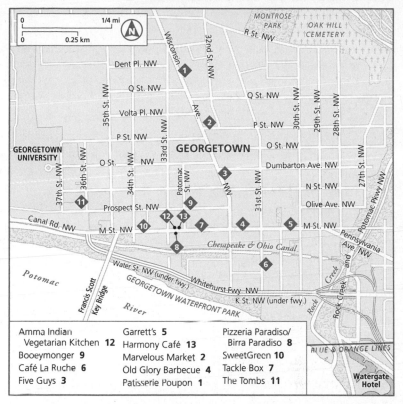

Amma Indian Vegetarian Kitchen **12**
Booeymonger **9**
Café La Ruche **6**
Five Guys **3**
Garrett's **5**
Harmony Café **13**
Marvelous Market **2**
Old Glory Barbecue **4**
Patisserie Poupon **1**
Pizzeria Paradiso/ Birra Paradiso **8**
SweetGreen **10**
Tackle Box **7**
The Tombs **11**

mimic other foods. If you're sharing with fellow diners, the garden salad with a light Asian dressing is a refreshing accompaniment to the other dishes. Don't see exactly what you want on the menu? Under the list of Chef's Specialties, one option is "Your Favorite Dish (ask for it)." Everything on Harmony's enormous menu costs less than $9, most less than $7, a couple dozen dishes less than $5. And that's at dinner. Lunch dishes are about $2 less.

3287¹/₂ M St. NW (btw. Potomac and 33rd sts.). ℰ **202/338-3881.** $4.95–$9.95. MC, V. Daily 11:30am–10pm. Georgetown Metro Connection bus from Dupont Circle or Rosslyn Metrorail station, or Metrobus D5 or 38B.

Old Glory Barbecue *AMERICAN* The cooks here tap the traditions of five U.S. regions to produce tasty ribs, brisket, pulled pork, pulled chicken, catfish, steak, and ham: Eastern Carolina, Southwest Texas, Savannah, Kansas City, and Lexington, KY. They even marinate and grill a vegetable skewer. The way to keep to your budget is to stick to the sandwiches. They're large, come with one large side dish and cost less than $10 with one exception. When you pick your side, you can stick with Southern traditions—collard greens, red beans, fried okra. Or you can reveal your Northern leanings and go with potatoes or slaw.

3139 M St. NW (btw. 31st St. and Wisconsin Ave.). ℰ **202/337-3406.** www.oldglory bbq.com. $8–$20. AE, DC, DISC, MC, V. Mon–Thurs 11:30am–2am; Fri–Sat 11:30am–3am; Sun 11am–2am. Circulator; Georgetown Metro Connection bus from Dupont Circle or Rosslyn Metrorail station; or Metrobus 31, 32, 36, 38B, or D5.

★ **Patisserie Poupon** *FRENCH*   Mouth-watering truffles, marzipan, tarts, petit fours, and sweet croissants will tempt you at this wonderful French bakery. But we cheapskates are drawn to the soups, sand-wiches, and quiches, which can be had here for less than $7.50. The sandwiches come on baguette or brioche and contain what you would expect—Brie, pâté, smoked salmon, or ham, for instance. Salmon finds its way into the quiches as well, as do asparagus, bacon, onion, tomatoes, and leeks. There's some seating inside and a patio out back.

1645 Wisconsin Ave. NW (btw. Q St. and Reservoir Rd.). ℰ **202/342-3248.** $5.25–$7.50. AE, MC, V. Tues–Fri 8am–6:30pm; Sat 8am–5pm; Sun 8am–4pm. Circulator or Metrobus 31, 32, or 36.

Tackle Box *SEAFOOD*   This is another spot that pushes the envelope of our definition of cheap, but it's so good we're going to recommend it anyway. For $9 you can get the Tackle Box Meal, which is one serving of fish and one side dish. Ten bucks buys you a salad with the fish, $13 the fish and two sides. A shrimp roll is $10, a clam roll $11. You must make many decisions here. The fish can be fried, grilled, or put in a taco. There can be a half-dozen kinds of fish to choose from and a dozen sides, including corn on the cob, a cornbread muffin, mac-and-cheese, and sweet-potato fries. Tackle Box also serves omelets, egg sandwiches, and breakfast pastries for less than $6.

3245 M St. NW (btw. Wisconsin Ave. and Potomac St.). ℰ **202/337-8269.** www.tackle boxrestaurant.com. $9–$19. AE, DC, MC, V. Daily 7am–10pm. Georgetown Metro Con-nection bus from Dupont Circle or Rosslyn Metrorail station, or Metrobus D5 or 38B.

★ **The Tombs** *AMERICAN*   One of the best college pubs you'll find anywhere, the Tombs stands at the edge of the Georgetown Univer-sity campus. Even more important to its quality, the Tombs sits in the basement of 1789 Restaurant, one of Washington's finest, and bene-fits from its relationships with 1789's chefs. Bill Clinton ate and drank here during his Georgetown years, as has nearly every other student who has wandered the campus since 1962. Faculty and townsfolk frequent the place, too. Brick walls, wooden tables, and sporting paraphernalia mark this as a classic college hangout. But the food is far from typical. The crab cakes are sweet, moist, and perfectly seasoned. The veggie burger is fat and juicy. The fries are tasty, salty, crisp on the outside and moist in the middle. The Tombs also serves full-course meals and 1789's pastries and wine.

1226 36th St. NW (at Prospect St.). ⓒ **202/337-6668.** www.tombs.com. $7.75–$17. AE, DC, DISC, MC, V. Mon–Thurs 11:30am–1:15am; Fri 11:30am–2:15am; Sat 11am–2:15am; Sun 9:30am–1:15am. Georgetown Metro Connection bus from Dupont Circle or Rosslyn Metrorail station, or Metrobus D5 or 38B.

7 Logan Circle

To find the restaurant reviewed below, see the map on p. 69.

Stoney's *AMERICAN*   No longer a dive, Stoney's still serves up the delicious famous grilled cheese sandwich. For 37 years, the bar operated out of a less-than-pristine space at 13th and L streets NW and became quite popular in the process. Redevelopment of that edge of Downtown forced owner Tony Harris to close in 2006, but he was able to reopen in Logan Circle later that year. The space now is cleaner and more attractive, but the large servings of food remain pretty much the same. The Super Grilled Cheese comes with tomato, bacon, onions, and a side of fries for $7.95. The regular grilled cheese with fries is $5.95. Also good: chili with cornbread and the many varieties of hamburgers.

1433 P St. NW (btw. 14th and 15th sts.). ⓒ **202/234-1818.** $5.25–$20. AE, MC, V. Mon–Thurs 11am–2am; Fri 11am–3pm; Sat 10am–3pm; Sun 10am–2pm. Metrobus 52, 53, or 54.

8 The National Mall

To find the restaurants reviewed below, see the map on p. 69.

★ **Cascade Café** *AMERICAN*   In addition to housing one of the world's great art collections, the National Gallery of Art offers two of the three best dining options on the Mall: this cafeteria in the concourse between the East and West buildings, and the Pavilion Cafe in the Sculpture Garden (see below). (The third is the Mitsitam Café in the National Museum of the American Indian, reviewed below.) At the Cascade, you select from a wide variety of items at several food stations in the cafeteria, then find a seat with a view of the waterfall that gives the cafe its name. The best deal here is the soup-and-sandwich combo for $7.25. Grab the rich and spicy wild mushroom soup if it's available.

4th St. and Pennsylvania Ave. NW. ℂ **202/712-7451.** $3–$15. AE, DISC, MC, V. Mon–Sat 11am–3pm; Sun 11am–4pm. Metro: Archives.

★ **Mitsitam Café** *AMERICAN INDIAN* The Native American–inspired food here is generally considered the best eating on the Mall. The menu changes seasonally and features items from various geographical regions in the Americas. You may have to search carefully to find main courses or sandwiches under $10, but you'll like what you find. Examples from recent menus: Peruvian roasted chicken, pulled pork empanadas from Meso-America, buffalo chili from Great Plains tribes.

4th St. and Independence Ave. SW. ℂ **202/633-1000.** $6.25–$26. AE, DISC, MC, V. Daily 10am–5pm; limited menu 3–5pm. Metro: L'Enfant Plaza.

Pavilion Café *AMERICAN* In the National Gallery of Art's Sculpture Garden, the Pavilion Café is a place for all seasons. We stepped into the glass-enclosed cafeteria one noon after a 7-inch snowfall, warmed ourselves with chili and tomato-herb bread, and gazed at the serene winter view outside. In winter, you can sit here and watch the ice skaters on the garden's frozen pond. In warm weather, you can eat at outdoor tables. Summer Fridays, jazz groups play here from 5 to 8:30pm. You get enormous salads here, and sandwiches so stuffed that a dining companion once complained of the tuna salad sandwich: "There's too much tuna."

7th St. and Constitution Ave. NW. ℂ **202/289-3360.** www.pavilioncafe.com. $6.25–$11. AE, DISC, MC, V. Memorial Day to Labor Day Mon–Thurs 10am–6pm, Fri 10am–8:30pm, Sat 10am–6pm, Sun 11am–6pm; Labor Day to mid-Nov and mid-Mar to Memorial Day Mon–Sat 10am–4pm, Sun 11am–5pm; mid-Nov to mid-Mar Mon–Thurs 10am–7pm, Fri–Sat 10am–9pm, Sun 11am–7pm. Metro: Archives.

9 Mount Vernon Square

To find the restaurants reviewed below, see the map on p. 69. Here you'll also find another branch of **Busboys and Poets** (p. 82).

Saints Paradise Cafeteria *AMERICAN*   Can there be a better place to eat soul food than in a church basement? The United House of Prayer for All People established this cafeteria for its members and later threw open the doors to all people, which seems appropriate. You will be served large portions of fried chicken, fried fish, meatloaf, barbecued ribs, collard greens, candied yams, mashed potatoes, fried potatoes, cabbage, biscuits, cornbread, sweet potato pie, and other traditional home cookin'. Breakfast starts at 4 bucks for two eggs, meat, fruit, and potatoes or grits. You get two sides with the main course at dinner. Children's meals cost $4.50. To avoid mealtime crowds, come for breakfast after 10am and for lunch after 2pm.

601 M St. NW (at 6th St.). *C* **202/789-2289.** $7–$11. Cash only. Mon–Fri 7am–7pm; Sat–Sun 8am–6pm. Metro: Mount Vernon Square.

10 Penn Quarter/Chinatown

To find the restaurants reviewed below, see the map on p. 69.

In this neighborhood, you'll also find branches of **Chopt** (p. 68), **Five Guys** (p. 68), **Nando's Peri-Peri** (p. 74), **Teaism** (p. 74), and **Vapiano** (p. 76).

Capital Q *BARBECUE*   Because this joint is in what's left of Washington's Chinatown, Capitol Q is required to display a sign in Chinese characters out front. But it's all Texas barbecue inside. The flatware is plastic, the plates are paper, and the "napkins" are rolls of paper towels set on each table. You order cafeteria style, then find table or counter space for yourself. (Best is at the window, where you can watch the Penn Quarter revelers wander by.) Proprietor Nick Fontana is a transplanted Texan who catered a party that Texan Dick Armey threw for 4,000 of his closest friends at a Republican National Convention when Armey was House majority leader. Texans are associated most with beef, but the pulled pork is good here, too. If you like spicy, order the spicy sauce on your meat and the spicy baked beans for a side. You'll need that plastic knife and fork to eat the giant sandwiches, most of which cost $6.50 to $7.50.

707 H. St. NW (btw. 7th and 8th sts.). *C* **202/347-8396.** www.capitalqbbq.com. $6.25–$26. AE, DC, DISC, MC, V. Mon–Thurs 11am–9pm; Fri–Sat 11am–10pm; Sun noon–8pm. Metro: Gallery Place.

More Meals on the Mall

You'll probably be spending lots of time in the museums and galleries along the National Mall, so it's good to know you can feed your face in the same places you're feeding your mind and feasting your eyes. The food spots tend to be open when the museums are. All are happy to add to your AE, DISC, MC, or V bills. Here are your options:

The **National Air and Space Museum** has a McDonald's fast food stand, Donatos Pizzeria, Boston Market (salads, sandwiches, rotisserie chicken, and so on), McCafé (McDonald's answer to Starbucks), and a seasonal outdoor kiosk (hot dogs, chips, hamburgers, soft drinks, ice cream). They're open 10am to 5pm.

You'll find two cafes in the **National Museum of American History.** The ground floor **Stars and Stripes Café** serves sandwiches, soups, salads, burgers, pizza, hot dogs, barbecue, and desserts. It's open daily 10am to 3pm. The **Constitution Café,** on the first floor, offers sandwiches, salads, soups, pastries, ice cream, specialty coffees, and soft drinks. Open daily 10am to 5pm.

The **National Museum of Natural History** has three indoor eateries plus outdoor carts in season. The **Fossil Café**'s main attractions are its tables, which have fossils embedded in the tops. The food offerings include sandwiches, salads, fruit, desserts, specialty coffees, soft drinks, and beer. It's open daily 10am to 5pm. At the **Atrium Café,** you can get barbecued brisket, rotisserie chicken, burgers, hot dogs, pizza, sandwiches, soups, salads, fruit, and desserts. It's open Monday through Thursday 11am to 3pm, Friday 11am to 4pm, Saturday 11am to 5pm, and Sunday 11am to 4pm. There's an **espresso, ice cream, and dessert bar** open daily 11:30am till 5pm, and seasonal outdoor carts that sell hot dogs, soft drinks, and ice cream daily 11am to 5pm.

The **Smithsonian Castle Café** offers sandwiches, wraps, panini, antipasti, soups, salads, pastries, ice cream, espresso, cappuccino, coffee, tea, soft drinks, beer, and wine daily from 8:30am till 5pm. Seasonal outdoor carts sell hot dogs, Italian sausages, soft drinks, and ice cream daily 11am to 5pm.

SPLURGE

CO CO. SALA *CHOCOLATE* Susan fell in love with this crazy place the first time we indulged ourselves here, so we figured we should tell you about it as a potential splurge. It's possible to cobble together a real dinner from Co Co. Sala's collection of small plates of salads, mac-and-cheese, seafood, and meats. But the point of this lounge/restaurant is to eat sweets. Just as Marcel's offers three-, four-, five-, and seven-course tastings of its exquisite French/Belgian cuisine, so Co Co. Sala tenders three-, four-, and five-course dessert tastings. You choose among four tasting themes—Asian, Italian, Aztec, or American, for instance. Three courses cost about $20, four $30, and five $40. The menu also suggests pairing each theme with specific cocktails, wines, coffees, and teas. Each course contains two to four small desserts. One Aztec course recently contained a hot chocolate soufflé, espresso gelato, chipotle truffle, and a "Kahlua soother." Three courses are plenty for most folk.

929 F St. NW (btw. 9th and 10th sts.). ✆ **202/347-4265.** www.cocosala.com. Small plates of savories, cheeses, and sweets $6–$18. AE, DISC, MC, V. Mon–Thurs 11am–10pm; Fri 11am–midnight; Sat 5pm–midnight; Sun 11am–3pm. Metro: Gallery Place.

Urfa Tomato Kabob *TURKISH* This small restaurant roasts seasoned beef, lamb, and chicken on vertical spits, then slices and serves them with a tomato sauce, all for very low prices. Sandwiches, for $6, are made with pita bread and lettuce, parsley, and onions. Meals and platters, which come with various sides, range from $7.30 to $11.

740 6th St. NW (btw. G and H sts.). ✆ **202/347-1178.** $6–$11. AE, MC, V. Daily 11am–11pm. Metro: Gallery Place.

11 Upper Northwest

You'll also find a branch of the **Booeymonger** deli (p. 77) here.

Cactus Cantina *TEX/MEX* This large and lively restaurant with lots of outdoor seating is just a couple of blocks north of the National Cathedral. It lives in Price family lore because Julie and some high school classmates were dining here one night when the second President Bush walked in with his wife, some friends, and a Secret Service entourage. You can follow the lead of those Texans and order cheese enchiladas for $8.25 (him) or fajitas (her). Unfortunately, the First

★ What's a Cheap Splurge?

It's not dirt cheap, but it's a way to experience some of the very best restaurants in Washington without breaking your bank. The secret is making a meal of the small plates that a growing number of DC chefs are preparing. Below we list several top restaurants where we've found that five small plates usually can make a meal for the two of us. If you're careful, you can spend less than $20 each on what becomes the equivalent of a main course.

Jaleo *SPANISH*   Superstar chef Jose Andres is the king of small plates in our town, and Jaleo is one of his digs. (Or, he is *"el rey,"* as they say in his native Spain?) Tapas—Spanish small plates—are the focus of this lively, colorful restaurant with walls of windows that look out onto bustling Penn Quarter sidewalks. Enjoy flamenco music while perusing an enormous menu. Our favorites include the spinach sautéed with pine nuts, apples, and raisons; roasted eggplant with red peppers and onions; and grilled asparagus. All cost just 6 bucks each. A bit more expensive—and, oh, so good—are Chorizo sausage with garlic mashed potatoes ($9) and garlic shrimp ($8.50). *480 7th St. NW (at E St.).* ✆ *202/628-7949. www.jaleo.com. Small plates $5.50–$12. AE, DC, MC, V. Mon 11:30am–10pm; Tues–Thurs 11:30am–11:30pm; Fri–Sat 11:30am–midnight; Sun 11:30am–10pm. Metro: Gallery Place.*

Oyamel *MEXICAN*   Another offering from Jose Andres in Penn Quarter, Oyamel provides the opportunity to graze on Mexican small plates—tacos (in handmade corn tortillas), *antojitos* (which Jose defines as "little dishes from the streets"), ceviches (seafood marinated in citrus juices), and *postes* (desserts). Some of our recommendations, all $7 or less: squash salad with crumbled cream cheese and crushed peanuts; meatballs in chipotle sauce with crumbled cheese and cilantro; and a taco filled with marinated chicken breast, guacamole, and grilled onions. The desserts are particularly seductive here. We especially like the traditional *tres leches* (three milks) cake flavored with rum and pineapple and accompanied by dark caramel ice cream; or the warm, rich chocolate cake with creamy *mole* sauce, frothed hot chocolate, vanilla ice cream, and a sprinkle of crushed peanuts, corn nuts, and cocoa beans. *401 7th St. NW (at D St.).* ✆ *202/628-1005. www.oyamel.com. Small plates*

$3–$12. AE, DISC, MC, V. Sun–Mon 11:30am–10pm; Tues–Thurs 11:30am–11:30pm; Fri–Sat 11:30am–midnight. Metro: Archives.

Rasika *MODERN INDIAN*   In the same Penn Quarter neighborhood, you'll find Rasika. The brains and talent behind the absolutely wonderful food here is chef Vikram Sunderam, who came to Washington from his native India via London's Bombay Brasserie. He starts with Indian recipes and alters them by substituting locally grown meats and produce for some traditional Indian ingredients. Once again, cheap splurgers concentrate on the small plates, especially vegetarian dishes. Whatever else you order, you must taste the *palak chaat,* a spectacular salad of crispy, deep-fried baby spinach, served with sweet yogurt and tamarind date chutney. At 9 bucks, it pushes our cheap splurge concept, but it is well worth it. *633 D St. NW (btw. 6th and 7th sts.). © 202/637-1222. www.RasikaRestaurant.com. Small plates $5–$12. AE, DC, DISC, MC, V. Mon–Thurs 11:30am–2:30pm and 5:30–10:30pm; Fri 11:30am–2:30pm and 5–11pm; Sat 5–11pm; Sun closed. Metro: Archives.*

Zaytinya *MEDITERRANEAN*   Yes, it's another Penn Quarter cheap splurge from Jose Andres. There's a reason he's starring on television and opening restaurants across the country. This is a spectacular place for eating an inexpensive meal. The dining room is two stories high in the front, with dark wood tables and chairs, white walls, and tiers of candles that cast soft light from the wall opposite the floor-to-ceiling windows. Here, again, cheapskates focus on small plates, this time Mediterranean *mezzes.* The zucchini-cheese patties are light and tasty, fried crisp on the outside but creamy within. *Fattoush* is a delightful salad made with tomatoes, cucumbers, red onions, and green peppers, and dressed in pomegranate vinaigrette. Also try the Adana Kebab—ground lamb, harissa hot sauce, grilled tomatoes, and sumac onions. For a refreshing dessert, order the muscat-soaked apricots with vanilla yogurt cream, apricot sorbet, and pistachio powder. It will cost you a grand total of $4. The other recommended dishes are $7.50 or less. *701 9th St. NW (at G St.). © 202/638-0800. www.zaytinya.com. Small plates $4–$12. AE, DISC, MC, V. Sun–Mon 11:30am–10pm; Tues–Thurs 11:30am–11:30pm; Fri–Sat 11:30am–midnight. Metro: Gallery Place.*

Lady's choice busts our cheapskate target. Five kinds of enchilada—served with rice, refried beans, lettuce, and tomato—qualify, as do a few other dishes. You can have a half dozen Mexican combo plates for $10 each. Kid-size Tex-Mex plates run $3.75 to $5.75.

3300 Wisconsin Ave. NW (at Macomb St.). ☎ **202/686-7222.** www.cactuscantina. com. $8.25–$17. AE, DC, DISC, MC, V. Mon–Thurs 11am–1pm; Fri–Sat 11am–midnight; Sun 10:30am–11pm. Metrobus 31, 32, 36, or 37.

★ **2 Amys** *PIZZA*   Another National Cathedral neighbor, 2 Amys goes Pizzeria Paradiso one better by obtaining the official *"Denominazione di Origine Controllata"* (DOC) certification from the Italian government. That means 2 Amy's DOC pizzas are made in a wood-burning oven in the traditional Neapolitan manner using specific ingredients and methods of preparation. They are wonderful, with thin, chewy crust, and we recommend them highly. The **Marinara** ($7.95) is topped with tomato, garlic and oregano; the **Margherita** ($12) with tomato, mozzarella di bufala cheese, and basil. The **Margherita Extra** ($13) adds cherry tomatoes. The pizzas are relatively small, so we tend to share one while ordering a couple of items from the "little things" menu. Tom likes the deviled eggs with pesto sauce. Susan prefers the *polpettini al forno* (meatballs) and the *suppli a telefono* (breaded rice balls stuffed with cheese and fried).

3715 Macomb St. NW (just west of Wisconsin Ave.). ☎ **202/885-5700.** www.2amys pizza.com. Pizza $7.95–$13, more with extra toppings. MC, V. Sun noon–10pm; Mon 5–10pm; Tues–Thurs 11am–10pm; Fri–Sat 11am–11pm. Metrobus 31, 32, 36, and 37.

12 U Street Corridor

To find the restaurants reviewed below, see the map on p. 69.

Bar Pilar *MODERN AMERICAN*   Here's another place for small plates, this one a lively, often crowded night spot in the U Street neighborhood. There's a large, changing menu here, much of it costing $6, almost everything in single digits.

1833 14th St. NW (btw. S and T sts.) ☎ **202/265-1751.** www.barpilar.com. Small plates $5–$10. AE, DC, MC, V. Daily 5pm–3am. Metro: U St.

★ **Ben's Chili Bowl** *AMERICAN*   Washington went into mourning on October 8, 2009, when Ben Ali, co-founder of Ben's Chili Bowl, died at age 82. Ben and his wife Virginia opened this neighborhood eatery in 1958, endured riots and Metrorail construction, and created a DC institution that their children now run. And we mean an *institution*.

Entertainers (Bill Cosby), politicians (Barack Obama), and everyday folk make the pilgrimage here to order Ben's famous half-smoke sausage with chili—a spicy challenge to the human digestive system that costs $5.20. Ben's offers standard lunch-counter fare along with some vegetarian dishes for those who don't think saturated fat is an essential food group. Breakfast starts at $4.65 for two eggs, along with potatoes or grits or apples, and toast or biscuit. Ben saw to it that there would always be a Ben by giving all his sons that for their middle name.

1213 U St. NW (btw. 12th and 13th sts.). (C) **202/667-0909.** www.benschilibowl.com. $3.25–$8.55. No credit cards. Mon–Thurs 6am–2am; Fri 6am–4am; Sat 7am–4am; Sun 11am–8pm. Metro: U St.

★ **Busboys and Poets** *AMERICAN*   Walk into this hip gathering spot and you'll find yourself in a restaurant, bookstore, theater, bar, coffeehouse, and Internet cafe rolled into one. Sandwiches—served with your choice of chips, fruit, salad, french fries, or sweet potato fries—start at $6.95, pizzas at $8.50. You also can get burgers, panini, soups, and full-course meals. Spinach-and-pesto lasagna with vegetables and garlic toast tastes good and is a good deal, too, at $9.95. Busboys serves breakfast until 11am. Weekends and holidays, you can get brunch until 3pm. We highly recommend the eggs Benedict or Florentine, served with home fries or grits. If you like entertainment with your food, check the website to see when the next poetry slam, documentary film, or folk guitar player is scheduled in the performance space next to the main dining room.

2021 14th St. NW (btw. U and V sts.). (C) **202/387-7638.** www.busboysandpoets.com. $6.25–$22. AE, DC, DISC, MC, V. Sun 9am–midnight; Mon–Thurs 8am–midnight; Fri 8am–2am; Sat 9am–2am. Metro: U St. Also in Mount Vernon Square at 1025 5th St. NW (btw. K and L sts.). (C) **202/789-2227.** Sun 9am–midnight; Mon–Thurs 8am–midnight; Fri 8am–1am; Sat 9am–1am. Metro: Mount Vernon Square.

U Street Café *AMERICAN*   Attractive digs, a great view, and delicious cheap food define this little cafe at the heart of the U Street action. Inside, you can sit at a table or at a counter by the large window, which looks onto the sidewalk where there is outdoor seating. The cafe serves breakfast till noon weekdays and 3pm weekends and offers tasty waffles all day. Two eggs with toast cost $4 and most waffles cost less than $6. All sandwiches are less than $7. The cheerful, friendly servers also whip up espressos, frappes, and an assortment of teas.

1301 U St. NW (btw. 13th and 14th sts.). (C) **202/332-1066.** $6–$7.50. AE, MC, V. Fri–Mon 7am–6pm; Tues–Thurs 7am–8pm. Metro: U St.

The memorial to president Franklin D. Roosevelt is free, open 24/7, and also includes a tribute to his dog, Fala.

EXPLORING WASHINGTON, DC

You could spend years exploring Washington and not spend a penny for admission to anything. In our other "Free & Dirt Cheap" books, we often run a chart listing the "free" days of various museums and attractions: In DC, with extremely rare exceptions, all the top sights in town are free. There are charges to a few worthwhile sights and activities, but you could skip all of those and still enjoy a robust visit that lasts as long as you wish. We're talking museums, galleries, monuments, memorials, parks, gardens, and the government buildings that are the reason this town exists. (Of course we all know that, in reality, there is no such thing as a free lunch—or

EXPLORING WASHINGTON, DC

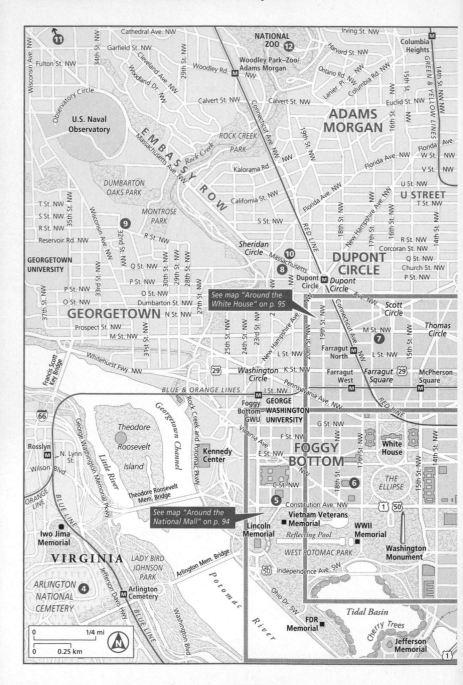

See map "Around the White House" on p. 95

See map "Around the National Mall" on p. 94

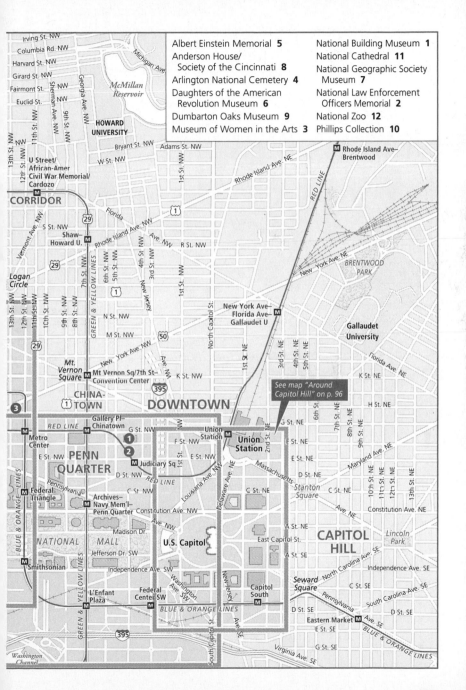

Albert Einstein Memorial **5**
Anderson House/
 Society of the Cincinnati **8**
Arlington National Cemetery **4**
Daughters of the American
 Revolution Museum **6**
Dumbarton Oaks Museum **9**
Museum of Women in the Arts **3**

National Building Museum **1**
National Cathedral **11**
National Geographic Society
 Museum **7**
National Law Enforcement
 Officers Memorial **2**
National Zoo **12**
Phillips Collection **10**

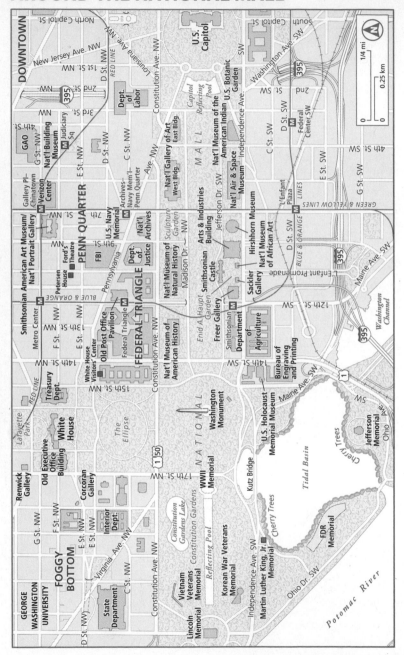

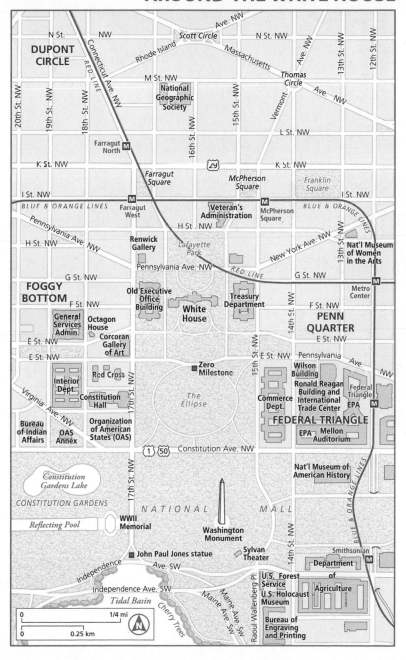

AROUND CAPITOL HILL

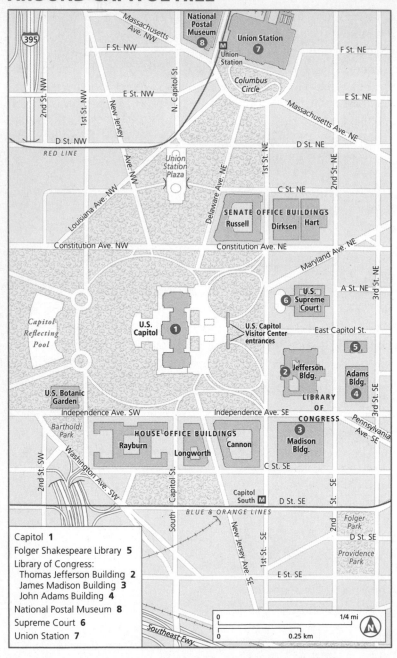

Capitol **1**
Folger Shakespeare Library **5**
Library of Congress:
  Thomas Jefferson Building **2**
  James Madison Building **3**
  John Adams Building **4**
National Postal Museum **8**
Supreme Court **6**
Union Station **7**

a free museum. If you live in the United States, you pay for most of these things with your taxes. So go get your money's worth!)

We generally stay away from the "greatest hits" in the "Exploring" chapters in the F&DC guides, because that's where the tourists hang out. But if there's one town in the United States where you *should* play tourist, this is it. In the ultimate company town of Washington, DC, that's where the action is. Watching laws being made, and the Constitution being interpreted up-close-and-personal, is something you won't see anywhere else, and for many of us who live here, it's our job to be part of the system, to report on it, or to try to change it.

We'll also show you more of the "hidden" attractions of DC in this chapter, and the places that the locals visit, along with some of the beautiful outdoor spaces and unusual monuments and other sites that seem to be around every corner.

1 Top 10 Free Things Not to Miss in DC

★ **1. The Capitol**   The 180-foot-high Capitol dome—topped with a statue titled *Freedom*—is the most-recognized symbol of American democracy, and the building serves as Congress's headquarters. The House and Senate meet in their separate chambers, and the offices of the most powerful congressional leaders are located here. You can get tickets from your U.S. representative and senators to watch lawmakers in action in the chambers, and you can take a guided tour. The building's interior is fascinating, and some of it seems more appropriate to a European monarchy than American democracy. Above the Rotunda, in the canopy of the dome, for instance, Constantino Brumidi's *The Apotheosis of Washington* portrays the first president as a godlike character flanked by such allegorical figures as Liberty, War, Victory, and Fame. The Capitol is filled with historic paintings, ornate decoration and statues of figures from American history. Start your visit at the Capitol Visitor Center, which is entered from the East Plaza near 1st and East Capitol streets. Here you'll find exhibits, gift shops, and a restaurant. Guided tours start here. While a limited number of tour passes are made available each day, you're smart to book ahead through your representative or senator or directly with the visitor center. Some lawmakers' aides—and even a few lawmakers themselves—will take constituents on a personalized tour if you ask. FINE PRINT If you do take a seat in the House or Senate visitors gallery, don't be surprised if nothing exciting happens. While the chambers fill for roll-call votes and during extremely important debates, there are usually only a few members on the floor. You can witness the surreal scene of a grandiloquent senator propounding profoundly on the greatest issues of the day, with only one or two other members, a reporter or two, a few congressional staffers—and the C-SPAN cameras—looking on.

1st and East Capitol sts. ℂ **202/226-8000.** http://tours.visitthecapitol.gov. Mon–Sat 8:30am–4:30pm. Closed Sun, Jan 1, Inauguration Day, Thanksgiving, Dec 25. Metro: Capitol South.

★ **2. White House**   Post-9/11 security continues to complicate Washington touring. To see the president's mansion, you have to request tickets from your representative or senator at least one month, but no more than six months, in advance. If you're not a U.S. citizen, you have to ask your embassy to arrange a tour. (Get embassy contact information here: **www.state. gov/s/cpr/rls/dpl/32122.htm**.) You'll see some of the public areas of the building, which is not only the president's home and office but also work space for the highest ranking presidential aides and the White House press corps. The best time to visit is when the place is decorated for Christmas. You'll also want to check out the **White House Visitor Center** which, strangely enough, is located in the Great Hall of the Commerce Department building. There, you'll find ranger talks, exhibits, a gift shop, and restrooms. FINE PRINT Tickets are limited, so request early. Tours can be canceled, so check the phone recording the day before and the morning of your

Congressional VIP Passes

Your U.S. representative and senators can give you passes to various government facilities—the Capitol, Supreme Court, Library of Congress, and so on. Sometimes they can arrange a VIP tour that shows you more than the regular tour. Sometimes they can just help you avoid standing in long lines with tourists who don't bother to plan ahead. When you've decided what you want to see, phone your legislators and ask what they can do for you. You can reach any congressional office at ℂ **202/224-3121.** You can also look up the latest information and contact info, both in DC and in your home state for your Senator or Representative at **www.senate.gov** or **www.house.gov**.

tour. You can't use restrooms in the White House, so tend to your needs at the Ellipse Visitor Pavilion, 15th and E streets NW.

Tours begin at 15th and E sts. NW. © **202/456-7041.** www.whitehouse.gov/about/ tours–and–events. Tues–Thurs 7:30–11am; Fri 7:30am–noon; Sat 7:30am–1pm. Closed Sun, federal holidays. Metro: McPherson Square. Visitor Center: 1450 Pennsylvania Ave. NW (btw. 14th and 15th sts.). © **202/208-1631.** www.nps.gov/whho/ index.htm. Daily 7:30am–4pm. Closed Jan 1, Thanksgiving, Dec 25. Metro: Metro Center.

★ **3. Supreme Court**   When you gaze upon the majestic Supreme Court building, you might think it's been standing here since the Romans ruled the world. In fact, The Supremes have only been in residence since 1935. Previously, they worked out of various locations in the Capitol. The best show at the court is the open-to-the-public, hour-long oral argument, during which attorneys for the competing parties try to make their cases while undergoing often-contentious (sometimes humorous) questioning by the justices. Beginning the first Monday in October, the arguments usually are held at 10 and 11am on alternate Mondays, Tuesdays, and Wednesdays, with some afternoon sessions added and longer intervals occurring between arguments in December and February. The arguments can be gripping debates about profound issues that command front-page news coverage. Or they can pick at arcane details of commercial contracts. Arguments usually conclude in late April, and the court usually announces its decisions between mid-May and late June, also in public sessions. Two lines form in front of the court for first-come, first-served seating. One is for those who want to sit through an entire argument, the other for those who just want a three-minute taste. You

Equal Justice from the Side Entrance

In May 2010, the Supreme Court closed its grand front entrance to the arriving public. Visitors will no longer walk up the marble steps to enter the building under the facade that says "Equal Justice Under Law." Instead they will go through a side entrance and be subject to security screenings. Upon leaving the building, visitors will be able to walk down the marble steps. Justice Stephen G. Breyer called the change "unfortunate" and said he believed it was not needed. Justice Ruth Bader Ginsburg said she agreed with Breyer.

Going Through Security (Get Used to It)

We understand why it's happened, but we'll never be happy with the ramp-up of security measures in Washington. When we first moved here, the Capitol was open to the public all the time. When Congress was out of session, anyone could use the Capitol parking lot. The first time Tom flashed his press pass at the White House, the fellow in the guardhouse became irritated that this new Washington correspondent didn't know how to reach through the gate to unlatch it so the guard didn't have to come outside.

To enter most government buildings now, you have to pass through metal detectors and put your bags through X-ray machines—if you're allowed to carry bags with you. There are lists of items you can't take into buildings. The Capitol bans weapons, explosives, pointed objects, bags larger than 14x13x4 inches, cans, bottles, food, beverages, aerosol containers, and non-aerosol sprays. The White House adds handbags, cameras, recording devices, tobacco products, personal grooming items and pens (!)—pointed object, we guess. Similar restrictions, often with smaller lists, apply elsewhere. If you take any banned items with you, you can't go in and there's no place to store them. These lists are subject to change, so you should ask about prohibited items when you request tour tickets. (**White House** list: www.whitehouse.gov/about/tours-and-events. **Capitol** list: www.visitthecapitol.gov/Visit/Visitor Safety and Policies.)

also can check out the exhibits on the ground floor, attend a lecture in the courtroom when the justices aren't using it, watch a film about the court, browse the gift shop, and eat in the cafeteria.

1 1st St. NE (at Maryland Ave.). ✆ **202/479-3211.** www.supremecourtus.gov. Mon–Fri 9am–4:30pm. Lectures when court not in session on the half-hour 9:30am–3:30pm. Closed Sat, Sun, federal holidays. Metro: Capitol South.

★ **4. Arlington National Cemetery**   Few sights are as emotionally moving as the 300,000 simple white grave markers that march with military precision across Arlington's hills and valleys. They dramatically remind visitors of the enormous human toll of American warfare, past and present. More than 300,000 veterans and their dependents are interred here, nearly 40,000 in above-ground columbaria. Stop first at the **visitor center,** pick up a map, then take the short walk to the memorial for women veterans. You can hike the large, hilly cemetery, but most people choose to ride the **Tourmobile,** which is boarded at the visitor center. (You'll have to pay a fee to board the Tourmobile, though admission to the Cemetery itself is free.) The Tourmobile stops at the major sights, and you can get off and on at your leisure. The top sights include Arlington House, where Confederate Gen. Robert E. Lee once lived; the graves of President John F. Kennedy, his widow Jacqueline Kennedy Onassis, their two infants who died before the president, and his brother Robert F. Kennedy, who was assassinated during his own presidential campaign in 1968; and the Tomb of the Unknowns, were an unidentified veteran of World War I, World War II, and the Korean War are interred. (There are no unidentified remains from the Vietnam War.) You'll encounter breathtaking views of Washington during your visit. After you return to the visitor center, you can take a 10-minute walk to the **Marine Corps Memorial,** which portrays the immortal photograph by Joe Rosenthal of Marines raising the U.S. flag on Iwo Jima during World War II. FINE PRINT Remember that Arlington is a cemetery, so conduct yourself accordingly. Nearly 30 burials occur every day, so one likely will be taking place while you visit.

In Arlington, across Memorial Bridge from the Lincoln Memorial. © **703/607-8000.** www.arlingtoncemetery.org. Tourmobile $7.50, 65 and older $6.50, 3–11 $3.75, younger free. Parking $1.75/hr. for the first 3 hr., $2 each additional hour. Apr–Sept daily 8am–7pm; Oct–Mar daily 8am–5pm. Tourmobile Apr–Sept daily 8:30am–6:30pm; Oct–Mar daily 8:30am–4:30pm. Guard change at Tomb of Unknowns Oct–Mar every hour on the hour, Apr–Sept also on half-hour. Metro: Arlington Cemetery.

★ **5. Abraham Lincoln Memorial**   Barack Obama's inaugural concert was just the latest of many landmark events conducted at the feet of the Civil War president. When Marian Anderson was refused permission to perform at Constitution Hall in 1939 because of her race, the great singer performed here instead. Martin Luther King, Jr., delivered his "I Have a Dream" speech in 1963. Major political demonstrations have used the memorial as a backdrop. After climbing 57 steps, you confront the 10-foot pedestal upon which stands a 19-foot-high statue of the seated Lincoln. He's surrounded by 50-foot columns and walls displaying the Gettysburg Address and Lincoln's second inaugural address. With Lincoln at your back, you get a spectacular vista of the National Mall, past the World War II Memorial and the

Washington Monument all the way to the Capitol. From the memorial's back, you can see the perpetual flame on John Kennedy's grave in Arlington National Cemetery.

West end of the National Mall at 23rd St. (btw. Constitution and Independence aves.). ℂ **202/426-6841.** www.nps.gov/linc. Always open. Rangers on duty daily 9:30am–11:30pm. Metro: Foggy Bottom or Metrobus 13A, 13B, 13F, or 13G.

★ **6. Thomas Jefferson Memorial**　This is Tom (Price's) favorite memorial, partly because Jefferson is his favorite president. (And not because they have the same first name!) The memorial also boasts a marvelous setting, with a spectacular view of the Washington Monument and the White House across the Tidal Basin. The scene is gorgeous in spring when the cherry trees blossom. It's awe inspiring after dark, when Jefferson's 19-foot-tall statue is dramatically illuminated and other of Washington's lighted landmarks glow in the distance. The memorial's columned rotunda suggests Jefferson's designs for his Monticello home and the University of Virginia, which he founded. Jefferson quotations are carved into the memorial's interior.

East Basin Dr. SW on southeast side of the Tidal Basin. ℂ **202/426-6841.** www.nps. gov/thje. Always open. Rangers on duty daily 9:30am–11:30pm. Metro: Smithsonian.

★ **7. Vietnam Veterans Memorial**　More people visit the Vietnam Veterans Memorial than the nearby memorials to World War II and Korean War vets. In fact, among National Park Service sites in DC, only the Lincoln Memorial draws more traffic. That's probably because many of those who fought—and fought against—the Vietnam War are still alive, and the controversies that raged around that war have never really been put to rest. It's also because the simple monument carries so much power. Depending on your age and your circumstances, it can be the most emotional spot in Washington. It's a black granite V carved into the ground and carrying the names of more than 58,000 U.S. troops who were killed in the war or remain missing. Like the war, the simplicity of the memorial itself became controversial. To appease those who wanted a more traditional monument, the memorial was expanded to include a flagpole, a statute of three soldiers, and a statue of three female military nurses tending to a wounded soldier. As at most Park Service sites, rangers are available to discuss the memorial and help if you're looking for individual names. Here, you're also likely to run into Vietnam-era vets who are willing to talk about their experience.

Bacon Dr. near Constitution Ave. NW, just northeast of the Lincoln Memorial. ℂ **202/426-6841.** www.nps.gov/vive. Always open. Rangers on duty daily 9:30am–11:30pm. Metro: Foggy Bottom or Metrobus 13A, 13B, 13F, or 13G.

★ **8. National Gallery of Art**   One of the world's great art museums, the National Gallery owns more than 100,000 works from the Middle Ages to the present day. Magnificent pieces are on exhibit throughout both of the gallery's buildings—which are connected by a subterranean passageway with an airport-style moving walkway—and the museum is always mounting special exhibitions, and almost always is a stop for the most important traveling exhibitions. The West Building is a treasure chest of European art from the 13th into the early 20th centuries and American art from the 18th to the early 20th. Here you will find, among many others, Raphael, Rembrandt, El Greco, and the only da Vinci painting in the Western Hemisphere. Architect I.M. Pei designed the starkly modern East Building, which, appropriately, houses the gallery's 20th-century and contemporary art. An immense Calder mobile dominates the soaring central court. You'll also see works by Matisse, Miró, Picasso, Pollock and others here. Across 7th Street from the West Building is the gallery's outdoor Sculpture Garden which contains some whimsical creations and—in winter—an ice-skating rink. The gallery offers a large number of educational programs, from audio tours in six languages, visitors guides in nine languages, guides to individual galleries in five languages, a variety of guided tours (including foreign language tours) throughout the day, lectures, films, concerts, and activities for children and teens. For details visit **www.nga.gov/programs/index.shtm**.

Constitution Ave. NW (btw. 3rd and 7th sts.). ℂ **202/737-4215.** www.nga.gov. Mon–Sat 10am–5pm, Sun 11am–6pm. Closed Dec 25, Jan 1. Metro: Archives.

★ **9. National Museum of American History**   After a 2-year closure for remodeling, this museum, sometimes billed as "The Nation's Attic," reopened in late 2008 as a vastly changed institution. For some time, the museum has been moving beyond being a mere collection of things. Now it's taken a further leap of using those artifacts to tell the story of America. An exhibit titled "America on the Move" shows how the planes, trains, and automobiles on display changed our cities and suburbs. This museum owns more than 3 million objects and displays about 5,000 at any one time. Here you find the profound with the trivial, artifacts of great historical importance with pop art.

Here's an 18th-century mousetrap. There's C3PO, the "Star Wars" droid. Go see Julia Child's kitchen, a North Carolina lunch counter where students staged sit-ins during the 1960s Civil rights movement, the original Star-Spangled Banner, a Dumbo car from Disneyland, Clara Barton's ambulance, Dorothy's ruby slippers, George Washington's military uniform, Muhammad Ali's boxing gloves, and on and on seemingly forever. Docents lead tours of the museum's highlights at 10:15am and 1pm daily. Look for "Docent on Duty" signs which tell when brief tours of specific exhibits will be conducted.

Constitution Ave. (btw. 12th and 14th sts.). ⓒ **202/633-1000.** www.americanhistory. si.edu. Daily 10am–5:30pm. Closed Dec 25. Metro: Smithsonian.

★ **10. Library of Congress**   Opened in 1801 with 740 books and three maps, Congress's library was destroyed by the British in 1814. It was replenished with Thomas Jefferson's private collection of 6,487 volumes in 1815. Today it is the world's largest library, with 142 million items (on 650 miles of shelves), including books, newspapers, magazines, films, photographs, posters, prints, drawings, maps, sheet music, and sound recordings. In addition to operating Congress's lending library, the staff here conducts research for legislators and administers the nation's copyright system. Although you can't borrow the books, you can do research. You also can tour the library's main building—an ornate Italian Renaissance structure named for Jefferson. Make sure you check out the changing exhibits, watch a film, or attend a concert. Tour highlights: the circular Main Reading Room, with domed ceiling 160 feet above the floor; the Great Hall, which soars 75 feet from marble floor to stained glass ceiling; and historical artifacts such as the Gutenberg Bible and the Giant Bible of Mainz.

1st St. SE (btw. E. Capital St. and Independence Ave.). ⓒ **202/707-8000.** www.loc. gov. Mon–Sat 8:30am–4:30pm. Tours Mon–Sat 10:30, 11:30am, 1:30, 2:30, 3:30pm; Sat no 3:30pm tour; on federal holidays, tours start at 9:30am. Closed Sun, Jan 1, Thanksgiving, Dec 25. Metro: Capitol South.

2 Other Free Museums

Daughters of the American Revolution Museum   The DAR complex is most famous—or infamous—for Constitution Hall, which today stages a variety of performances but which in 1939 barred a concert by Marian Anderson. The famed African-American singer then made civil rights history by performing instead at the Lincoln

Memorial on Easter Sunday with the support of First Lady Eleanor Roosevelt. Also here, however, are a library and a museum which focuses on furnishings and decorative arts. You can take a guided tour of the "Period Rooms," which are furnished and decorated as they would have been at a particular time in U.S. history. Among them are a Pilgrim dwelling, an upper-middle-class Victorian parlor, a Beaux Arts board room (which the DAR board uses), an 18th-century tavern, and an attic filled with toys and dolls. FINE PRINT When a guide isn't available, you can visit the rooms on your own.

1776 D St. NW (btw. 17th and 18th sts.). ☎ 202/628-1776. www.dar.org. Mon–Fri 8:30am–4pm; Sat 9am–5pm; Sun closed. Period Room guided tours on the hour and half-hour Mon–Fri 10am–4:30pm; Sat 9am–4:30pm. Tours are free for individuals, $3 per person for groups of 10 or more. Self–guided tours Mon–Fri 9:30am–4pm; Sat 9am–5pm. Metro: Farragut West.

Folger Shakespeare Library   The largest collection of items related to Shakespeare will be found not in England, but on Washington's Capitol Hill, across 2nd Street from the Library of Congress. The Folger's interests are not confined to Shakespeare, however. Other artistic artifacts from the 13th century to the present are within the collections, which include 256,000 books, 60,000 manuscripts, 250,000 playbills, and 200 oil paintings, as well as drawings, water colors, prints, photographs, costumes, films, and musical instruments. Among the museum's most prized possessions is the only known quarto (small, inexpensive publication) of *Titus Andronicus,* which Shakespeare wrote in 1594. The library has 79 copies of the First Folio, the first collected edition of Shakespeare's plays, which was published in 1623, seven years after his death. A copy of the Second Folio, once owned by a college in Spain, testifies to the Spanish Inquisition, which censored parts of the publication, including the entire play *Measure for Measure.* The Folger houses 55,000 English-language books printed before 1700 and another 30,000 printed during the 18th century. The library's Elizabethan Theatre—where plays, concerts, and other presentations are staged—is designed to evoke the courtyard of an English inn of Shakespeare's time, where traveling troupes of players would perform. The theater is the site for performances of Early English music (before the 19th century) by the resident Folger Consort. Outside, the Elizabethan Garden grows plants that were popular during Shakespeare's lifetime, and contains sculptures of characters from his plays. Docents lead **tours** of the building

Monday through Friday at 11am and 3pm and Saturday at 11am and 1pm. April through October, you can take a guided tour of the garden on the third Saturday of the month at 10 and 11am.

201 E. Capitol St. (at 3rd St.). ℂ **202/544-4600.** www.folger.edu. Mon–Sat 10am–5pm. Closed Sun, federal holidays. Metro: Capitol South.

★ **Holocaust Memorial Museum**   Prepare to be emotionally drained when you leave this remembrance of Hitler's attempt to annihilate the Jewish people and to persecute and kill millions more. Multimedia exhibits document this obscene chapter of human history. Upon entering, each visitor picks up an identity card of a Holocaust victim, which personalizes the museum experience. The self-guided tour begins with the rise of Nazism. Aboard a freight car that was used to transport Jews to the Treblinka extermination camp, visitors listen to recordings of survivors. Another section is dedicated to the liberation of the concentration camps and to the non-Jews who, at great risk, hid Jews. The museum recommends that no one younger than 11 visit the permanent exhibits, for which you must obtain tickets. Other exhibits can be entered without tickets, and the museum recommends several for younger children: **Daniel's Story,** the multimedia Wexner Center, the Children's Tile Wall, and the Hall of Remembrance. The museum is about hope and heroism as well as suffering. In some respects, the most disturbing programs here are those that remind us that genocide is not just a historic artifact but a recurring event. And the museum itself was the target of a hate-inspired attack from an 88-year-old neo-Nazi who shot and killed a security guard on June 10, 2009.

FINE PRINT March through August, you must obtain a first-come, first-served free pass that allows you to view the permanent exhibits at a specific time that day. They're distributed, beginning at 10am, at the 14th St. entrance. For $1 each, you can buy advance tickets online at **https://tix.cnptix.com/tix/ushmm?eventid=21322**. For $2, you can order by phone at ℂ **877/808-7466.**

100 Raoul Wallenberg Place SW (south of Independence Ave.). ℂ **202/488-0400.** www.ushmm.org. Daily 10am–5:20pm. Closed Yom Kippur, Christmas. Metro: Smithsonian.

★ **National Air and Space Museum**   As former Ohio residents, we had a special fondness for the Milestones of Flight Hall by this museum's Mall entrance. There, you could stand beside the *Friendship 7* capsule, in which John Glenn became the first American to orbit Earth, while gazing upon Neil Armstrong's Columbia command module, which first carried men to the moon, and the airplane in which Orville and Wilbur Wright became the first men to fly. Those few feet of museum space showed how four guys, who lived within 160 miles of each other in the Buckeye State, took us from "man cannot fly" to "man can walk on the moon" in just 65 years! The Wright brothers have their own exhibit hall as we write this, but someday their craft will be reunited with Glenn's and Armstrong's. This place is just jampacked with significant artifacts and exhibits that teach the history and science of flight. You can see Charles Lindbergh's ocean-crossing *Spirit of St. Louis,* Chuck ("The Right Stuff") Yeager's sound-barrier-breaking X-1, a space station, a space rock, and oh so much more. For fees, you can take rides that simulate a space walk or F-18 fighter plane flight, or test your piloting skills on a flight simulator. You also can watch an IMAX movie or a planetarium show (sometimes free). Because the Air and Space Museum is on so many visitors' agendas, arriving when the doors open or late in the day is wise in spring and summer. On holiday weekends and school vacations, it's usually packed with more kids than you realized had been born this century. FINE PRINT The museum displays even more aircraft and spacecraft at an **annex** by Dulles Airport. See p. 132 for details.

Btw. Independence Ave. SW, Jefferson Dr., and 4th and 7th sts. ℂ **202/633-1000.** www.nasm.si.edu. Films, simulators, planetarium $7.25–$13. Daily 10am–5:30pm. Closed Dec 25. Metro: L'Enfant Plaza.

National Geographic **Museum**   The great magazine of exploration comes to life here. Because the National Geographic Society explores the universe, you can find exhibits on just about anything. Changing exhibits reveal the discoveries of recent society-sponsored expeditions, highlights from the organization's history, and the findings of others. As we write this, the museum is displaying 15 of the life-size terra-cotta warriors that were buried with China's first emperor two millennia ago and were discovered near the city of Xi'an in 1974. You also can expect to see fine examples of the magazine's spectacular photography. FINE PRINT Admission to the museum is free, but there can be charges for special exhibits—such as the terra-cotta warriors.

1145 17th St. NW (at M St.). ℂ **202/857-7588.** http://events.nationalgeographic.com/events/locations/center/museum. Mon–Sat 9am–5pm; Sun 10am–5pm. Closed Dec 25. Metro: Farragut North.

★ **National Museum of the American Indian**   The limestone exterior of this museum was designed to evoke a stone mass carved over time by wind and water. Inside you'll find 10,000 years worth of artifacts from all over the Americas. Leaders of Indian organizations were intimately involved in planning the museum, including choosing its name. The museum's displays and programs deal with the present as well as the past. One ongoing exhibit—"Our Lives"—explores the contemporary experiences of eight Indian communities in the United States, Canada, and the Caribbean island nation of Dominica. Recent temporary exhibits have delved into the interactions of Indians and blacks and have displayed contemporary Indian art. The museum's **Mitsitam Cafe,** serving traditional Indian foods, is the most interesting place to eat on the Mall. Its name means "let's eat!" in the Delaware and Piscataway Indian language. This museum also has some of the most interesting shopping in town.

Independence Ave. SW (at 4th St.). (Ⓒ) **202/633-1000.** www.nmai.si.edu. Daily 10am– 5:30pm. Closed Dec 25. Metro: L'Enfant Plaza.

★ **National Museum of Natural History**   This is not just a collection of dinosaur bones and stuffed animals. We humans also are part of natural history and command a great deal of prominence in the exhibits here. The newest section of the museum—scheduled to open shortly before this book rolls off the presses—is the Hall of Human Origins, which will tell the story of human evolution. Visitors will enter the hall through a "time tunnel" which will depict how humans and the environment have changed over the last 6 million years. Among the hall's contents: life-size models of early human faces, an interactive "human family tree," a Neanderthal skeleton, and depictions of the milestones in human development (walking upright, growing a larger brain, and learning to use tools, to speak, and to write). This is the third major hall the museum has opened since 2003, so there's lots new here and much use of new and interactive technology. **The Ocean Hall,** opened in 2008, contains a 1,500-gallon coral reef aquarium. You *will* find stuffed animals—274 of them—in the **Hall of Mammals,** which opened in 2003. And all the old favorites are still around: the huge African elephant in the Rotunda, dinosaurs, the moon rock, the 45.5 carat Hope Diamond. Kids love the **Insect Zoo** (where they can pet a tarantula and hold a giant hissing cockroach) and the **Discovery Room** (which is full of hands-on activities). FINE PRINT You can walk among live butterflies and exotic plants in the **Butterfly Pavilion,** but it will cost

Why It's Called the "Smithsonian"

Bear with us a moment as we explain how the Smithsonian Institution is named after one James Macie. At least that's what he was called after his out-of-wedlock birth in France in 1765 to an English couple—Hugh Smithson (also known as Hugh Percy), the Duke of Northumberland, and Elizabeth Hungerford Keate Macie, a niece of the Duke of Somerset. James later took his father's name and became a noted scientist—the first person to isolate zinc carbonate, or smithsonite. No one knows for sure why Smithson left his half-million-dollar fortune "to found at Washington, under the name of the Smithsonian Institution, an establishment for the increase and diffusion of knowledge among men." He never visited the United States while alive and (though some DC tour guides say otherwise) wasn't a particular fan of the American form of government. In fact, when Smithson died in 1829, his primary heir was a nephew whose offspring would have inherited the estate. But the nephew died in 1835 without issue, legitimate or otherwise. Thus the Smithsonian was born. Smithson's remains were brought to America in 1903, and he was interred in a crypt near the Smithsonian Castle's north entrance.

you $5 ages 2 to 12, $6 ages 13 to 59, and $5.50 ages 60 and older. Except on Tuesday, when it's free. IMAX tickets run $7.25 and $12.50 depending on your age and what's showing.

Btw. Constitution Ave. NW, Madison Dr., and 9th and 12th sts. © **202/633-1000.** www.mnh.si.edu. Daily 10am–5:30pm. (Sometimes extended hours in spring and summer.) Closed Dec 25. Metro: Smithsonian.

National Postal Museum   Hands-on stuff makes this another popular place with kids. Telling the history of stamps and the postal service, it delivers along the way a large slice of American history. Tour a Southern Railway mail car, look up at mail planes, discover the real story of the Pony Express, and observe the evolution of the mail truck. The museum is located in the old City Post Office Building, which operated from 1914 through 1986.

2 Massachusetts Ave. NE (btw. N. Capitol and 1st sts.). © **202/633-5555.** www.postalmuseum.si.edu. Daily 10am–5:30pm. Closed Dec 25. Metro: Union Station.

Washington with Kids

Oh yes, kids. You'll see *lots* of them at the major attractions in Washington, DC. It's not just local children on field trips from schools, but young people from all over the country, many of whom are making a long-awaited and worked-for trip to Our Nation's Capital. So if you're the sort of person who doesn't care for a double stroller parked next to you at the museum cafeteria, or would like to look at a picture without having someone run into your kneecap, try to plan your sightseeing during the week, and in the late afternoon.

But if you're someone who's always been a free-and-dirt-cheap type, and is now raising a family this way, we've tried to indicate places where you and the next generation might have the most fun, stay, and eat most cheaply (and feel welcome).

Washington is one of the more kid-friendly cities in the country, and if you have some with you, one of the best ways to entertain them is to just let them run around places that are designed to interest and educate them while you sit and watch. That makes all of Washington's many parks prime real estate for kid entertainment. The best and biggest would be the National Mall, which to a small child will seem to stretch to infinity. Leave any Mall museum, make for the grass, and let the children run to their hearts' content. If the wind cooperates, add a kite to the equation. The Air and Space Museum sells quite a few. Off the mall, you'll seldom be far from a patch of green.

Nearly every museum in town has some kid-centric stuff: special exhibits, workbooks, guides, activities. Here are a few more specific suggestions:

● **Dumbarton Oaks Gardens:** Cheapskate parents bring children here between November 1 and mid-March. They're open Tuesday through Sunday from 2 to 5pm except federal holidays and in bad weather. And they're free. You don't get to see the flowers and trees bloom. That starts mid-March and ends in October, when you have to pay to get in. But there's lots of room for the children to run and benches on which you can sit (p. 118).

● **Carousel on the Mall:** What child doesn't like a merry-go-round? In nice weather, you'll find a wonderfully restored 19th-century carousel spinning and playing its music across Jefferson Drive from the Smithsonian Castle.

- **Discovery Theater:** Just west and south of the Castle, in the S. Dillon Ripley Center, this theater stages programs specifically for children. Tickets usually cost $5 for children, $6 for adults. © **202/ 633-8700;** www.discoverytheater.si.edu.

- **National Gallery of Art Sculpture Garden:** Across 7th Street from the Gallery's West Building, several whimsical installations tickle the fancy of kids and grownups.

- **National Air and Space Museum:** Kids tend to be fascinated by airplanes and spaceships, so much of this museum is child-friendly. Especially for kids: a paper-airplane contest. Check the information desk for time and location (p. 106).

- **National Museum of African Art:** Ask about story-telling times (p. 115).

- **National Museum of American History:** The hands-on Spark Lab and Invention at Play exhibit turn children into scientists and inventors (p. 103).

- **National Museum of Natural History:** Dinosaurs always draw *oohs* and *ahhs.* At the Insect Zoo, children can pet a tarantula, hold a giant hissing cockroach, and slither through a replica of a termite mound. Hands-on activities abound in the Discovery Room (p. 108).

- **National Postal Museum:** Interactive exhibits make this small museum surprisingly popular with children (p. 108).

- **National Zoo:** This is 500 acres of thrills for kids. But Kids Farm is made specially for them. They can pet or groom cattle, donkeys, and goats, check out chickens and ducks, and play with interactive educational displays. Kids 3 to 8 can crawl through Prairie Playland—which mimics the nearby prairie dog village—popping their heads up through openings and looking around just like the prairie dogs do (p. 129).

3 More Monuments and Memorials

ALWAYS FREE

Albert Einstein Memorial   The man who may have been the world's greatest scientist looks whimsical, happy, and inviting in this memorial located appropriately on the grounds of the National Academies, across Constitution Avenue from the Mall. Sculptor Robert Berks' lumpy style imbues the bronze statue with more warmth than you'd expect from 4 tons of metal. The great physicist is depicted sitting on steps, and children love to climb up and sit in his lap. In one hand, he holds a paper with mathematical equations summarizing his most important scientific contributions. A map of the universe—about which he offered so many accurate analyses—spreads out at his feet. Einstein quotes are engraved on the steps, including one about his "joy and amazement at the beauty and grandeur of this world."

Constitution Ave. NW (btw. 21st and 22nd sts.). Always open. Metro: Foggy Bottom or Metrobus L1, H1, or N3.

Korean War Veterans Memorial   Walk among 15 soldiers, two Marines, Navy medic and Air Force observer—ghostly and larger than life—who are frozen in perpetual patrol in a field of juniper. Before Vietnam, this undeclared war helped to drive a once-popular president (Truman) from office, took more than 50,000 American lives, and left the nation wanting to forget rather than memorialize. Finally, on the 42nd anniversary of the armistice that ended the fighting—but which has not yet officially sealed the peace—this memorial was dedicated on July 27, 1995, by the presidents of the United States and South Korea, Bill Clinton and Kim Young Sam.

French Dr. SW and Independence Ave. (southeast of the Lincoln Memorial). ℭ **202/ 426-6841**. www.nps.gov/kowa. Always open. Rangers on duty daily 9:30am– 11:30pm. Metro: Foggy Bottom or Metrobus 13A, 13B, 13G, or 13F.

National Law Enforcement Officers Memorial   More than 18,000 names are engraved on the blue-gray marble walls of the National Law Enforcement Officers Memorial in Judiciary Square. They honor all the federal, state, and local officers killed in the line of duty since New York City Sheriff's Deputy Isaac Smith became the first known U.S. law-enforcement fatality on May 17, 1792. Supporters are raising funds to build a National Law Enforcement Museum across the street from the memorial in the 400 block of E St. NW. In the meantime, you can explore interactive exhibits about law enforcement at the memorial's visitor center about 3 blocks away.

E St. (btw. 4th and 5th sts.). ℭ **202/737-3400.** www.nleomf.com. Always open. Judiciary Square Metrorail Station. Visitor center: 400 7th St. NW (at D St.). Mon–Fri 9am–5pm; Sat 10am–5pm; Sun noon–5pm. Metro: Archives.

U.S. Navy Memorial   The global reach of the U.S. Navy is symbolized by the 100-foot-diameter granite map of the world that is the memorial's centerpiece. Other elements include fountains, pools, masts, 26 bronze reliefs that depict important moments in U.S. naval history, and a bronze statue of a young sailor who has thrust his hands into his coat pockets as his eyes gaze into the distance. Metal from eight Navy ships—from the 18th-century *Constitution* (Old Ironsides) and *Constellation* to the nuclear submarine *Seawolf*—was mixed in the bronze. The adjacent **Naval Heritage Center** contains exhibits about Naval history.

701 Pennsylvania Ave. NW (at 7th St.). ℭ **800/821-8892** or 202/737-2300. www. navymemorial.org. Memorial always open. Heritage center: Daily 9:30am–5pm. Closed Thanksgiving, Dec 25, Jan 1. Metro: Archives.

★ **Franklin Delano Roosevelt Memorial**   Roosevelt said he wanted a memorial the size of his desk. You can see it on the National Archives grounds at Pennsylvania Ave. and 9th St. NW. But that didn't prove to be enough. So, in 1997, this memorial was dedicated: four open-air "rooms," on 7.5 acres of land, that tell the story of Roosevelt's four presidential terms. Among the sculpture here: a man listening at a radio to a "fireside chat," through which Roosevelt spoke directly to the American people; men in a Depression breadline; Roosevelt with his dog Fala; and First Lady Eleanor Roosevelt. Note how Fala's statue shines where visitors pet it. The memorial opened without a depiction of Roosevelt in a wheelchair, an image he hid during his life. Advocates for the disabled howled, and a statue of the president in a wheelchair was added. You can see a wheelchair he used, and other memorabilia, in the information center.

W. Basin Dr. SW (at Ohio Dr.). ℭ **202/426-6841.** www.nps.gov/fdrm. Always open. Rangers on duty daily 9:30am–11:30pm. 1.6-mile walk from Smithsonian Metrorail Station.

★ **George Washington Monument**   In addition to honoring our first president, this towering marble obelisk offers the most spectacular view of the nation's capital from its 555-foot peak. The ride to the top takes just 70 seconds. You can stare out the windows as long as you like. You descend at a slower speed so that you can view the monument's interior, especially the commemorative stones which were donated in Washington's honor by the 50 states, Indian tribes, foreign governments, and private organizations. On summer evenings, military bands perform here, and the monument provides a gleaming exclamation point for the 4th of July fireworks. Construction began in 1848 and wasn't completed until 1884, the 36-year gap caused first by a depletion of funds and then by the Civil War. By the time there was enough money to finish the project, the marble used in the early construction couldn't be matched perfectly, hence the two-tone effect you see today. FINE PRINT You can get free time-specific tickets for riding the elevator on the day of your visit at the Washington Monument Lodge, near 15th Street and Madison Drive, beginning at 8:30am. One person may get up to six tickets. Tickets disappear quickly in spring and summer, and the line sometimes starts forming by 7am. You can buy tickets in advance by calling ✆ **877/444-6777** or on the Internet at **www.recreation.gov**. The charge is $1.50 per ticket, plus 50¢ per order. April through September, you should book months ahead.

Btw. Constitution Ave. NW, Independence Ave. SW, and 15th and 17th sts. ✆ **202/ 426-6841;** advance tickets ✆ 877/444-6777. www.nps.gov/wamo; advance tickets www.recreation.gov. Daily 9am–5pm; Memorial Day through Labor Day weekend till 10pm. Metro: Smithsonian.

World War II Memorial   Just as the Vietnam Veterans Memorial was criticized for its minimalism, controversy surrounded the World War II Memorial because of its size, complexity, and location. Because it sits in the middle of the Mall between the long-standing Lincoln Memorial and Washington Monument, critics complained that it would disrupt the hallowed view from Lincoln's seat to the Capitol dome, which had been interrupted only by Washington's thin obelisk. Critics also argue that it's too big with too many elements. The giant plaza bakes in the summer. (Come in spring or fall.) The memorial contains pillars, wreaths, arches, fountains, pools, stars, eagles, quotations, and bas reliefs. The final rap is that the memorial gets the symbolism wrong: There's a tall pillar with a wreath for each state and territory that fought in the war, which emphasizes separatism when in fact the country was never more unified. The beauty of

America, of course, is that each visitor can decide for himself. You can check Lincoln's view. You can study the new memorial up close.

17th St. NW (btw. Constitution and Independence aves.). © **202/619-7222.** www. nps.gov/nwwm. Always open. Rangers on duty daily 9:30am–11:30pm. Metro: Smithsonian or Circulator.

4 Galleries & Art Museums

ALWAYS FREE

Freer and Sackler Galleries of Art   Although these two galleries comprise the Smithsonian's museum of Asian art, perhaps the most stunning item on display is by American James McNeill Whistler, in the Freer. It's an entire room—the Peacock Room—that Whistler painted without the permission of its owner. The brilliant colors and intricate patterns—and the many peacocks—will knock you over, even if you wouldn't necessarily want the decoration for *your* dining room. Take the Freer **tour** (noon daily except Wed and federal holidays) to learn the story behind this bizarre artistic act.

The Freer also displays a world-renowned collection of art from Asia and the Near East. Highlights include Chinese paintings, Japanese folding screens, Korean ceramics, Buddhist sculpture, and Indian and Persian manuscripts. In the Sackler—connected by an underground exhibition space—highlights include early Chinese bronzes and jades, Chinese paintings and lacquer ware, ancient Near Eastern ceramics and metal ware, South and Southeast Asian sculpture, and Islamic arts. The galleries also mount temporary exhibits of contemporary Asian art.

Btw. the Smithsonian Castle and Independence Ave. SW.© **202/633-1000.** www. asia.si.edu. Daily 10am–5:30pm. Closed Dec 25. Metro: Smithsonian.

Hirshhorn Museum and Sculpture Garden   If modern and contemporary art is your thing, then the Hirshhorn is your museum. All the top guns are here: Picasso, Benton, Christo, Close, Gorky, Hopper, Miró, O'Keeffe, Warhol, Bacon, DeKooning, Matisse, Rauschenberg . . . you get the—uh—picture. The Hirshhorn cannot show all 12,000 works in its collection, so it mounts temporary exhibitions, often built around themes. Across Jefferson Drive is the sunken Sculpture Garden, with more than 60 works by Rodin, Moore, Koons, Calder, and others (a particularly neat place in winter when the statues are draped in snow). More sculpture is displayed on the plaza surrounding the museum, including the striking, 60-foot-high "Needle Tower" by Kenneth Snelson.

Independence Ave. (at 7th St. SW). ☎ **202/633-4674.** www.hirshhorn.si.edu. Daily 10am–5:30pm; Plaza 7:30am–5:30pm; Sculpture Garden 7:30am–dusk. Closed Dec 25. Metro: L'Enfant Plaza.

National Museum of African Art   Both traditional and contemporary art from throughout Africa is displayed here. Among the indefinite exhibits are the ceramics hall, which showcases traditional and modern pottery and other ceramics, and the Disney-Tishman collection of traditional art from sub-Saharan Africa. The Eliot Elisofon Photographic Archives contain more than 300,000 photos that document African arts, people, and history of the last 120 years.

950 Independence Ave. SW (midway btw. 7th and 12th sts.). ☎ **202/633-4600.** www.nmafa.si.edu. Daily 10am–5:30pm. Closed Dec 25. Metro: Smithsonian.

National Portrait Gallery   The Portrait Gallery and the Smithsonian American Art Museum (p. 117) share the Old Patent Office Building, a columned Greek Revival structure in Penn Quarter which no less an artist than Walt Whitman called "the noblest of Washington buildings." President Andrew Jackson laid the cornerstone for this "temple to the industrial arts" in 1836, and it's become an important historical structure. That's appropriate, because the Portrait Gallery really is more about history than about art. Congress established it to collect portraits of folks who have made "significant contributions to the history, development and culture of the people of the United States." All the presidents are here, of course, and many other powerful political leaders. But there also are significant contributors from other aspects of American life—Calvin Klein, for example, and Mia Hamm, Toni Morrison, Pocahontas, Frederick Douglass, Lucille Ball, Janis Joplin, Miles Davis, Jackie Robinson, Susan B. Anthony, Cesar Chavez, Rosa Parks, and Shari Lewis with Lamb Chop. The portraits come in many media, not just oil on canvas. Check out cartoonist Pat Oliphant's sculpture of president George H.W. Bush, appearing possibly naked, leaning forward to pitch a horseshoe. FINE PRINT The gallery and the art museum do not simply divide this building in half. Some galleries belong to one, some to the other, and some space is shared. To tell where you are, look at the label that describes the art work. In the art museum, the artist's name appears first. In the portrait gallery, it's the subject.

8th St. NW (btw. F and G sts.). $\textcircled{C}$ **202-633/8300.** www.npg.si.edu. Daily 11:30am–7pm. Closed Dec 25. Metro: Gallery Place.

Renwick Gallery   Not as overpowering as the Old Patent Office Building, this Second Empire structure, across Pennsylvania Avenue from the White House, is striking in its own right. It was completed in 1874—to plans by noted architect James Renwick, Jr.—to house the art collection of William Wilson Corcoran. (Renwick also designed the Smithsonian's Castle and St. Patrick's Cathedral in New York. Corcoran later moved his collection to larger quarters just down 17th St.) Inside the Renwick, you'll find rotating displays of the gallery's collection of American crafts and decorative arts from the 19th century to today. Among the more interesting are Larry Fuente's *Game Fish,* with its glittering scales of game pieces, buttons, and beads, and Albert Paley's *Portal Gates,* made from forged steel, brass, copper, and bronze.

1661 Pennsylvania Ave. NW (east of 17th St.). $\textcircled{C}$ **202/633-7970.** www.americanart. si.edu/renwick. Daily 10am–5:30pm. Closed Dec 25. Metro: Farragut West.

Smithsonian American Art Museum   Here you find, in a magnificent setting, all kinds of American art from colonial times to today. The museum holds 41,500 pieces by more than 7,000 artists. Because of the recent renovation (see National Portrait Gallery review for more info), the galleries are extremely well-lighted, so it's easier to appreciate the art than it is in many other museums. The collection covers the gamut of what American artists have produced, including works by such notables as Charles Willson Peale, Gilbert Stuart, James McNeill Whistler, Robert Rauschenberg, Peter Paul Rubens, Georgia O'Keefe, Thomas Hart Benton, and Grandma Moses. You can trace photography from its 19th-century birth to the present and peruse traditional and contemporary folk art from many ethnic groups. One of the most eye-popping pieces is a gigantic folk-art installation, covered with aluminum foil, titled "Throne of the Third Heaven of the Nations' Millennium General Assembly." It's in the 1st floor west wing. Don't miss it.

8th St. NW (btw. F and G sts.). $\textcircled{C}$ **202/633-7970.** www.americanart.si.edu. Daily 11:30am–7pm. Closed Dec 25. Metro: Gallery Place.

SOMETIMES FREE

National Museum of Women in the Arts   The world's only museum dedicated to women artists is housed in an ornate palace originally built for one of the most famous all-male organizations in the world— the Masons. Now the former temple houses more than 3,000 pieces created by women from the 16th century to today. Included are paintings, sculpture, photography, and pieces made by 18th- and 19th-century women silversmiths. FINE PRINT You can get in free the first Sunday of every month. If you're 18 or younger, admission is always free.

1250 New York Ave. NW (at 13th St.). ℂ **800/222-7270** or 202/783-5000. www. nmwa.org. Admission $10; students and seniors $8; under 18, free. Mon–Sat 10am– 5pm, Sun noon–5pm. Closed Jan 1, Thanksgiving, Dec 25. Metro: Metro Center.

Phillips Collection   Opened in 1921 as America's first museum of modern art, the Phillips also displays the works of earlier artists who influenced the modern masters. Thus, museum founder Duncan Phillips acquired El Greco's *The Repentant St. Peter,* painted around 1600, because the collector considered the artist to be the "first impassioned expressionist." This is a very personal space and collection. Phillips founded the museum, with his mother Eliza Laughlin Phillips, in his home. He built the collection with his wife Marjorie, and ran the museum until his death in 1966. The facility has been expanded several times, but the 19th-century Georgian Revival mansion continues to house galleries. The Phillips is noted for impressionist and post-impressionist paintings. Its most famous piece is Renoir's *Luncheon of the Boating Party.* You'll also run into van Gogh, Monet, Degas, Gauguin, Cézanne, Rothko, Matisse, de Kooning, Hopper, O'Keeffe, and others. There's another personal mark left by Duncan and Marjorie. He was a baseball fan and held box seats behind the Washington Senators' dugout. She would sketch during games, and her 1951 painting, "Night Baseball," hangs in the old mansion. FINE PRINT Pricing is complicated here. If you're 18 or younger, you get in free. The permanent collection is free to everyone Tuesday through Friday, though contributions are accepted.

1600 21st St. NW (at Q St.). ℂ **202/387-2151.** www.phillipscollection.org. Admission: Free Tues–Fri. Sat–Mon: $10 adults; $8 students and seniors; 18 and under free. For special exhibits: $12 adults; students and seniors $10. Tues–Sat 10am–5pm; Sun 11am–6pm; Thurs 11am–8:30pm. Closed Mon, Jan 1, July 4, Thanksgiving, Dec 25. Metro: Dupont Circle.

5 Historical Sites

ALWAYS FREE

Dumbarton Oaks From the early days of the Republic until the founding of the United Nations, this mansion played prominent roles in American history. Now it reaches further into the past, supporting scholarship in Byzantine and Pre-Columbian studies, gardens and landscape, as well as being a museum of Byzantine and Pre-Columbian art. Built in 1801, Dumbarton Oaks provided housing for John C. Calhoun while he was a prominent senator in the second quarter of the 19th century. During World War II, the mansion hosted the Dumbarton Oaks Conversations—diplomatic negotiations that laid the foundations for the U.N. Today, the museum displays Byzantine art from the 4th to the 15th centuries and Pre-Columbian objects produced by Aztecs, Mayans, and other peoples of the Americas before the arrival of Europeans. Up to 15 visitors can take a guided tour of rooms not open to the public at 3pm Saturdays. FINE PRINT Dumbarton Oaks also has large, interesting gardens, but they're free only when nothing blooms, November 1 to mid-March.

Museum: 1703 32nd St. NW (btw. R and S sts.). ✆ **202/339-6401.** www.doaks.org. Tues–Sun 2–5pm. Closed federal holidays. Metrobus 31, 32, 36, D1, D2, D3, or D6; Circulator. Gardens: R St. NW (at 31st St.). ✆ **202/339-6401.** www.doaks.org/gardens. Nov 1 to mid-Mar Tues–Sun 2–5pm. Free. Mid-Mar to Oct 31 Tues–Sun 2–6pm. Admission $8 adults, children and seniors $5, children 2 and under, free. Closed Sun, federal holidays, in bad weather. Metrobus 31, 32, 36, D1, D2, D3, or D6; Circulator.

Ford's Theatre & Peterson House The place where actor John Wilkes Booth shot President Abraham Lincoln is a functioning theater again, and you can attend performances as well as tour the historical site. Ford's did not function as a theater from the night Lincoln was assassinated in 1865 until it was renovated and reopened in 1968. Another extensive renovation of the theater—and of the Lincoln Museum in the basement—was carried out from 2007 to 2009. The museum now reaches beyond the assassination to tell about Lincoln's life as president. Artifacts most relevant to the theater include the clothing Lincoln wore that night; the .44 caliber Derringer that Booth fired; the dagger, compass, diary, and two revolvers Booth carried; items taken from Booth's conspirators; and first lady Mary Todd Lincoln's opera glasses case. Exhibits also address Lincoln's campaigns and his initial train trip to Washington, part of which Barack Obama replicated for his inauguration. Across the street, you can visit Peterson House, where Lincoln died. FINE PRINT Visitors must have timed tickets to enter the theater. You can obtain up to six same-day tickets for free at the box office beginning at 8:30am. Advance tickets can be purchased from Ticketmaster for $2.50 each. The theater closes to tours during performances and rehearsals, the museum during performances. Peterson House remains open.

511 10th St. NW (btw. E and F sts.). ℭ **202/426-6924.** www.nps.gov/foth. Performance and advance tour tickets ℭ 202/397-7328; www.ticketmaster.com. Performance information ℭ 202/347-4833; www.fords.org. Advance tickets $2.50. Performance prices vary. Daily 9am–5:30pm. Petersen House 9:30am–5:30pm. Closed Dec 25. Theater closed to tours during performances, rehearsals. Metro: Metro Center.

6 Government Buildings

ALWAYS FREE

Bureau of Engraving and Printing   Harry Truman may have said the buck stops in the White House, but it starts here, where printers and engravers make money, postage stamps, Treasury bonds, and White House invitations. No free samples! But you can purchase a souvenir (such as uncut or shredded currency) in the **visitor center,** where you also can play with interactive displays. On the guided tour, you can watch as money and other documents are engraved and printed. FINE PRINT March through August, you must get free timed tickets on the day you tour. The ticket booth on Raoul Wallenberg Place (15th St.) opens at 8am, but people line up as early as 5:30am, especially in April when the Cherry Blossom festival and school field trips are underway. Usually all tickets are distributed by 8:30am. Without tickets, you can skip the tour and enter the visitor center through the tour entrance on the 14th Street side.

14th and C sts. SW. ℭ **866/874-2330** or 202/874-2330. www.moneyfactory.gov. Sept–Mar Mon–Fri 8:30am–3:30pm; Apr–Aug till 7:30pm. Tours every 15 min. Sept–Mar 9–10:45am and 12:30–2pm; Apr–Aug 9–10:45am, 12:30–3:45pm, and 5–7pm; ticket booth (on Raoul Wallenberg Place) 8am till tickets gone. Closed Sat–Sun, federal holidays, Dec 25–Jan 1. Metro: Smithsonian.

✯ **National Archives**   If you haven't visited the Archives since the major renovations of the last decade, you won't recognize the place. Previously, visitors squinted to glimpse documentary treasures behind thick glass. Now, it's much easier to view the documents, and U.S. history is explained with multimedia presentations, interactive exhibits, and other state-of-the-art technologies. The Declaration of Independence, the Constitution of the United States, the Bill of Rights, a 1297 version of the Magna Carta, and numerous other historical documents are displayed here. In the Charters of Freedom Hall, visitors for the first time can see all four pages of the Constitution at once. Multimedia exhibits display documents and

Roosevelt's Other Memorial

President Franklin Roosevelt said the only memorial he wanted was a marker the size of his desk, and initially that's what he got. You can see the marble block on the northwest corner of the National Archives grounds at 9th Street NW and Pennsylvania Avenue The Roosevelt Memorial we reviewed earlier (p. 113) is quite a bit larger.

make their historical importance easier to understand. "Documents" today include photographs, films, audio recordings, video recordings, and digital media. Watch Harry Truman deliver the first televised presidential address, about a 1947 international food crisis. At the Archives gift shop, you can buy copies of documents as well as books, CDs, and games based on the institution's collections. Beyond being a tourist attraction, the Archives is the nation's record-keeper (official name: National Archives and Records Administration), and it has facilities around the country. Holdings include Indian treaties, the Emancipation Proclamation, slave ship manifests, Japanese surrender documents from World War II, the Louisiana Purchase Treaty signed by Napoleon Bonaparte, and much more. The collection contains 9 billion printed or written pages, 20 million photographs, 365,000 reels of film, 110,000 videotapes, billions of machine-readable data sets, and 7.2 million maps, charts, and architectural drawings. Anyone can conduct research here. FINE PRINT Waits of an hour or more may be encountered during March, April, May, Thanksgiving weekend, and the week between Christmas and New Year's. To skip the lines, make advance reservations by phone or on the Internet.

Constitution Ave. NW (at 9th St.). ✆ **866/272-6272** or 202/357-5000; reservations ✆ 877/874-7616 or 202/357-5450. www.archives.gov; reservations www.recreation. gov. Daily Mar 15 to Labor Day 10am–7pm, last admission 6:30pm; day after Labor Day to Mar 14 10am–5:30pm, last admission 5pm. Closed Thanksgiving, Dec 25. Metro: Archives.

State Department   If you've ever wondered why the State Department is sometimes referred to as Foggy Bottom, it's not because of the opaque language diplomats often employ. (That's just an appropriate coincidence.) Foggy Bottom happens to be the name of the neighborhood—prone to fog and industrial smoke in the 19th century—where the department's headquarters stands. The department occupies a plain gray box here, and the drab corridors inside are even duller. But tourists can't really see them anyway (state secrets, you know). What you can see—on a **guided tour** for which you must make reservations—are the Diplomatic Reception Rooms, where the secretary of state and other high-ranking officials entertain visiting dignitaries. The rooms are interesting for what occurs in them, for their spectacular architecture, for their collection of Revolutionary era arts and furniture (Thomas Jefferson's desk, for instance), and for the view from the eighth-floor terrace outside. They're on display only by guided tours for which reservations must be made, usually three months in advance. Don't be spooked by the "authorized users only" warning at the website. The tour is not recommended for children younger than 12.

2201 C St. NW (at 22nd St.). ✆ **202/647-3241.** www.state.gov/www/about_state/diprooms/index.html. Tours Mon–Fri 9:30, 10:30am, 2:45pm. Metro: Foggy Bottom or Metrobus L1, H1, or N3.

7 Awesome Architecture

ALWAYS FREE

⭐ **Anderson House**   In our opinion, this is Washington's most mind-boggling hidden gem. The first time we saw it, we were stunned. We had driven and ridden buses past it uncountable times and never noticed it behind its stone wall. The Beaux Arts exterior is enough to knock you out. But it's inside that you're truly blown away by architecture, decoration and furnishing that seem more appropriate to a European palace than a Washington home—even a Washington mansion. Its 50 rooms were built between 1902 and 1905 by wealthy diplomat Larz Anderson III and his wife Isabel, to serve as their *winter home* where they entertained the elite of Washington and the diplomatic corps. Guests included U.S. presidents and visiting kings and queens. The interior features towering rooms, floor-to-ceiling murals, large crystal chandeliers, carved-wood walls and doors, gilded ceilings, ornate iron staircases, intricate marble floors, a winter garden over-looking a reflecting pool, French furniture, Flemish tapestries, Asian decorative arts, antiquities, the Andersons' eclectic collections of art from around the world, and artifacts from the American Revolution, including armaments and paintings by Gilbert Stuart, Charles Willson Peale, and James Peale. The Society of the Cincinnati, to which Anderson belonged, makes its headquarters here. It was formed by Revolutionary War officers and is continued by their descendents.

2118 Massachusetts Ave. NW (btw. 21st and O sts.). © **202/785-2040.** www.society ofthecincinnati.org. Tues–Sat 1–4pm; tours quarter-past each hour. Closed Dec 25, Jan 1, Thanksgiving, and during some society events. Metro: Dupont Circle.

National Airport   If you fly in or out of here, you have the opportu-nity to study some fascinating architecture. First you have the histori-cally interesting old Terminal A. State-of-the-art when it opened in 1941, this terminal combined Art Deco, Streamlined Moderne, Colo-nial Revival, and Stripped Classical styles. The National Park Service termed it a reflection of a debate about whether future American architecture would be modern or neoclassical. Here, it turned out to be both. The new terminal also offers picture-window views of Wash-ington landmarks. Because of heightened security, only ticketed pas-sengers are allowed access to the gate concourses. But, if you're not a passenger, you can see much of the interesting stuff from outside those security checkpoints. When entering the terminal, the first thing you notice is the roof with 54 domes designed to suggest Thomas Jefferson's contributions to architecture. Works by 30 artists are incorporated into the floors, walls, windows, and other elements of the terminal in various materials, including stained glass, marble, terrazzo, cast bronze, painted steel, porcelain, enamel, paint on board, paint on canvas, and hammered aluminum and copper. As a practical, functioning airport, it's easy to navigate and has an unusu-ally good collection of eating and shopping spots. In 1998, Republi-cans in the GOP-controlled Congress added their hero's name to the place, producing the rather lengthy official moniker "Ronald Reagan Washington National Airport." FINE PRINT You can save a buck an hour on parking using the economy lot and taking the shuttle bus to the airport.

Off George Washington Memorial Pkwy. in Arlington, VA. © **703/417-8000.** www. metwashairports.com/national. Always open. Parking $3–$4/hr., $12–$36/day. Metro: Ronald Reagan Washington National Airport.

Old Post Office   This post office did not win universal admiration for its architecture when it opened as the city's largest and tallest government building in 1899. Its busy Romanesque style led one senator to describe the place as "a cross between a cathedral and a cotton mill." You can ride the elevator 270 feet to the clock tower's observation deck for a great **view** without the long lines of the Washington Monument. Visible are Capitol Hill, the White House, the Mall, and even such Virginia landmarks as Arlington National Cemetery, the Pentagon, the U.S. Air Force Memorial, and National Airport. The tower— now the third tallest building in Washington—contains the Bells of Congress, a Bicentennial gift from London that replicates the Westminster Abbey bells. They are rung by the National Cathedral's Washington Ringing Society on federal holidays, days of national mourning, the opening and closing of congressional sessions, and Thursday nights for practice. No longer a post office, the building houses the National Endowment for the Arts, the National Endowment for the Humanities, the Advisory Council on Historic Preservation, a handful of shops and fast-food stands, and a soaring atrium where musicians often perform for free.

1100 Pennsylvania Ave. NW (at 12th St.). © **202/606-8691.** www.nps.gov/opot. Memorial Day through Labor Day, Mon–Wed and Fri–Sat 9am–8pm; Thurs 9am–7pm; Sun and federal holidays 10am–6pm. Rest of year Mon–Sat 9–5pm; Sun and federal holidays 10am–6pm. Closed Thanksgiving, Dec 25, and Jan 1. Observation deck sometimes closed during inclement weather. Last ride up 15 min. before closing. Metro: Federal Triangle.

Smithsonian Castle   The first Smithsonian Institution building is one of the most remarkable sights in Washington, if only because it seems so out of place: It resembles a 12th-century Norman castle in the 21st century. On the other hand, the structure suggests the Old World is not an inappropriate symbol for an institution that was founded with a bequest by James Smithson, a Brit who never set foot in the United States. The Castle was constructed of red Maryland sandstone in 1855 and was designed by noted architect James Renwick, Jr., whose other works include the Smithsonian's Renwick Gallery, near the White House, and St. Patrick's Cathedral in New York. Today, it houses the institution's administrative offices and serves as the Smithsonian visitor center. Waiting to orient you to the institution's multitude of offerings are two information desks, a 10-minute video overview, interactive information screens in six languages, a scale model of Washington's monumental core, a tactile map of the same with Braille labels, and display cases with a sampling of objects from all the Smithsonian museums. You can also get a bite to eat here. And you can visit Mr. Smithson, who is buried in a crypt near the north entrance. Guided tours are offered on an irregular basis. Check at an info desk.

1000 Jefferson Dr. (at 10th St. on the Mall). © **202/633-1000.** www.si.edu/visit/ infocenter/sicastle.htm. Daily 8:30am–5:30pm. Closed Dec 25. Metro: Smithsonian.

Union Station A bustling transportation hub when it opened in 1908, Union Station has regained its status as one of the busiest places in town. The train is the best way to travel in the Washington–New York corridor today. Hordes of subway travelers use the Metrorail station daily. Maryland and Virginia commuter trains converge here. Cabs line up outside. Tour buses and Metrobuses come and go. More than 32 million people pass through this place every year. The building is, indeed, a railroad palace. Located on the edge of what had been a rough Capitol Hill shantytown known as Swampoodle, it was designed in grand Beaux Arts–style by Daniel Burnham, who gathered inspiration from the Diocletian Baths and the Arch of Constantine in Rome. When construction was completed in 1908, Union Station occupied more land area than any other U.S. building and there was no bigger train station in the world. Presidents really used the President's Room (now home to B. Smith's Restaurant), and kings, queens, and other world leaders passed through with regularity. Airplanes and interstate highways drove the station into a long decline. But a monumental renovation campaign led to a spectacular reopening in 1988, and now you can gaze upon the grandeur that welcomed travelers a century ago—with a lot of new amenities. A fountain and a statue of Columbus stand outside the building, along with a replica of the Liberty Bell called the Freedom Bell. Inside, sculptures of Roman soldiers by Augustus Saint-Gaudens stand guard over the Main Hall, which features a 96-foot high barrel-vaulted ceiling. The East Hall boasts stenciled skylights. At its east end, be sure to peek into B. Smith's to see the soaring ceilings and ornate architecture of the President's Room.

50 Massachusetts Ave. NE (at 1st St). © **202/289-1908.** www.unionstationDC.com. Always open. Metro: Union Station.

FREE (WITH SUGGESTED DONATION)

National Building Museum   If visiting impressive buildings piques your interest in architecture, then you want to pay a visit to the National Building Museum, which is dedicated to architecture, design, engineering, construction, and urban planning. The building here is fascinating in its own right. Designed in 1881 and opened in 1887, it was constructed to house the Pension Bureau, a predecessor of today's Department of Veterans Affairs. Among the building's most striking features is a 3-foot-high terra-cotta frieze of Civil War soldiers that wraps around the entire exterior. The **Great Hall**—316 feet long, 116 feet wide, and up to 159 feet high—has a central fountain and eight 75-foot-tall Corinthian columns that are painted to look like marble and are among the tallest interior columns in the world. Its monumental dimensions and spectacular appearance make the Great Hall a popular site for major events, including presidential inaugural balls. The focus of the museum is on the building process, architectural styles, and construction techniques. A long-term exhibit is "Washington: Symbol and City," which tells the story of how the nation's capital grew to its current form. Staff frequently conduct hands-on activities for children. Phone or check the website for scheduled activities. In the Building Zone, kids can erect their own structure. You can take a guided tour of the Building Museum building daily at 11:30am and 12:30 and 1:30pm. Also call or check the website for guided tours of the exhibits. FINE PRINT The museum does not charge admission, but it does suggest a $5 donation.

401 F St. NW (btw. 4th and 5th sts.). ℰ **202/272-2448.** www.nbm.org. Mon–Sat 10am–5pm, Sun 11am–5pm; Building Zone till 4pm. Closed Jan 1, Thanksgiving, Dec 25, and for rare special events. Metro: Judiciary Square.

Washington National Cathedral   Officially named the Cathedral Church of Saint Peter and Saint Paul, this Episcopal house of worship frequently does serve as the National Cathedral it's always called. In 1907, President Theodore Roosevelt joined the bishop of London in laying the foundation stone, which came from a field near Bethlehem. The cathedral was founded to serve all faiths. It's been the site of presidential inaugural prayer services and funerals. Services to celebrate the end of World War I and World War II were held here. Martin Luther King, Jr., delivered his last Sunday sermon here on March 31, 1968, a few days before his assassination. The tomb of the only president buried in DC, Woodrow Wilson, is near the Space Window, which is embedded with a shard of moon rock from the Apollo XI moon landing in 1969. Standing on a high hill, the cathedral's towers rise higher than anything else in Washington and can be seen throughout DC and into the Virginia suburbs. It's the world's sixth-largest cathedral and the seat of the Episcopal bishop of Washington. You can find much to see and do here, outside as well as inside. When you arrive, ask about joining the half-hour highlights tour. You can rent an **audio tour** ($4) or wander about on your own. Take the elevator to the **Pilgrim Observation Gallery** for a 360-degree view of the city. Youngsters 10 and older enjoy the gargoyle tour. (Bring binoculars and look for Darth Vader.) The Cathedral offers too many tours to detail here. Get information at the website. Whatever you do, be sure to check out the gardens as well as the interior. FINE PRINT The real business of the church—weddings, funerals, worship services, and the like—takes precedence. So programs and tours may be canceled. Phoning or checking the website is wise before you visit. Also note: While there's no charge to enter the cathedral, you're asked to donate $5 per adult, $3 for seniors, students, and those in the military, or $15 per family. Many tours and activities also come with fees.

3101 Wisconsin Ave. NW (btw. Massachusetts Ave. and Woodley Rd.). © **202/537-6200.** www.nationalcathedral.org; tour information www.nationalcathedral.org/visit/index. shtml. Mon–Fri 10am–5pm; Sat 10am–4pm; Sun 1–4pm. Highlight tours Sun 1–2:30pm; Mon–Fri 10–11:30am, 12:45–4pm; Sat 10–11:30am, 12:45–3:30pm. Parking Mon–Fri $4/hr., max $16; Sat $5 flat rate; Sun free. Metrobus 31, 32, 36, and 37.

8 Parks/Gardens

ALWAYS FREE

Enid A. Haupt Garden Between the Smithsonian Castle and Independence Avenue, this is actually a collection of gardens that grow above the underground sections of the Arthur M. Sackler Gallery of Asian Art, the National Museum of African Art, and the S. Dillon Ripley Center's International Gallery. The **Parterre** is a large flower bed, lined with benches, in which designs are formed with the dirt, grass, shrubs, and flowers. The **Moongate Garden** was inspired by the Temple of Heaven in Beijing. It features a circular granite "island" and granite walkways that bridge the water. Also of interest are the cast iron gates at Independence Avenue Called the Renwick Gates, they were based on an 1849 drawing by James Renwick, Jr., architect of

Feeding Your Face As Well As Your Soul

The National Cathedral is a bit off the standard tourist path, but you can grab a good lunch or dinner at two neighborhood restaurants:

- ● **2 Amys:** This place serves the best pizza in town—real Neapolitan pizza, with thin, chewy crust. It's a great spot for kids (p. 87).

- ● **Cactus Cantina:** A large, boisterous Tex-Mex spot with an outdoor dining area, where our daughter once encountered President Bush II and his entourage (p. 87).

Also, it's not cheap, but another alternative, if you feel like a splurge, is the Cathedral's **Tour and Tea,** usually offered every Tuesday and Wednesday. An in-depth Cathedral tour begins at 1:30pm and ends in the Pilgrim Observation Gallery at 2:45pm. There, you take in the view of Washington while consuming English tea with finger sandwiches, cookies, and scones with clotted cream—for 25 bucks. Make a reservation—highly recommended—at ℂ **202/537-8993** or www.national-cathedral.org/visit/tourAndTea.shtml. The Cathedral also occasionally serves "Teddy Bear Tea" for kids. Ask at the phone number above, or e-mail **tea@cathedral.org**.

the Castle and other notable buildings. The 4.2-acre park is a pleasant place to rest when you're touring the National Mall. **Guided tours,** from the Castle's south patio, are offered from May into the fall on Wednesdays at 1pm. The garden is named for the woman who endowed it, an heir to the Annenberg publishing fortune and a one-time editor and publisher of *Seventeen* magazine.

Btw. Independence Ave. SW and the Smithsonian Castle. ℂ **202/663-1000.** www.gardens.si.edu/horticulture/gardens/Haupt/hpt_home.htm. Sept to mid-May daily 7am–5:45pm; mid-May to Aug till 9:15pm. Metro: Smithsonian.

Lafayette Square With shade trees, benches and the White House and Washington Monument (in the distance) for a view, Lafayette Square is a pleasant place to bring food and drink that you purchase at one of the many nearby food spots. Once part of the White House North Lawn, it's now separated from the president's mansion by Pennsylvania Avenue and a security fence. In fact, this is a place where DC's heightened security smacks you hard upside the head. Pennsylvania Avenue is closed to motor vehicles, and barriers, and guards abound. Shut out that unhappy 21st-century fact, and you can pretend you're visiting a 19th-century town square. To the west are historic houses. The **Decatur House,** at the northwest corner of the square, was built in 1818 for Navy Commodore Stephen Decatur, Jr., and later was the home of President Martin Van Buren and Henry Clay, who served as U.S. representative, Speaker of the House, Senator, and Secretary of State. You can check out an ethnically diverse collection of statues: Marquis de Lafayette, for whom the square is named, the Comte Jean de Rochambeau, French general in the American Revolution; Thaddeus Kosciusko, Polish engineer who helped to fortify American facilities during the Revolution; Baron Frederich von Steuben, German military leader who trained Revolutionary War soldiers; and President Andrew Jackson on horseback. The park attracts lunching workers from nearby office buildings, resting tourists, and a diverse collection of demonstrators who like to display their signs at the president's door. Over the centuries, the land has accommodated a farmhouse, an apple orchard, a cemetery, a racetrack, slave auctions, a zoo, and a camp for soldiers during the War of 1812. According to the National Park Service, it's also home to "the highest density of squirrels per square acre ever recorded."

Bordered by Pennsylvania Ave. NW and 15th, 17th and H sts. www.nps.gov/history/nr/travel/wash/dc30.htm. Metro: McPherson Square. Always open.

★ **National Zoological Park**   It's all happening at the zoo. This definitely is the top kid-pleaser in town, and a pretty fun place for most grownups as well. We can't even begin to tell you all you can see here: lions and tigers and bears, *oh my,* and a whole lot more. Some 2,000 animals occupy various kinds of exhibits scattered around the 163-acre park. Grab a map and schedule of events at the Education Building near the Connecticut Avenue entrance. Zookeepers conduct demonstrations and give talks throughout the park. It's always fun to be around at feeding time and when the elephants and seals put on performances. Some highlights: The **giant pandas** have been the most popular zoo residents, especially since the in-zoo birth of Tai Shan (tie-SHON) in 2005. Unfortunately, Tai Shan moved to China in early 2010, and it's possible his parents, mother Mei Xiang and father Tian Tian, will leave us as well. The zoo leases the adults from China, and China owns the rights to their offspring. There were hopes that the couple might produce another cub before the lease was to expire at the end of 2010, and that they and their new child would be allowed to stay awhile longer. The **Invertebrates House**—from octopi and lobsters to cockroaches and ants—resembles the bar scene from *Star Wars*. At the Think Tank, you can watch as scientists test apes' ability to use and understand word symbols. Outdoors and 50 feet overhead, the apes use lines strung between towers to commute between the Think Tank and the **Great Apes House.** The Amazon River Basin's tropical habitat is recreated in **Amazonia.** (It's a great place to warm up in the winter.) Little boys in particular seem to love the **Reptile Discovery Center.** In the **Pollinarium,** hummingbirds and butterflies flit about, pollinating plants. At the **Kids Farm,** children can pet and groom domestic animals and play with interactive educational displays. Kids 3 to 8 can crawl through **Prairie Playland**—which mimics the nearby prairie dog village—popping their heads up through openings and looking around just like the prairie dogs do. FINE PRINT Parking starts at $10 and costs $20 if you stay more than 3 hours. Metrobuses stop at the main entrance. The zoo is a half-mile from the Cleveland Park Metro Station and a third of a mile from Woodley Park Metro station—longish, but doable, walks.

3001 Connecticut Ave. NW (north of Cathedral Ave.). ℂ **202-673-4821.** www.nat zoo.si.edu. Nov–Mar daily 10am–5pm; Apr–Oct to 6pm. Closed Dec 25. Metro: Cleveland Park and Woodley Park. Metrobus L1, L2, or L4. Parking $10 first hour, $15 2–3 hr., $20 more than 3 hr.

United States Botanic Garden   About 4,000 plants are on display inside the Conservatory, which you might call the nation's greenhouse. More grow in the National Garden, just outside the Conservatory, and across Independence Avenue in Bartholdi Park. The park also contains the Bartholdi Fountain, created for the 1876 International Centennial Exhibition in Philadelphia by Frederic Auguste Bartholdi, the French designer of the Statue of Liberty. You can take a **guided tour** of the conservatory Mondays and Thursdays at noon, and of the National Garden Mondays at 5:30pm in summer. Call ℂ **202/730-9303** to get a tour over your cellphone. Or you can just wander around on your own. The garden traces its origin to 1816. It moved to its current site in 1933 and underwent a major, major, major renovation from 1997 to 2001. The National Garden opened in 2006. The conservatory is particularly appealing in winter, when it serves as a tropical respite from the cold. It's a great place to visit in

Zoo Tips: When You're Visiting the Animals

- Tip 1: This is a large, hilly place. You'll be temped to walk for hours. Dress accordingly. You can bring in food and drink if you like, or purchase them at several locations around the park.

- Tip 2: The best time to see animal activity is early morning or around dusk. Midday, many are napping and/or hiding away from zoo-goers.

- Tip 3: If you eat at the Zoo's **Maine Cafe,** go all the way to the back of the dining room and you'll find tables at windows that overlook nearby zoo facilities.

- Tip 4: Despite Its name, Woodley Park–Zoo is not the best Metrorail station to use on the way to the zoo. Coming to the zoo, use the **Cleveland Park** station and walk south on Connecticut Avenue from the East Side exit. When leaving the zoo, walk south on Connecticut to the Woodley Park–Zoo Metro station. The distance is about the same, and you spend more time walking downhill.

the Christmas season, when poinsettias, trains, and child-friendly displays (Snow White's cottage, the Owl and the Pussycat's beautiful pea green boat) brighten holiday spirits.

100 Maryland Ave. SW (at 1st St.). ✆ **202/225-8333.** Telephone tour ✆ **202/730-9303.** www.usbg.gov. Daily 10am–5pm. Metro: Federal Center Southwest.

9 Top Sites (If You Have a Car)

ALWAYS FREE

Clara Barton National Historic Site   The founder of the American Red Cross lived here from February 28, 1897, until she died in her bedroom on April 12, 1912, at the age of 90. Until she resigned as Red Cross president in 1904, the house also served as Red Cross headquarters and a warehouse for disaster supplies. Hard as it is to believe, when this became a national historical site in 1975 it was the first dedicated to the accomplishments of a woman. You can see the interior only on a guided tour. To get here, drive west on M Street NW out of Georgetown, then

FREE Capital Views

Here are some of the best of the Capital's many marvelous views:

- From the **Capitol Reflecting Pool,** between the Mall and the Capitol (p. 97), you can get a great look at the Capitol itself.

- The best long-range view of Mall monuments and the august buildings of the federal government is from the porch of Arlington National Cemetery's **Arlington House** (p. 99), once the home of Robert E. Lee, who tried and failed to destroy the nation that the capital still governs.

- From the nearby **U.S. Marine Corps War Memorial** (commonly called the Iwo Jima Memorial; p. 101), you can see an imposing alignment of the Capitol, Washington Monument, and Lincoln Memorial.

- The steps of the **Thomas Jefferson Memorial** (p. 101) offer a gorgeous view of the Tidal Basin (especially at cherry blossom time), the Washington Monument, and the White House beyond.

- For a bird's-eye view of monumental Washington, take the elevator to the top of the **Washington Monument** (p. 113).

- The **Lincoln Memorial** (p. 101) offers a spectacular view of the entire Mall, all the way to the Capitol in the distance.

- It's not as lofty as the Washington Monument, but an elevator ride up the **Old Post Office clock tower** (1100 Pennsylvania Ave. NW at 11th St.; p. 123) gives you a nice view of Downtown, Capitol Hill, the White House, monuments and memorials on the Mall, and even such Virginia sights as Arlington National Cemetery, the Pentagon, the U.S. Air Force Memorial, and National Airport.

- For the highest view of DC, take the elevator to the Washington National Cathedral's **Pilgrim Observation Gallery** (p. 127).

- For a water view, stroll the river walk at **Washington Harbour** (p. 254) below Thomas Jefferson and K streets NW in Georgetown. Washington is especially attractive after dark, when many of the white-stone buildings, monuments, and memorials are illuminated and DC truly is an alabaster city gleaming.

turn left on Canal Road, which becomes Clara Barton Parkway. Follow the signs to the Clara Barton National Historic Site, which is about 6½ miles from the M-Canal intersection. Because of traffic patterns, you should return to DC by turning right out of the Clara Barton parking lot onto MacArthur Boulevard. Follow MacArthur until it ends at Foxhall Road. Bear right on Foxhall, then turn left where Foxhall ends at Canal Road, and you'll be on your way into Georgetown. You can also get here by public transit (see instructions below). FINE PRINT Don't leave Washington before 10:15am weekdays, when a portion of Canal Road is inbound only. Be sure to follow the MacArthur Boulevard route back to DC between 2:45 and 7:15pm, when the traffic pattern is reversed.

5801 Oxford Rd., Glen Echo, MD (southwest of MacArthur Blvd.). 𝄞 301/320-1410. www.nps.gov/clba. Daily tours on the hour 10am–4pm. Closed Thanksgiving, Dec 25, Jan 1. Parking free. Via public transit: Montgomery County Ride-On Bus 29 from Friendship Heights Metrorail Station.

★ **Franciscan Monastery** Since 1217, the Franciscan friars have been charged with preserving Christian holy sites. In the late 19th century, in keeping with that charge, they decided to build copies of some of those sites in the United States so Americans could visit them. Scattered within the monastery's serene and beautiful gardens are replicas of the Grotto of Gethsemane Shrine in Jerusalem; the tomb of Mary; the house in Cairo where Jesus's family lived during their Egyptian exile; the Ascension Chapel, which crusaders built on Mount Olivet near Jerusalem; Lourdes Grotto in France; and the church in Assisi, Italy, where the Franciscan Order was founded. Inside the monastery's Memorial Church of the Holy Sepulchre are copies of the Grotto of the Nativity in

Why Drive in the District?

We always recommend against driving in DC. The traffic's lousy, so are many of our drivers, and our mass transit system can take you almost anywhere you want to go. Still, there are some worthwhile attractions that are relatively easy to reach by automobile. We'll just call this section—as members of Congress do in the *Congressional Record*—a "revision and extension of our remarks." You'll notice that we're really not suggesting that you drive *in* central DC, just that you can use your car to reach attractions that are mostly outside the city. We'll also note public transportation options when they're not greatly more difficult than driving.

Bethlehem, Jesus's tomb, and catacombs with crypts containing the remains of two saints. The Byzantine-style church itself is beautiful with stained glass windows, marble alters, impressive artwork, and a dome. The gardens, with trees soaring overhead and benches scattered about, offer quiet spots for contemplation or just relaxation. From central DC, drive northeast on Rhode Island Avenue, turn left on 13th Street NE, then turn right on Quincy Street The monastery is on the left, a free parking lot on the right.

1400 Quincy St. NE (btw. 13th and 14th sts.). ℂ **202/526-6800.** www.myfranciscan. org. Daily 10am–5pm. Guided tours Mon–Sat at 10 and 11am; 1, 2, and 3pm; Sun at 1, 2, and 3pm. By public transit: Metrobus H6 from Brookland Metrorail Station.

★ National Air and Space Museum Udvar-Hazy Center   When your job is to display aircraft and spacecraft, you face some space limitations in the heart of a city. That's why the Smithsonian opened this enormous annex at Dulles International Airport in 2003, nearly quintupling the museum's display area. Here there's room for more and larger vehicles, including the Space Shuttle *Enterprise,* the first shuttle, which was used in tests; the Lockheed SR-71 Blackbird reconnaissance plane, the fastest and highest-flying jet aircraft ever built, with a top speed over 2,200 mph at altitudes exceeding 85,000 feet; and the Boeing B-29 Superfortress *Enola Gay,* which dropped the first atomic bomb on Japan during World War II. Altogether, more than 160 aircraft, 150 large space artifacts, and 1,500 smaller items are displayed. As on the Mall, this annex has an IMAX theater and simulators (which charge an admission fee). There's also an observation tower where you can watch the planes at the airport and learn about air traffic control. Knowledgeable docents enrich the visitor's experience by explaining displays and answering questions. To get here, drive west on Constitution Avenue to westbound I-66. Take I-66 about 22 miles to exit 35B, then go north on Virginia Rte. 28. After 5.3 miles, get on the Air and Space Museum Parkway, and follow the signs to the Udvar-Hazy Center. FINE PRINT Admission to the museum is free, but you'll pay $15 for parking.

14390 Air and Space Museum Pkwy., Chantilly, VA, off Virginia Rte. 28, south of the airport's main entrance. ℂ **202/633-1000.** www.nasm.si.edu. Films, simulators $7.25–$13. Daily 10am–5:30pm. Closed Dec 25. Parking $15.

National Arboretum   One of the best places to get away from Washington's hustle and bustle is the National Arboretum, which really is more remarkable for its flowers than its trees. The best time to visit is from late April into late May, when the azaleas are in full riot, and crabapples, dogwoods, peonies, roses, and irises also bloom. If you can't make it then, though, don't worry: The arboretum always has something to show off, such as magnolias in early spring and holly berries in winter. Some manmade items will grab your attention as well, such as 22 sandstone columns that were removed from the Capitol during a renovation and now stand here like an ancient ruin. Stop at the Administration Building to pick up a map and guide, and to find out what's blooming. If the azaleas are in flower, you absolutely must drive Azalea Road. You won't believe the cascade of colors! This is a great place for cheapskates to save restaurant expenses by packing a picnic. From downtown DC, go northeast on New York Avenue to Bladensburg Road (about 2 miles from N. Capitol St.). Turn right onto Bladensburg and go 4 blocks to R Street. Turn left on R, then continue 2 blocks to the Arboretum entrance.

R St. NE (east of 24th St.). (✆ **202/-245-2726.** www.usna.usda.gov. Daily 8am–5pm. Closed Dec 25. Parking free.

★ **Rock Creek Park**   We can barely scratch the surface of the many, many, many things you can do at this marvelous, through-the-heart-of-the-city park, which winds its way from the Potomac River near the Kennedy Center all the way to DC's most northern tip. Write or phone the park headquarters for a map/brochure, explore the park's website, or ask for the publication at other National Park Service sites in the Washington area. When you get here, you can find information desks at the **Nature Center** (5200 Glover Rd. NW, south of Military Rd.) and **Peirce Barn** (Tilden St. at Beach Dr.). Both places offer numerous programs for children. The Nature Center also contains exhibits on plants, animals, and habitats in the park. It's the starting point for guided and self-guided nature walks. The center's hands-on **Discovery Room** appeals to youngsters, as does the planetarium's kid-oriented shows Wednesdays at 4pm. The planetarium focuses programs on children 5 and older Saturday and Sunday at 1pm, and on kids 7 and older those days at 4pm. The park accommodates a wide range of outdoor activities, including hiking, horseback riding, bicycling, picnicking, golf, tennis, and boating. The 4,000-seat **Carter Barron Amphitheatre** (p. 156) offers numerous outdoor performances in season, both paid and free. To enter the park from central DC, drive northwest on Virginia Avenue to Rock Creek Parkway and turn right.

FINE PRINT Rock Creek Parkway and Beach Drive are major commuter routes during workday rush hours. South of Connecticut Avenue, the parkway is one-way south Monday through Friday from 6:45 till 9:30am, and one-way north 3:45 to 6:30pm. In return, from 7am to 7pm on holidays, and from 7am Saturday to 7pm Sunday, Beach Drive is closed to motor vehicles from Broad Branch Road to Military Road, from Picnic Grove 10 to Wise Road, and from West Beach Drive to the DC–Maryland border. Then, walkers, runners, rollerbladers, and bicyclists clog the roadway.

Mailing address: 3545 Williamsburg Lane NW, Washington, DC 20008. ✆ **202/895-6070.** www.nps.gov/rocr. Outdoor facilities daily during daylight. Nature Center Wed–Sun 9am–5pm; closed Thanksgiving, Dec 25, Jan 1. Peirce Barn daily noon–5pm; closed Thanksgiving, Dec 25, Jan 1. Parking free.

Theodore Roosevelt Island National Memorial T.R., the great conservationist, would have approved of this memorial. Wander about this little island in the middle of the Potomac River, and you can forget that bustling Georgetown and DC's Northern Virginia suburbs are just beyond the tree line. The 89 acres of woods contain 2.5 miles of trails, and a memorial plaza with an outsized statue of Roosevelt. It's a pleasant respite which is actually inside the city limits. It also helps to dramatically illustrate how the Republican Party has changed since it was led at the beginning of the 20th century by this man, who arguably was our most environmentalist president and the scourge of big business. Drive west on Constitution Avenue and continue straight across the Theodore Roosevelt Memorial Bridge (I-66 and U.S. 50) to the George Washington Memorial Parkway (northbound). The Roosevelt Island parking lot is to your right immediately after you enter the parkway. Don't miss it! The only entrance is from the northbound lanes.

George Washington Memorial Pkwy. ✆ **703/289-2500.** www.nps.gov/this. Daily 6am–10pm. Free parking.

George Washington Memorial Parkway Like its Rock Creek cousin, the GW Parkway has become a major commuter route, with cars speeding along way too fast or locked in a bumper-to-bumper creep. But, it is a PARKway with many interesting nooks and crannies to explore, along the south and west bank of the Potomac River, from I-495 northwest of DC to George's Mount Vernon mansion. Again, we can give you only the highest of highlights. Write, phone, or e-mail parkway headquarters to ask for a map/brochure to be mailed to you. Otherwise, look for it at National Park Service facilities along the parkway or at park service sites in the DC area. Some spots worth a stop, from north to south:

- **Turkey Run:** 700 acres of forest and hiking trails.

- **Fort Marcy:** Earthenwork remnant of one of many forts that surrounded Washington during the Civil War. Access from northbound lanes only.

- **Marine Corps War Memorial:** Oversized sculpture of famous World War II photo of Marines raising U.S. flag during battle for Iwo Jima. Walk a fifth of a mile from Arlington National Cemetery Parking lot ($1.75/hour for 3 hr., $2 each additional hour; p. 99).

- **Netherlands Carillon:** 50-bell, 127-foot tall carillon given by Dutch in gratitude to United States after World War II. In May and September, free concerts are presented from 2 to 4pm on Saturdays and national holidays. June through August, the concerts start at 6pm. You can climb the tower to check out the view and watch the carillonneur perform. Automated concerts daily noon and 6pm. Walk a fifth of a mile from Arlington National Cemetery Parking lot ($1.75/hour for 3 hr., $2 each additional hour; p. 99).

- **Gravelly Point:** Popular spot to watch airplanes take off and land at National Airport. If you have a boat, put it in the Potomac here and view Washington's landmarks from the water. It's also a good point to park your car and get on Mount Vernon Bicycle Trail. Access from northbound lanes only.

- **Daingerfield Island:** Another good place to picnic, access bike trail, rent a bike, or boat.

- In Alexandria, the parkway runs through the city as **Washington Street.**

- **Dyke Marsh:** 380-acre tidal marsh, floodplain, and swamp forest comprises largest remaining freshwater tidal wetlands in Washington area. Attracts bird-watchers.

- **Fort Hunt:** Batteries here guarded river approach to Washington from 1898 to 1918. Large picnic grounds. Good place to access bike trail from south. Julie learned to ride bike on lightly used roads here.

To enter the parkway from DC, drive west on Constitution Avenue and continue straight across the Theodore Roosevelt Memorial Bridge (I-66 and U.S. 50) to the George Washington Memorial Parkway (northbound). Or drive west on Independence Avenue, circle behind the Lincoln Memorial, and watch closely for signs to the Arlington Memorial Bridge. After you cross the bridge, turn right out of the traffic circle and then exit left to continue southbound or go straight to go northbound. The southbound route also is marked to National Airport. FINE PRINT Do *not* sightsee along the parkway during rush hour, when the road is clogged with commuters. Drive here on the weekend or from mid-morning until mid-afternoon during the week. Note that some spots are accessible only from the northbound or southbound lanes.

George Washington Memorial Pkwy. ℭ **703/289-2500.** www.nps.gov/gwmp; mailing address: George Washington Memorial Pkwy. Headquarters, Turkey Run Park, McLean, VA 22101.

PARKS WITH ADMISSION FEES

✷ **Chesapeake and Ohio Canal National Historical Park**   This park actually stretches along the old canal from Georgetown to Cumberland, MD. This review refers only to the section of the park at the Great Falls of the Potomac River in Maryland. We come here regularly to picnic, stroll the boardwalk out to the falls, and hike or ride bikes along the canal and into the bordering hills. The setting is beautiful. After substantial rain, the falls can be quite dramatic—or destructive. Floods have done substantial damage to the boardwalk from time to time. You can brush up on your history at the visitor center in the old Great Falls Tavern, which served canal boat passengers. You can bring a picnic or buy simple foods at the park refreshment stand. April through October, you can take an hour-long ride on a mule-pulled replica of an 1870s canal boat. Rangers in period clothing drive the mules, steer the boats, and describe what life was like along the canal, which operated from the first half of the 19th century through the first quarter of the 20th. To get to this park site, follow the directions to the Clara Barton house (p. 131), but stay on the Clara Barton Parkway until it ends at MacArthur Boulevard. Follow MacArthur to the left until it ends in the park. Because of traffic patterns, you should return to DC by staying on MacArthur until it ends at Foxhall Road. Bear right on Foxhall, then turn left where Foxhall ends at

Canal Road, and you'll be on your way into Georgetown. FINE PRINT Don't leave Washington before 10:15am weekdays, when a portion of Canal Road is inbound only. Be sure to follow the MacArthur Boulevard route back to DC between 2:45 and 7:15pm, when the traffic pattern is reversed. Hours for visitor center and boat rides can change. It's wise to call ahead to check.

11710 MacArthur Blvd., Potomac, MD. ☎ **301/767-3714.** www.nps.gov/choh. $5 pass admits all in one car for three days here and at Great Falls Park across the river in Virginia. Admission: $3 per individual walking or on bike. Daily in daylight. Visitor center daily 9am–4:30pm. Closed Thanksgiving, Dec 25, Jan 1. Boat rides older than 3 $5; Apr Thurs–Sat 11am, 1:30, and 3pm; May–Oct Wed–Sun 11am, 1:30, and 3pm.

Great Falls Park   When you get to the Potomac River at the C&O Canal Park, you can wave at the folks here—and vice versa. Here, on the Virginia side of the river, you see the same falls from different angles, can picnic and hike, and can check out some additional history. A substantial visitor center offers history and nature exhibits. Before he presided over the successful launch of a new nation, George Washington presided over a failed attempt to build a canal on this side of the Potomac. Remnants are visible. There are riding trails in the park, but it's BYOH (bring your own horse). Go west on M Street out of Georgetown, left on Canal Road, left over Chain Bridge, right on Virginia Rte. 123 (Chain Bridge Road), then right on Virginia Rte. 193 (Georgetown Pike). Turn right at Old Dominion Drive at the sign to the park. FINE PRINT Don't leave Washington before 10:15am weekdays, when a portion of Canal Road is inbound only. If you return to DC during evening rush hour, you'll run into a portion of Canal Road that is one-way coming at you. At that point, turn left on Arizona Avenue, drive to the top of the hill, then turn right on MacArthur Boulevard. Follow MacArthur until it ends at Foxhall Road. Bear right on Foxhall, then turn left where Foxhall ends at Canal Road, and you'll be on your way into Georgetown.

9200 Old Dominion Dr., McLean, VA (at Georgetown Pike). ☎ **703/285-2965.** www. nps.gov/grfa. $5 pass admits all in one car for 3 days here and at the C&O Canal Park site across the river in MD; $3 per individual walking, on bike, or on horseback. Daily 7am until dark. Visitor center daily 10am–5pm.

WORTH THE SPLURGE

★ **Mount Vernon**   The Mount Vernon Ladies' Association has been laboring since 1853 to preserve 500 acres of George Washington's

Savings for Seniors and Travelers with Disabilities

Who says there's no upside to growing older? When you turn 62, 10 bucks buys you the **Interagency Senior Pass,** which gets you into all federal recreation sites that charge an entrance fee for the rest of your life. That includes the national parks reviewed here along with all other sites managed by the National Park Service, Forest Service, Bureau of Land Management, Bureau of Reclamation, and Fish & Wildlife Service. Even better, if you drive into a site that charges a per-vehicle fee, everyone else in your vehicle gets in free, too. If the site charges per person, you can bring three other adults with you for free plus children younger than 16. The pass also gets you 50% discounts on "expanded amenity fees" for such things as camping, swimming, and using a boat launch. If you have a disability, you can get a free Interagency Access Pass at any age. It carries all the benefits of the senior pass. Passes are issued at fee-charging sites. To get the access pass, you must substantiate your disability with a doctor's statement, documentation issued by a federal agency such as the Veteran's or Social Security administration, or a document issued by a state agency such as a rehabilitation agency. For more information on the pass, and how to obtain one, visit **http://store.usgs.gov/pass/senior.html#obtain**.

plantation. In recent years, they've really outdone themselves. Since 2004: The estate acquired an orientation center, museum, and education center, with multimedia and interactive displays. Washington's distillery was reconstructed, and visitors can observe whiskey being made as Washington made it. A gardener's house was restored. The blacksmith shop was reconstructed. A log cabin, modeled after those that housed slaves, was built and is used to explain the lives of field hands. The main attraction, of course, is the house where George and Martha lived, which has been meticulously restored down to the original paint colors on the walls. Guides are stationed throughout the mansion to answer questions. Visitors also can explore gardens, a 16-sided barn, Mount Vernon's wharf, the slave burial ground, and

Washington's Tomb. Mount Vernon has activities for kids, including an "adventure map" with puzzles they solve by exploring the estate. The mansion contains original furnishings, other items owned by the Washington family, other 18th-century objects, and some reproductions. The gardens and farm fields are planted as they were when Washington lived here. Mount Vernon keeps farm animals similar to Washington's. More than 700 artifacts are displayed in the new museum, orientation, and education facilities. They include Washington's dentures (not made of wood). April through October, guided tours explore the lives of Mount Vernon's slaves at 2pm and the gardens at 11am. Mount Vernon commemorates **Presidents' Day,** the third Monday in February, by admitting visitors for free and hosting a wreath-laying at Washington's tomb, with music and military exercises by the U.S. Army Old Guard Fife and Drum Corps. From late November to mid-December, candlelight tours of the mansion are conducted from 5 to 8pm Friday through Sunday. Tickets go on sale November 1 and sell out quickly. You can eat here at a food court or the full-service Mount Vernon Inn Restaurant where waiters in colonial costume serve lunch and candle-lighted dinner. Three miles west, on Virginia 235, the distillery and Washington's gristmill are operated by workers in 18th century costume. To get to Mount Vernon, drive west on Independence Avenue, circle behind the Lincoln Memorial, and watch closely for signs to the Arlington Memorial Bridge. After you cross the bridge, turn right out of the traffic circle, then exit left to the southbound George Washington Parkway. (The route also is marked to National Airport.) The parkway ends at Mount Vernon.

3200 Mount Vernon Memorial Hwy. © **703/780-2000.** www.mountvernon.org. 5 and younger free; 6–11 $7, 62 and older $14, others $15. Daily Mar 9am–5pm; Apr–Aug 8am–5pm; Sept–Oct 9am–5pm; Nov–Feb 9am–4pm. Parking free. Fairfax Connector Bus 101 from Huntington Metrorail Station (timetable: www.fairfax-county.gov/connector/pdf/101.pdf). Mount Vernon Inn: © **703/780-0011.** www.mountvernon.org/visit/dining/index.cfm/pid/51. Lunch main courses $7.50–$12; dinner $15–$23. AE, DISC, MC, V. Lunch daily 11:30am–3:30pm; in winter till 2:30pm; reservations required Easter, Mother's Day, Thanksgiving; closed Christmas. Dinner Mon–Thurs 5–8:30pm; Fri–Sat till 9pm; dinner reservations recommended. Distillery and gristmill: 5513 Mount Vernon Memorial Hwy. (Virginia 235). © **703/780-3383.** $4 ($2 with Mt. Vernon admission), ages 6–11 $2 ($1.50 with Mt. Vernon admission), 5 and younger free. Apr–Oct 10am–5pm. Closed Nov–Mar.

The buxom redhead who lures partyers to Madam's Organ Blues Bar and Soul Food Restaurant (p. 173) also inspires one of the popular Adams Morgan nightclub's specials: Redheads drink Rolling Rock beer half-price all the time.

ENTERTAINMENT & NIGHTLIFE

Washington is not known for its nightlife. We're stereotyped as a workaholic town, full of people who rise early for working breakfasts, continue working at lunch and dinner, then head home to page through the latest public affairs book, paying special attention to the index to see if we know anyone listed. While some of us are, maybe, a *little* like that . . . most of us are pretty well-rounded folks. We partake of a great—and ever improving—cultural scene that features a world-class orchestra, opera, and a wide-ranging theater scene, and includes many other highly skilled performing arts companies. Lots of young people go to school and work in Washington, and

DC PERFORMING ARTS & SPORTS

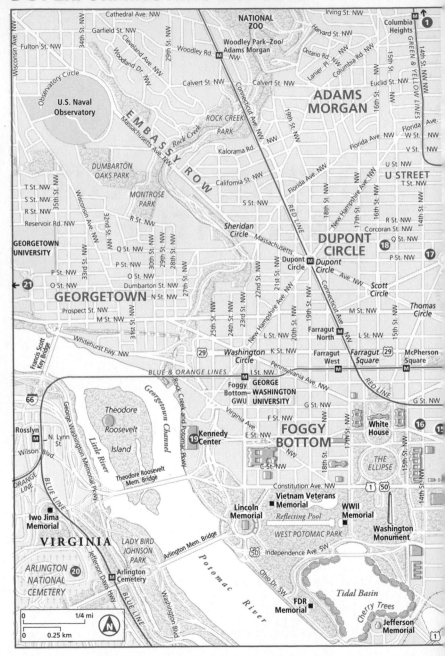

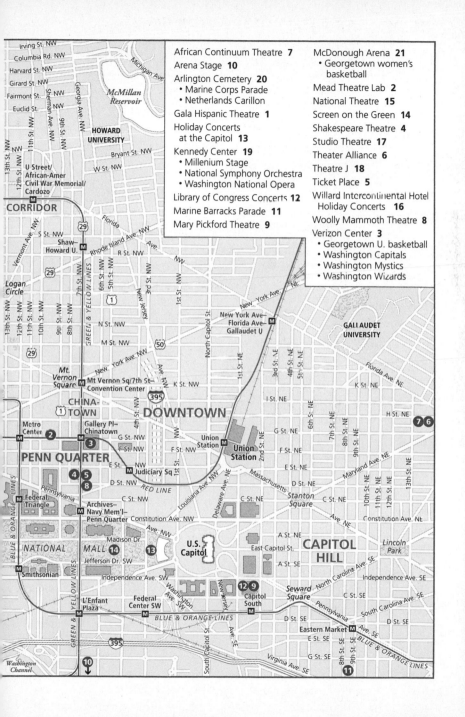

African Continuum Theatre **7**
Arena Stage **10**
Arlington Cemetery **20**
• Marine Corps Parade
• Netherlands Carillon
Gala Hispanic Theatre **1**
Holiday Concerts
at the Capitol **13**
Kennedy Center **19**
• Millenium Stage
• National Symphony Orchestra
• Washington National Opera
Library of Congress Concerts **12**
Marine Barracks Parade **11**
Mary Pickford Theatre **9**

McDonough Arena **21**
• Georgetown women's
basketball
Mead Theatre Lab **2**
National Theatre **15**
Screen on the Green **14**
Shakespeare Theatre **4**
Studio Theatre **17**
Theater Alliance **6**
Theatre J **18**
Ticket Place **5**
Willard Intercontinental Hotel
Holiday Concerts **16**
Woolly Mammoth Theatre **8**
Verizon Center **3**
• Georgetown U. basketball
• Washington Capitals
• Washington Mystics
• Washington Wizards

Surfing the Web for DC Theater

Believe it: Washington is one of the major theater towns in the country. To help navigate a huge and complex scene that runs from national touring companies, to famous regional houses, to the most avant-garde or experimental storefront theater, head for one of these URLs. You'll find everything you need to know about what's on, who's in it, and how it's been received:

- ● **DC Theatre Scene (http://dctheatrescene.com**) is a good-looking, informative site that covers the metro area theater scene from national touring productions, to the regional stalwarts, to the smaller independent companies. It offers reviews, podcasts, and a "Deal of the Day" covering discounts and "Pay What You Can" nights.

- ● **The League of Washington Theatres (www.lowt.org)** is the membership organization of professional theaters in the DC area, and its website offers a comprehensive list of and contact information for its members, as well as links to other theater resources.

- ● **The Helen Hayes Awards (www.helenhayes.org)** recognize the best work being done in Washington theater each year, and its website offers a detailed calendar of what's on in all the local theaters, as well as "Special Deals," including information on the free shows at the Helen Hayes Gallery of the National Theatre (p. 149).

they support a lively—and expanding—collection of clubs, bars, and concert venues that focus on popular entertainment. With the arrival of Major League Baseball's Washington Nationals in 2005, we now have a full complement of professional sports teams.

Cheapskates will be happy to know that a great deal of DC entertainment can be had for free or at low prices. Just as government support makes many museums, galleries, monuments, and memorials free, so there are subsidies for free concerts and other forms of entertainment. Many theaters and other performing arts venues offer some free or deeply discounted performances in the hope of luring new patrons into regular attendance. Volunteer to usher or provide other services to performing arts organizations, and you can attend shows for free. Like many cities, Washington has a half-price tickets service where venues offer unsold passes at the last minute. And, we're happy to say, happy hours abound in bars all over town!

1 All the World's a Stage: DC Theater

★ **Arena Stage**   Since its founding in 1950, Arena Stage has built a distinguished record. It was the first regional theater to transfer a production to Broadway, the first regional theater invited by the U.S. State Department to tour behind the Iron Curtain, and the first regional to win a Tony. The theater focuses on American plays, both the classics and new productions. Its newly expanded digs were scheduled to open in time for the 2010–11 season. Tickets usually range from $47 to $74, but there are several discounts available for cash-poor theater mavens. Full-time **students** can get 35% off regular prices by phone or at the box office. Each Monday, theater buffs **30 and younger** can buy tickets to that week's performances for $10. Between 90 and 30 minutes before curtain, **half-price rush tickets** are sold at the box office. **"Family Fun Packs"** are sold by phone or at the box office for $100; the C-note buys you two adult tickets and two for children 5 to 18. If, like Arena Stage, you live or work in DC's

Before & After the Show at Arena Stage

A program called **The Salon** features Artistic Director Molly Smith and other artistic staff in a series of in-depth conversations with the playwrights, actors, directors, designers, and audiences. The Salon takes place from 7 to 8 pm, in the theater of each production, in most cases on the Monday before opening nights. The program is free to theater subscribers, and $3 for the general public. Reserve through the Sales Office at ℂ **202/488-3300.** In addition, **post-show conversations** provide background information and backstage anecdotes about productions and an opportunity for the audience to interact with the actors from the shows. The talkbacks are scheduled on selected Tuesday and Thursday evenings and selected matinees, and there's no additional charge (than the ticket price) to attend.

Southwest quadrant, you can buy **$20 tickets** to one designated performance of each production. The dates are marked with "sw" on Arena's online calendar. 1101 6th St. SW (at Maine Ave.). ℂ **202/488-3300.** www.arenastage.org; calendar www.arenastage.org/season/calendar. Metro: Waterfront.

Capital Fringe Festival   The Fringe enables local and touring theater and musical artists to present their work exactly as they wish. The Capital Fringe Festival hosted its first performances in July 2006, and has rapidly become a local theatrical institution. An abbreviated fall festival was presented in 2009 with two reprises from the summer and one new production. Capital Fringe, the organization that manages the festival, hopes to add a spring event as well. During the summer festival, more than 100 productions are presented—most about five times each—in a dozen venues over about 15 days. Genres have included cabaret, comedy, dance, drama, experimental, and musical theater. Tickets cost from about $10 to $15, and there are various passes available which drop the price of shows even lower. The 2010 festival will be held from July 8 to July 25. ℂ **202/737-7230.** www.capfringe.org.

GALA Hispanic Theatre   Founded to preserve and promote Hispanic culture in the United States, *Grupo de Artistas Latino Americanos* (Group of Latin American Artists) also helped to save a grand old American movie palace that had been crumbling for three decades. The four-story Mediterranean Revival Tivoli Theatre, built in 1924, closed in 1976. In 2005, a renovation turned the giant building into a shopping center and created a new 270-seat theater for GALA. GALA presents classical and contemporary Spanish-language plays from Spain and throughout the Americas, as well as programs of music, dance, poetry, and film. As at operas, English translation is projected above the stage. GALA's children's theater—called **GALita**—stages bilingual programs. Some of the theater's programs are free. For most performances, prices vary from $15 to $30. Student and military tickets often are available for half to two-thirds full price. A limited number of $18 "Rush Tickets" are sold at the box office on Thursday and Friday from 6:30 to 7:15pm before each main-stage presentation. **FREE** You can get in free by volunteering to usher or help with other administrative duties. Being able to speak Spanish is desirable but not

Get Your Discount Tickets Here!

The **Cultural Alliance of Greater Washington** sells tickets to a wide variety of performances for 62% of face value. Many of the tickets can be purchased online at **www.ticketplace.org**. Some require a visit to the Ticket Place **office** at 407 7th St. NW (btw. D and E sts.), near the Gallery Place and Archives Metro stations. While the emphasis is on same-day tickets, some advance-sale tickets are available as well. The office is open Wednesday through Friday 11am to 6pm, Saturday 10am to 5pm, and Sunday noon to 4pm. It's closed Monday and Tuesday. Ticket Place doesn't sell tickets by phone but does provide recorded information at © **202/842-5387.** Ticket Place accepts American Express, MasterCard, and Visa, but not cash, checks, or travelers checks. Sign up for e-mail alerts to find out what's on at **www.patron mail.com/pmailweb/PatronSetup?fid=1748**.

required. FINE PRINT This neighborhood is improving, but crime remains a problem. The walk to the theater from the Metrorail station is just a block through a revitalized commercial area, but stay alert. 3333 14th St. NW (at Park Rd.). © **202/234-7174.** www.galatheatre.org. Metro: Columbia Heights.

National Theatre   Opened in 1835, the National Theatre was burned and rebuilt five times during the 19th century. It was rebuilt again in 1922 and underwent a major interior renovation in 1984. Each time, the original foundation remained in use. Since its opening, every president has attended a production here. Many notable actors have performed here as well. The National is a touring house for big national productions, so tickets aren't cheap. It *does* sell a limited number of half-price tickets at the box office—usually for Tuesday, Wednesday, or Sunday matinees—to patrons 65 and older, full-time students, military personnel below the rank of E4, and holders of a District of Columbia Human Services Card that demonstrates income below $775 a month. What endears the National to the cheapskate is the National's **Helen Hayes Gallery,** where **free shows**—usually music or dance—are staged at 6 and 7:30pm Mondays, and **free children's**

Washington's Thriving Indie Theater Scene

It's impossible for this book to review all of Washington's many professional and independent theaters. Take a look at "Surfing the Web for DC Theater," p. 146, for links to comprehensive information about what's on in the District. Here's just a taste of some of the theatrical activity going on in DC:

- **African Continuum Theatre Company** produces classic American plays (*A Raisin in the Sun*) and premieres by African-American playwrights. Its mission is to stage professional caliber performances for the general public so the public can better understand and appreciate African-American culture. Atlas Performing Arts Center, 1333 H St. NE (btw. 13th and 14th sts.). ℂ **202/529-5763.** Tickets ℂ **202/529-5763.** www.africancontinuumtheatre.com. Tickets (at $20–$30 full-price) are available at www.boxofficetickets.com. Take the H St. NE Shuttle (p. 171) or Metrobus X1, X2, or D8.

- **Theater J** aims to produce thought-provoking plays and musicals that explore urban Jewish culture. Sometimes with people of other faiths, Theater J sponsors forums to engage in what the organization terms "frank, humane conversations about conflict and culture." There's a regular schedule of Artistic Director Roundtables, Peace Cafés, and Cast Talk Backs, as well. Ticket prices range from $25 to $55 depending on the show and the time and date of the performance. You can get a discount if you're 65 or older, or 35 or younger. 1529 16th St. NW (btw. Q and Church sts.). ℂ **202/777-3210.** www.washingtondcjcc.org/center-for-arts/theater-j. Metro: Dupont Circle or Metrobus S1, S2, S4, or S9.

shows are held at 9:30 and 11am Saturdays. You can also see **free films** at 6:30pm Mondays during the summer. Tickets are distributed first-come, first-served a half-hour before curtain. The children's programs are intended for kids 4 and older, who must be accompanied by an adult. 1321 Pennsylvania Ave. NW (btw. 13th and 14th sts.).

- **Mead Theatre Lab** is part of the Flashpoint arts incubator (an organization which supports, hosts and develops arts organizations of all kind), this 75-seat, flexible performance space provides a venue for emerging artists and theatrical organizations to produce theater, dance, performance pieces, readings, and workshops that explore new and challenging ideas. Tickets range from $10 to $20. 916 G St. NW (btw. 9th and 10th sts.). ✆ **202/315-1305.** www.flashpointdc.org/venues/theatre_lab.html. Metro: Gallery Place.

- **Theater Alliance** was founded to focus on the experiences of Washington's diverse population. Now theater-in-residence at the 100-seat **H Street Playhouse,** the Alliance received a 2009–10 Helen Hayes Award nomination for Best New Play for the world premiere of *Bread of Winter* by Victor Lodato and has also received the Joseph Keller Award for Outstanding Community Service. The company offers various discounts, including "I Pay What I Can" performances, $15 tickets for theater professionals, and even some free tickets to people who live in the neighborhood. 1365 H St. NE (btw. 13th and 14th sts.). ✆ **202/399-7993.** Tickets ✆ 202/339-7993 ext 2. www.theateralliance.com. H St. NE Shuttle (p. 171) or Metrobus X1, X2, or D8.

- Styling itself the "home to Washington's edgiest artists," **Warehouse** has two theaters, a music venue, a 50-seat film-screening room, a gallery, and a bar/cafe in what was at one time a hardware store and warehouse. 1021 7th St. NW (btw. K St. and New York Ave.). ✆ **202/783-3933.** www.warehousetheater.com. Metro: Mount Vernon Square.

✆ **202/628-6161.** Tickets ✆ **800/447-7400.** Free programs ✆ 202/783-3372. www.nationaltheatre.org; children's programs: www.nationaltheatre.org/saturday/saturday.htm; Mon night programs: www.nationaltheatre.org/monday/monday.htm; summer films: www.nationaltheatre.org/cinema/cinema.htm. Metro: Metro Center.

★ **Shakespeare Theatre Company**   This critically acclaimed troupe offers numerous ways to see Shakespeare and other classical theater performances at a discount. Financially, the best deal is the annual **Free for All,** during which performances are (as you might expect) free. Plays were staged outside at Carter Barron Amphitheater in Rock Creek Park, and we never had trouble getting tickets, which were available the morning of the performance. In 2009, however, the company moved the production inside to **Sidney Harman Hall** in Penn Quarter and made tickets available the night of the performance. That proved to be so popular that you had to get in line 4 hours before curtain to get a seat. Free for All's schedule and venue have bounced around, so we recommend starting to phone or check the theater's website in May for details. The theater offers the following discounts for many—though not all—performances. Call for details. **Young Professionals** (ages 21–35): tickets for $10 to $30. Tuesdays at 10am, $10 tickets are made available for upcoming performances; use promotional code 2010 online, by phone or at the box office. **Age 60 and older:** Half off Wednesday noon matinees, 20% discount at other times. **Military:** 20% discount. **Students:** Half-price first week of run; $10 tickets and half off other tickets, when available, an hour before performance. Some $20 tickets are always available at Sidney Harman Hall performances. In the fall, the company participates in the League of Washington Theatres' annual **Free Night of Theatre** promotion (p. 153). FINE PRINT The company performs in two Penn Quarter venues. There may be service fees on some of these deals. Students must show a full-time student ID. Lansburgh Theatre: 450 7th St. NW (btw. D and E sts.). Sidney Harman Hall: 610 F St. NW (btw. 6th and 7th sts.). ℂ **877/487-8849** or 202/547-1122. www.shakespearetheatre.org. Metro: Gallery Place.

★ **Studio Theatre**   Founded on a shoestring in 1978 and moved in 1987 to an area that hadn't recovered from the 1968 riots, Studio Theatre has grown large and prosperous while helping its Logan Circle neighborhood as well. Over the years, Studio has converted two auto dealerships and other buildings into four theaters and become nationally recognized for staging high-quality contemporary plays, other cutting-edge presentations, and some revivals. Its 2009–10 season, for instance, included David Mamet's *American Buffalo,* the drag

FREE Free Night of Theater

Each fall, the **League of Washington Theatres** takes part in the fabulous national program that's called "Free Night of Theatre." But it's much more than that: In 2009, that "night" extended from October 6 to November 23! More than 30 theaters participated, including such organizations as the Shakespeare Theatre Company, Washington National Opera, Arena Stage, Folger Theatre, Ford's Theatre, Signature Theatre, Studio Theatre, and the Woolly Mammoth Theatre Company. Check the league's website (**www.lowt.org**) in September for information. In the past, tickets became available online October 1 at noon. The hot tickets disappear quickly. We got the tickets we wanted in 2009—to see *Ariadne auf Naxos* at the Washington National Opera. But, even though Tom hit the website at the crack of noon, he had to spend about a half-hour trying different dates before he found one that was available.

artist Lypsinka in James Kirkwood's *Legends,* and George S. Kaufman and Howard Teichmann's half-century-old *Solid Gold Cadillac.* Studio's commitment to actor-audience intimacy is demonstrated by its manner of growth—to four theaters, each with just 200 seats. Tickets usually run $25 to $69. Except for Saturday evenings, **$5 discounts** are available to students, military members, and patrons 62 and older. When available, **Rush tickets** sell for $30 a half-hour before curtain. **Student Rush** tickets cost $19. On "Studio District Nights," tickets cost $10 for people who live or work in the neighborhood bounded by Florida Avenue NW and 11th, 17th, and N streets. And to see a show absolutely **free,** you can usher or fill some other volunteer position. For more information on who and what is needed, visit **www.studiotheatre.org/opportunities/form.php?employ=usher**, phone the theater, or send an e-mail to usher@studiotheatre.org. 1501 14th St. NW (at P St.). ☎ **202/332-3300.** www.studiotheatre.org. Parking $5 at Colonial Parking garage on P St. (btw. 16th and 17th sts.). Dupont Circle Metrorail Station or Metrobus 52, 53, 54, or G2.

Woolly Mammoth Theatre Company This risk-taking troupe has earned critical acclaim for its plays and its playhouse, and is one of the foremost avant-garde/experimental companies in the country. Its new digs opened in 2005 with great accommodations for the playmakers and great seats for the playgoers. Nearly half of Woolly's plays are premieres, and most others are re-imaginings of new or classic works. Artistic Director Howard Shalwitz described the 2009–10 season thus: The plays seek to "engage in a provocative dialogue with our community . . . gain new perspective on economics, war, race, love, and commitment . . . ask big questions: Are the old divisions between capitalism and socialism breaking down? What is the role of the individual in times of upheaval?" The dialogue goes beyond the plays to pre- and post-performance panel discussions and social gatherings. Tickets usually cost $27 to $62. If you're **25 or younger,** you can get into most performances for $15. Woolly sells a few **"Stampede Seats"** for $15 2 hours before curtain for most shows. **"Pay-What-You-Can"** tickets are sold 90 minutes before curtain at the first two performances of each run (cash or check only). Volunteer ushers get in **free.** Sign up by sending an e-mail to **sarahb@woollymammoth.net**. 641 D St. NW (at 7th St.). ℂ **202/393-3939.** www.woollymammoth.net. Metro: Gallery Place.

2 DC on the Silver Screen

Filmfest DC Every spring for a quarter century, Filmfest DC has brought the world of film to Washington. For 11 days, more than 100 movies of all genres are screened in theaters around town. Special focus is given to a couple of countries or geographical regions of the world. Directors and actors participate in workshops, Q&A sessions, and other programs. While many of the films and their directors and actors operate beneath the radar of pop culture, superstars also participate. Among past Filmfest participants are Cicely Tyson, Morgan Freeman, Sigourney Weaver, Peter Bogdanovich, John Malkovich, and Sydney Pollack. Check the website for this year's schedule. Some programs are **free,** but films usually cost $10. You can buy four tickets for $30 and 10 for $80. A service fee is added on advance sales. Sales at the door are by cash or check only. ℂ **202/274-5782.** Tickets ℂ 800/955-5566. www.filmfestdc.org and www.tickets.com.

★ **Mary Pickford Theater** FREE   As the world's largest library, the Library of Congress has quite a film and video collection, which it taps for free screenings at this theater, named for the great actress and producer of the early 20th century. Pickford, who is widely remembered for her little-girl looks, was a founder of United Artists and the Academy of Motion Picture Arts and Sciences. Films and television programs shown here range across the full scope of the craft, from classic features to documentaries on a wide variety of topics. In other programs, authors discuss film-related books and directors screen and discuss their films. The theater seats just 60, so it's a good idea to phone for reservations up to 1 week in advance. The library's Music Division sponsors some screenings with musical themes, which is why you need to check two websites. Room 302, James Madison Building, 101 Independence Ave. SE (btw. 1st and 2nd sts.). ℂ **202/707-5677.** www.loc.gov/rr/mopic/pickford and www.loc.gov/rr/perform/concert. Metro: Capitol South.

Screen on the Green FREE   For about a month each summer, a giant screen rises on the National Mall and Washingtonians bring blankets and lawn chairs to watch free movies. In the past, the films have rolled on Mondays at sundown, and the screen's been erected on the Mall between 4th and 7th streets. Check the website or phone for details. The National Mall. ℂ **877/262-5866.** www.nationalmall.org. Metro: Smithsonian.

3 Classical Music & Concerts

Capitol Holiday Concerts FREE   The West Lawn of the Capitol becomes a concert venue at 8pm on the Sunday of Memorial Day and Labor Day weekends, and on July 4. The Independence Day concert is a real blowout that's televised nationally over public TV stations. It's hosted by a well-known celebrity, and some nationally known entertainers join the National Symphony Orchestra and other performers. The *1812 Overture,* accompanied by cannons, ushers in the National Mall fireworks, making for quite an audio/visual finale. Celebrities and guest musicians also join the symphony in the other holiday concerts, but they're somewhat lower-key affairs which attract families with blankets and lawn chairs. On July 4, people arrive hours ahead of time to get a decent spot to sit. Hint: To see the shows with smaller crowds, come for the **dress rehearsal** at 3:30pm the day before. West Lawn of Capitol. ✆ **800/444-1324** or 202/467-4600. www.kennedy-center.org/nso/programs/summer. Metro: Union Station or Capitol South.

Carter Barron Amphitheatre On pleasant summer nights, this is a wonderful place to take in an outdoor concert. Many of the performances are **free** and feature Washington-area talent. *The Washington Post* sponsors a series of free concerts built around themes: Latin Night, Reggae Night, Ska Night, and so forth. The military jazz bands have performed here for free, as has the Blues Alley Youth Orchestra, which is a project of DC's premier jazz club (p. 170). Performers at 2009's paid concerts (tickets $24) included Ashford & Simpson, Ohio Players, and the Stylistics. Free tickets to the *Post*-sponsored events are distributed the day of the performance starting at 8:30am at *The Post,* 1150 15th St. NW (btw. L and M sts.), and starting at noon at the Carter Barron box office. Tickets for the paid programs can be purchased at the box office starting at noon the day of the performance, or in advance online (for an additional fee). The other free events don't require tickets. Colorado Ave. (southwest of 16th St.). ✆ **202/426-0486.** www.nps.gov/rocr/planyourvisit/cbarron.htm. Tickets ✆ 202/397-7328. www.ticketmaster.com. Parking free. Metrobus S1, S2, S4, or S9.

Library of Congress Concerts `FREE` The library's collections of sheet music and musical instruments play roles in some of the many concerts it's been presenting for more than 80 years. One 2009 concert, for instance, was played from the autograph score of Mendelssohn's *Octet* on period instruments. Classical music predominates, but the concerts draw on a variety of musical genres from around the world and feature top-notch musicians. The Juilliard String Quartet has performed here for more than 45 years. Chris Hillman—of the Byrds, the Flying Burrito Brothers, and the Rock and Roll Hall of Fame—gave a lecture and performance in 2009. The Zemlinsky Quartet, from the Czech Republic, performed at another concert that year. The annual series also contains lectures and films. The events occur in various venues around the library's buildings—and some outside of it—so you need to check the website for details. `FINE PRINT` The concerts are free, but advance tickets carry a Ticketmaster service charge of $2.75 per ticket plus $2 per order. Folks line up at the door

90 minutes before some performances in hope of landing a free seat. Children must be at least 7 to attend. Library of Congress buildings, near Independence Ave. and 1st St. SE. ✆ **202/707-5502.** www.loc. gov/rr/perform/concert. Advance tickets ✆ 202/397-7328; www.ticket master.com. Metro: Capitol South.

★ **Marine Corps Parades** FREE   The solemnity and color of Marine Corps ceremony are on display on summer evenings at the **Marine Barracks** on Capitol Hill and at the **Marine Corps War Memorial** (better known as the Iwo Jima Memorial) near Arlington National Cemetery. The parades feature the Marine Corps Band, Silent Drill Team, and Drum and Bugle Corps. Each location has its own drawing power. At the memorial, the ceremonies occur by the giant sculpture of Marines raising the U.S. flag on Mount Suribachi during the bloody World War II battle for the Japanese island of Iwo Jima. Three of the six men who raised the flag never left the island. The barracks, opened in 1801, are the oldest active Marine Corps post and are home to the "President's Own" band. FINE PRINT The barracks parade begins at 8:45pm Fridays, and guests who made reservations online should arrive by 8. At 8:15pm, unclaimed seats in the parade ground grandstand are given to those lined up at the Main Gate. No food or beverage is allowed except water and baby food. Reservations aren't needed for the parade at the memorial, which begins at 7pm Tuesdays. Bring blankets or lawn chairs, because there is no seating. **Barracks:** 8th St. SE (at G St.). www.mbw.usmc.mil/parades.asp. Free parking and shuttle at 1201 M. St. SE (east of 12th St.). Metro: Eastern Market. **Memorial:** North of Arlington National Cemetery. www. mbw.usmc.mil/parade_sunsetdefault.asp. Parking at cemetery $1.75/ hr. Metro: Arlington Cemetery. Free shuttle to and from Cemetery Visitors Center.

★ **Military Band Concerts** FREE   Military bands have been performing on the Capitol grounds since at least 1863. That's when the Marine Corps Band—whose most famous unit, The President's Own, is stationed at the Marine Barracks on Capitol Hill—began to offer free concerts at the Capitol. Now, bands from all the services perform all over town throughout the year. And they don't restrict themselves to military or classical music. **The Airmen of Note,** the **U.S. Army Blues,** and the **Navy Commodores** play jazz, for instance. The Navy Band has units that focus on country and popular music. From June through August,

★ Performing Arts Central

You'll bump into the **John F. Kennedy Center for the Performing Arts** several times in this section. It's a living memorial to the martyred president, multiple performance venues, and a tourist attraction in its own right. President Eisenhower signed legislation creating a "national cultural center" in 1958. After Kennedy's 1963 assassination, Congress designated the center as his memorial. It opened in 1971 with a performance of Leonard Bernstein's "Requiem" for Kennedy. The center contains a concert hall, opera house, movie theater, and other facilities. It's home to the National Symphony Orchestra and the Washington National Opera, and it hosts numerous local and traveling troupes in all the performing arts. Check the website (**www.kennedy-center. org/calendar**) to see what's playing during your visit. You'll find a drop-down menu that lets you search by genre: ballet, comedy, dance, children, lectures, music (chamber, choral, classical, jazz, popular), performance art, puppetry, storytelling, theater, and musicals. Ticket prices vary widely depending on the show, and there are freebies. See our separate review of the **Millennium Stage** (p. 159), where there's a free performance every day. Become a Kennedy Center volunteer, and you'll get an occasional free or discounted ticket, discounts at the **KC**

the Marine, Navy, Air Force, and Army bands take turns performing at the Capitol's West Front at 8pm Monday, Tuesday, Wednesday, and Friday, except for a few days around July 4. The Marine Band performs at the Sylvan Theatre, near the Washington Monument, on Thursday at 8pm. The Navy Band plays at the Navy Memorial, Pennsylvania Avenue at 7th Street, at 8pm Tuesday, and at 12:30pm Memorial Day, July 3, and Labor Day. The Army Band performs the *1812 Overture*—with cannons!—at the Sylvan Theatre in August. The Army, Navy, and Air Force bands play holiday concerts in December at Constitution Hall, 1776 D St. NW (btw. 17th and 18th sts.). Free tickets are required for the Constitution Hall performances. They are distributed at the Constitution Hall box office in early November, and they run out quickly. The National Park Service publishes a comprehensive calendar of summer

Café cafeteria and the gift shops, and $2 parking. Volunteer info: **www.kennedy-center.org/support/volunteers**.

The hallways outside the performance venues are truly grand. More than 40 nations donated building materials and works of art. The center is open daily from 10am until 30 minutes after last performance. There are two restaurants, but the best way to eat cheap here is to bring a picnic and grab a table on the third-floor terrace when the weather is nice. **Free** guided tours are offered every 10 minutes Monday through Friday from 10am to 5pm and Saturday to Sunday 10am to 1pm. The center is at 2700 F St. NW (at New Hampshire Ave.). For information, phone ℂ **800/444-1324** or 202/467-4600, or surf to www.kennedy-center.org. FINE PRINT Parking is a flat $18. A **free shuttle bus** runs between the center and the Foggy Bottom Metro Station every 15 minutes Monday through Friday from 9:45am to midnight, Saturday 10am to midnight, Sunday noon to midnight, and federal holidays 4pm to midnight. Look for signs to the left as you get off the station escalator. **Metrobus 80** connects the center with Union Station, Gallery Place, Metro Center, McPherson Square, Farragut North, and Farragut West Metro stations.

concerts at **www.nps.gov/ncro/PublicAffairs/SummerintheCity.htm**. Phone or check the bands' websites for details. Army ℂ **703/-696-3718**; www.usarmyband.com. Marines ℂ **202/433-4011;** www.marineband. usmc.mil. Navy ℂ **202/433-2525;** www.navyband.navy.mil. Air Force Band ℂ **202/767-5658;** www.usafband.af.mil.

Millennium Stage FREE Every day of the year, you'll find a free concert at 6pm on this stage in the Kennedy Center's Grand Foyer. All genres make appearances here—music, dance, comedy, puppets, theater, and all manner of other performers. You probably don't know many of these folks, but the occasional headliner has shown up— Peter Yarrow, Bobby McFerrin, Patti Smith, Norah Jones, the Pointer Sisters, Earl Scruggs, and Asleep at the Wheel among them. Regular appearances are made by members of top DC groups, such as the

National Symphony Orchestra, the Washington National Opera, and military bands. FINE PRINT You don't need tickets, but seating is limited and first-come, first-served. Parking is very much *not* free, being a flat charge rather than an hourly rate. 2700 F St. NW (at New Hampshire Ave.). ℂ **800/444-1324** or 202/467-4600. www.kennedy-center.org/programs/millennium. Parking $18. Free shuttle bus from and to Foggy Bottom Metrorail Station every 15 min. Metrobus 80 connects with Union Station, Gallery Place, Metro Center, McPherson Square, Farragut North, and Farragut West Metro stations.

★ **National Symphony Orchestra** The acoustics are so good in the Kennedy Center's Concert Hall that the cheapest seats offer a great place to watch and listen to the world-class National Symphony Orchestra. Over the course of the year, the symphony presents classical, popular, and seasonal concerts, as well as a series especially for families with young children. Normally, tickets range from $20 to $85, and we always hand over a Jackson. The family concerts cost $18. The NSO plays **free outdoor concerts** around the Memorial Day, July 4, and Labor Day holidays. (See Capitol Holiday Concerts review, p. 155.) Also check the Millennium Stage (p. 159) website for free performances by NSO personnel. One hour before the *Kinderkonzerts* (designed for children 4 and up), the orchestra conducts a "Petting Zoo," during which kids can go up to the stage and handle instruments. Kennedy Center **volunteers** occasionally get free or discounted tickets, and $2 parking. 2700 F St. NW (at New Hampshire Ave.), in the Kennedy Center for the Performing Arts. ℂ **800/444-1324** or 202/467-4600. www.kennedy-center.org/nso. Parking $18. Free Kennedy Center Shuttle from Foggy Bottom Metrorail Station.

Netherlands Carillon Concerts FREE In May and September, free concerts are played on this 50-bell carillon from 2 to 4pm on Saturdays and national holidays. June through August, the concerts start at 6pm. You can climb the 127-foot tower, which is near the Marine Corps War Memorial, to watch the carillonneur perform, and take a bird's-eye look at Washington. You can listen to automated concerts daily at noon and 6pm. North of Arlington National Cemetery. ℂ **703/289-2500.** www.nps.gov/archive/gwmp/carillon.htm. Parking at cemetery $1.75/hr. Metro: Arlington Cemetery. Walk .2 mile.

Twilight Tattoo FREE Wednesday evenings in May and June at Fort McNair, the U.S. Army presents a military pageant that traces Army history from the Revolutionary War. Participants include the Army Band, the Old Guard Fife and Drum Corps, the Army Drill Team, the Army Blues jazz ensemble, and units of the 3rd Infantry Regiment (the Old Guard) in historical uniforms. Bleacher seating is first come, first-seated. The pageant starts at 7pm and lasts an hour. FINE PRINT In inclement weather, phone after 3:30pm to see if the pageant is still on. 4th St. SW (at P St.). ② **202/685-2888.** www.twilight.mdw.army.mil. For free parking, enter 2nd St. gate south of P St. From Waterfront Metrorail Station, walk 2 blocks south on 4th St. to pedestrian gate.

★ **Washington National Opera** The Washington Opera added "National" to its name a few years back. Perhaps these folks now should call themselves the Washington International Opera. The last performance we attended—for free, of course (more about that in a moment)—the seven major characters were played by two Swedes, a Brit, a Russian, an Israeli, and two Americans. Maybe that comes with being world class, which—especially since renowned tenor Placido Domingo took charge of the organization—this opera certainly is. It's also become a leader of the free-theater movement. Early every autumn, a performance is **simulcast for free** on the enormous screen at the Washington Nationals' baseball park. You can get VIP tickets for prime seating, but they're not necessary. In the fall, the opera participates in the League of Washington Theatres' annual **Free Night of Theatre** promotion (p. 153). **National Opera Week** in late fall brings a week's worth of freebies—performances of opera music, educational lectures, programs for children, and events around the community. Beginning in August, check the opera's website for info about free offerings. On the home page, click on "E-Updates and Promotions" to be notified about special events. FINE PRINT Lots of people bring little kids to the Nationals Park performance, because parents can sit on blankets on the outfield grass and the children can run around to their hearts' content. If you're not bringing little kids, *do not* sit in the outfield. The children's running and shouting will disrupt your enjoyment of the opera. In the stands, sit at least 15 rows up from the field so you don't get neck cramps from looking up at the screen. 2700 F St. NW (at New Hampshire Ave.), in the Kennedy Center for the Performing Arts. ② **800/876-7372** or 202/295-2400. www.dc-opera.org. Parking $18. Free Kennedy Center Shuttle from Foggy Bottom Metro Station.

Willard Intercontinental Hotel Lobby FREE Every December, this deluxe hotel transforms its ornate lobby into a venue for free holiday concerts. Call it the "Cheapskates in Luxury" Program. Local ensembles perform in a wide variety of musical styles from 5:30 till 7:30pm every day of month except for a few around Christmas itself. The 2009 program included early music ensembles, a madrigal ensemble, *a capella* groups, a women's barbershop quartet, a colonial chorus singing 18th-century music, and a group performing in Renaissance costume. 1401 Pennsylvania Ave. NW (at 14th St.). ✆ **202/628-9100.** www.washington.intercontinental.com. Metro: Metro Center.

4 Dance

Dance Place Education and youth-outreach share importance with performance at Dance Place, which plays host to four resident companies. The organization regards itself as a community arts centers, a theater, a haven for at-risk youth, and a school—for children and adults. Its education efforts focus on training adults in modern and West African dance and children in creative movement. Adults can study for **free** in exchange for working in the theater. **Student interns,** some of whom get free housing, learn arts administration as well as dance. Performances span the genres ranging from contemporary, postmodern, tap, and ethnic, to performance art, and special programs for children and families. Dance Place's resident companies include two modern troupes—one that focuses on traditional and contemporary West African dance and music—and a youth step team. Touring artists also appear here. Past performers have included Karen Finley, famous for her outrageous performances (and for being de-funded by the NEA), and Blue Man Group before they became superstars and a franchise. When there's a charge for a program, tickets typically cost $22 to $30, with **discounts** available to artists, students, K-12 teachers, and patrons 2 to 17 and 55 or older. You can also see the show for **free** by volunteering to usher. 3225 8th St. NE (btw. Kearney and Jackson sts.). ✆ **202/269-1600.** www.danceplace.org. Parking free. Metro: Brookland.

Washington Ballet You could say these dancers are on perpetual tour—within Washington. They take over the Warner Theatre for much of December for their annual performances of *The Nutcracker*. They also perform at the Kennedy Center, the Shakespeare Theatre

Company's Sidney Harman Hall, the Atlas Performing Arts Center on Capitol Hill, England Studio Theatre in Alexandria, and The Town Hall Education, Arts & Recreation Campus (THEARC) near the Maryland border in Southeast DC. The company performs both classical and contemporary works, and does not take itself so seriously that it can't do humor as well. Note the 2009–10 season's "Shoogie, the Tail of My Wiener Dog." Tickets to the ballet's performances range from $24 to $130. **Volunteers** are invited to **open rehearsals** and are **given tickets.** Various venues. ℭ **202/362-3606.** www.washingtonballet.org.

5 Spectator Sports

Washington has a full complement of pro sports teams, and some major college teams as well. You're not going to find cheap seats for a team that's at the top of the standings, but there are ways to see some contests that won't cost you a fortune, and some downright bargains available if you know where to look (and sit).

Washington Capitals Hockey
The Caps used to offer the best deal in local pro sports—10-buck "Eagles Nest" seats in the top rows in the end zone. Alas, now they've acquired Alex Ovechkin—arguably the best hockey player on the planet—and are making serious runs for the Stanley Cup, selling out Verizon Center, and raising their ticket prices. The cheapest seats now are $35 (ouch), and they're available for fewer than a third of the games. A fifth of the time, the cheapest seats are $65! The rest of the time, they're $50. Plus you have to add on Ticketmaster's usual extortionary "convenience" and delivery charges. (Can anyone explain why Ticketmaster will

NHL up Close for Free

Capitals owner Ted Leonsis has worked to make his operation friendly and transparent to fans, despite the rapid rise of ticket prices. You can watch the **Caps practice for free** at Kettler Capitals Iceplex, 627 N. Glebe Rd. (btw. N. Randolph St. and Wilson Blvd.), in Arlington, VA, near the Ballston Metrorail Station. When they're not on the road, the Caps usually practice at 10am on game day, 11am the day after a game, and 10:30am other days. The Caps post exceptions to that schedule on their website. Click "schedule" on the Home page (**http://capitals.nhl.com**).

mail the tickets to us for free but charges us to print them on our own computer with our own ink, paper, and electricity?) What's a cheap-skate hockey fan to do? Hit **StubHub** (**www.stubhub.com**), the online ticket exchange. We've seen Caps tickets for as low as $10 there. We've used it. It works. Verizon Center is a great hockey venue. There are no bad seats, and we happen to like the end zone. Just bring your binoculars. FINE PRINT You can't bring food or drink inside. F St. NW (btw. 6th and 7th sts.). ✆ **202/266-2200.** Tickets: ✆ **202/397-7328.** http://capitals.nhl.com. Metro: Gallery Place.

Washington Mystics Basketball   Look up in the Verizon Center rafters and you'll see banners celebrating the Wizards' (then Bullets) 1978 NBA championship and several lower-level titles won by the Wiz and the NHL Caps. The Mystics are represented in the rafters, too, but their banners read "WNBA Attendance Champions." The Mystics may have had just two winning seasons in a dozen years and have advanced beyond the Women's National Basketball Association's Eastern Conference semifinals just once, but they do draw fans. The impact on ticket prices is kind of strange. If you're willing to *sit* in the end zone rafters, you actually can watch an NBA game for less ($10) than a WNBA game ($17). Come on down, however, and the Mystics become a (relative) bargain. Their most expensive courtside seats are $125, the Wizards' $2,250. Lower-level corner seats are $35 at Mystics games, center seats $60. Less desirable seats go for $20 to $30. The WNBA season runs from early May to late August. Despite the Mystics' popu-larity, you usually can buy tickets at the door. *Hint:* There's *always* some kind of discount or package available (sometimes through local businesses or fast-food franchises): Call or stop by the box office to find out about the latest offers, and keep an eye on StubHub. Verizon Center, F St. NW (btw. 6th and 7th sts.). ✆ **202/266-2200.** www.wnba.com/mystics. Metro: Gallery Place.

★ **Washington Nationals Baseball**   One good thing about having a losing team is that tickets can be dirt cheap. The Nats lost more than 100 games in both 2008 and 2009. As a result, tickets in the upper, upper, upper deck in far left field cost just 5 bucks. They have to be purchased at the park on game day, but they're usually not hard to get. *Sigh.* The players look like toys from way up here, but you can see the entire field. (Bring your binoculars.) These seats also happen to have the best view to outside the park: Gaze on the Capitol dome or the Washington Monument if the action on the field gets too ugly. There are picnic tables closer to the field on this deck. The Nats allow you to bring food (but no drinks, except still-sealed bottled water) inside. So pack a picnic, dine at the picnic tables, and save money while getting a bit closer to the play. There are no bad seats in this new ballpark as far as we can tell, and we've sat in quite a few and wandered around the park as well. You can sit in the upper deck behind home plate for $18. The $30 seats along the baselines are darn good. Food and beer aren't cheap, but at least there are some good local restaurants represented, including Ben's Chili Bowl's half-smokes, Five Guys' burgers, and the Hard Times Café's varieties of chili. N St. SE (at Half St.). © **202/675-6287.** http://washington.nationals.mlb.com. Metro: Navy Yard.

Washington Redskins Football Despite a decade of on-field futility, the Redskins remain a Washington obsession. The team claims to have 160,000 names on a waiting list for general admission season tickets, but there are reasons to be skeptical of that. We put ourselves on the list about 10 years ago, just to see what it would bring. At first there were repeated offers to buy premium seats that start at about $600 a game. The last few years have brought weekly e-mails for *hoi polloi* tickets at the face value of below $50. Thousands of tickets have been available on StubHub each week, and some have sold for $35 or less. To get on the waiting list, click "Season Ticket Waitlist" on the Redskins' home page. FINE PRINT FedEx Field is fine for watching football, but it's in the middle of nowhere. Taking the Metro necessitates a 1-mile walk, and greedy owner Dan Snyder charges $40 for parking that's so far from the stadium you have to ride a shuttle bus after you've left your car. 1600 FedEx Way, Landover, MD (west of I-495/I-95 Exit 17). © **301/276-6800.** www.redskins.com. Metro: Morgan Blvd.

Washington Wizards Basketball The ever socially responsible Abe Pollin (much missed after his death at age 85 in 2009) changed his team's name from Bullets to Wizards to put forth a less violent image. Unfortunately, it's not had a favorable impact on the won-lost column, as the Wiz consistently chug along in mediocrity. Upper level end zone seats go for as little as $10. Basketball, however, doesn't view as well from the rafters as hockey does. We've found somewhat better—but still high up—seats on StubHub for less than $10. We're

Free Market for Tickets

You'll notice we frequently refer to **StubHub.com** as a source for cheap tickets. It's an online market where folks sell tickets they no longer want. Many are season ticket holders who don't want to go to every game (or concert or play or . . .) and help pay for the events they do attend by selling some of their tickets, sometimes for more than they paid for them. You'll find hard-to-get tickets here at prices far above face value. But you'll find bargains, too, because season ticket holders get discounts or because they're desperate to sell. We've found StubHub easy to use. You buy online and the tickets either are delivered to you or you pick them up someplace near the event. ℂ **866/788-2482.** www.stubhub.com.

not willing to shell out $250 for the lower-level good seats near center court. This wouldn't be considered cheap, but if you really want to see an NBA game reasonably close up and center, you can find StubHub seats from time to time for less than $100. Verizon Center. F St. NW (btw. 6th and 7th sts.). ℂ **202/661-5050.** www.nba.com/wizards. Metro: Gallery Place.

COLLEGE SPORTS

The **University of Maryland** and **Georgetown University** play big-time, as in Division I, frequently going to "The Big Dance" college basketball, and Maryland plays big-time BCS football as well. Except for Maryland men's basketball, tickets usually are readily available, and they cost less than most seats at NBA and NFL games. These schools also field men's and women's teams in many other sports, as do most of the region's higher education institutions.

Georgetown University   The Hoyas are regular competitors in the NCAA Division I men's basketball tournament, including as a No. 3 seed in 2010 (Their 2010 run ended abruptly when they lost in the first round to our alma mater, Ohio University!). (See p. 257 for the answer to your question: "What the heck is a Hoya?") Before 2010, they had won one national championship and played in the Final Four five times. They are a member of the Big East Conference, which generally guarantees some Top 20 and Top 10 matchups. The 2010 season also was good for the women's basketball team, which took a No. 5 seed into the Division I tournament. The men play most of their games at **Verizon Center** in Penn Quarter against the likes of West

Virginia, Notre Dame, Syracuse, and Duke. The women play on campus at **McDonough Arena**. Women's tickets are $10. Men's range from $10 to $75. Verizon Center; F St. NW (btw. 6th and 7th sts.). McDonough Arena; on campus. ℭ 202/687-4692. www.guhoyas. com.

University of Maryland The Terrapin women won the NCAA Division I basketball championship in 2006, the men in 2002. The men entered the 2010 tournament as a No. 4 seed, while the women failed to make the tournament for the first time since 2003 (they've been a perennial power in women's DI hoops since the mid-'80s. Men's basketball tickets can be hard to come by, especially when they play a hated ACC rival such as Duke. Your best shot at getting a seat comes when students leave town for the winter semester break (or to know, date, or be a student). The Terrapins football team took off like a hare at the beginning of coach Ralph Friedgen's tenure, winning 10 or 11 games in 2001, 2002, and 2003, appearing those years in the Orange, Peach, and Gator bowls, and winning top-20 national rankings. Things haven't gone so well since, and they won just two of 12 games in 2009. They play in the powerful Atlantic Coast Conference against such opponents as Florida State, Georgia Tech, Virginia Tech and Miami. Football tickets cost $30 to $48, men's basketball $30 to $50, women's basketball $6 to $12. **Cole Field House** and **Byrd Stadium,** both on campus in College Park, MD ℭ **800/462-8377.** www. umterps.com.

6 Live Music & Dance Clubs

✯ **Black Cat** This place is four, four, four clubs in one. Best known is the large **Mainstage** concert and dance hall, where the greatest indie and alternative groups—and others—perform. Among those who have trod these boards: the Decemberists, Radiohead, Flaming Lips, Foo Fighters, Korn, The White Stripes, Yeah Yeah Yeahs, and Pete Seeger. Cover charges here tend to be in the $10 to $20 range. The 200-seat **Backstage** presents lesser-known musicians as well as DJ dances, poetry readings and films. Cover charges usually are $5 to $10, and some events are free. There's **no cover** at the **Red Room Bar**—which offers pool, pinball, and a jukebox—or the **Food for Thought restaurant,** which serves vegans, vegetarians, and carnivores

DC LIVE MUSIC, CLUBS & BARS

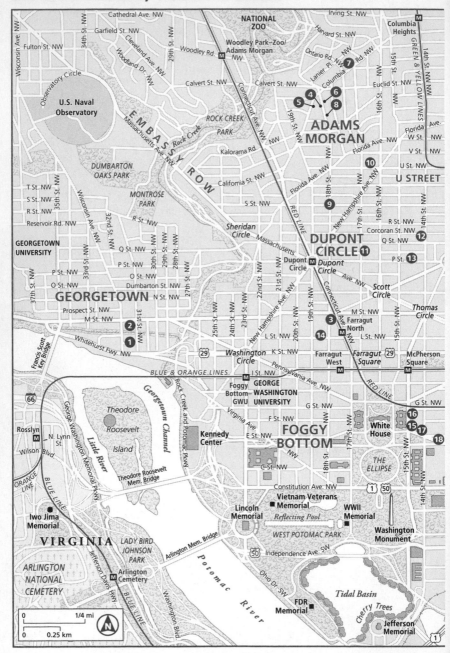

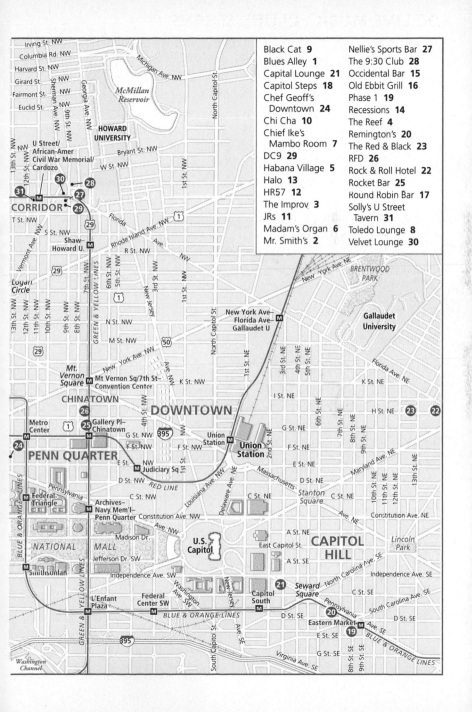

Black Cat **9**
Blues Alley **1**
Capital Lounge **21**
Capitol Steps **18**
Chef Geoff's
  Downtown **24**
Chi Cha **10**
Chief Ike's
  Mambo Room **7**
DC9 **29**
Habana Village **5**
Halo **13**
HR57 **12**
The Improv **3**
JRs **11**
Madam's Organ **6**
Mr. Smith's **2**

Nellie's Sports Bar **27**
The 9:30 Club **28**
Occidental Bar **15**
Old Ebbit Grill **16**
Phase 1 **19**
Recessions **14**
The Reef **4**
Remington's **20**
The Red & Black **23**
RFD **26**
Rock & Roll Hotel **22**
Rocket Bar **25**
Round Robin Bar **17**
Solly's U Street
  Tavern **31**
Toledo Lounge **8**
Velvet Lounge **30**

alike. To get an idea of the broad range of events presented here, consider: the concert by Chopteeth Afrofunk Big Band, the No Control Punk Rock Slam Dance Party, and Bad Taste Film Night. The Black Cat celebrated Christmas 2009 with the James Brown Death-Mas Holiday Bash, which commemorated Brown's Christmas Day death. Every Old Year is blown out and New Year blown in by Peaches O'Dell and her swing band, playing music from the 1920s through the '50s. Beer and wine cost $4 to $7. Appetizers, salads, and sandwiches are $3 to $7. Meat dishes top out at $10. It's all organic, fairtrade, and certified cruelty free. You can avoid the ticket service-charge by buying in cash at the box office. Black Cat's shows are open to all ages, but the club requests that patrons younger than 18 come with an adult. 1811 14th St. NW (north of S St.). ⓒ **202/667-4490.** www. blackcatdc.com; tickets www.ticketalternative.com/Venues/399.aspx. Metro: U St.

SPLURGE

★ **Blues Alley** Washington's top jazz club is not cheap. This is a supper club, with dinner entrees ranging from $19 to $25 and latenight eats from $9 to $12. Tickets cost $18 to $45 or more, depending on the performer. Plus, there's a $10 minimum. But, if you like the artist who's performing, it can be worth the splurge. Blue Alley is a small club with excellent acoustics and there's not a bad seat in the house. It's a nationally known venue. All the top touring artists come here: Dizzy Gillespie, Charlie Byrd, Stanley Turrentine, Ahmad Jamal, and Ramsey Lewis cut live albums at the club. The club's menu of upcoming performers in 2010 included Jamal, Larry Coryell, Gil Scott-Heron, and Mose Allison. You're wise to buy tickets in advance. Seating is first-come, first-seated. The best way to get the best seats is to buy tickets to the early show and arrive early for dinner. Shows start at 8 and 10pm, and doors open for diners at 6pm. Check the club's online calendar to see what's coming. We did and found a free concert by the U.S. Army Blues jazz band. They were cutting an album and were terrific. (Of course we went!) 1073 Wisconsin Ave. NW (to the left in the alley south of M St.). ⓒ **202/337-4141.** www. bluesalley.com. Circulator; Georgetown Metro Connection bus from Dupont Circle or Rosslyn Metrorail station; or Metrobus 31, 32, 36, 38B, or D5.

DC Night Life Basics

Some essential knowledge about nightlife in the District:

- **Metrorail does not run round the clock.** The system closes at midnight Sunday through Thursday and 3am Friday and Saturday. But the stations don't close simultaneously. When you leave a station to begin your night on the town, check the sign at the kiosk and note when the last train leaves. Give yourself plenty of time to get to the station at the end of the night, or you may find yourself having to hail a cab. Be aware: DC cabs, plentiful as grains of sand during business hours, make like Cinderella's coach at night. Note also: Metrorail charges higher rush-hour fares after 2am.

- Some nightlife neighborhoods—notably, Adams Morgan, the U Street Corridor, and H Street NE—are **still transitioning** from their earlier down-at-the-heels lives. After dark, stick to crowded commercial streets. And don't stay till the bars close. It seems the most common time for violence around the main drags is when drunks pour out of the bars, get into fights, and innocent bystanders get hurt. Actually, sticking to the busy commercial streets after dark is good practice on all neighborhoods—especially if you're alone. And, as one Adams Morgan innkeeper told Tom: "Use your urban street smarts."

- H Street NE—which remains closest to its earlier life—runs a **free shuttle** to different venues in the neighborhood from 5pm until midnight Sunday through Thursday and till 3am Friday and Saturday. It picks up near the Gallery Place Metrorail Station, at 781 7th St. NW (south of H St.). Look for the van with the green and white "H ST. NE" logo.

Chief Ike's Mambo Room   Before he was a presidential aide and a TV news star—when he was just a young congressional staffer from Ohio—George Stephanopoulos was among those who frequented Chief Ike's. What you find here is three bars on two floors and an outdoor patio. Bands play Wednesday and Thursday. DJs spin for dancing Friday and Saturday. Monday is Trivia Night. It's happy hour all night Monday and Tuesday. Chili, burgers, nachos, gumbo, and— for a change of pace—turkey-and-brie sandwiches—sell for $7.50 to $9.50. There's an occasional cover charge of $5 to $10. The benefits of the happy hours change. 1725 Columbia Rd. NW (btw. Ontario and Quarry rds.). ✆ **202/332-2211.** www.chiefikesmamboroom. com. Circulator or 96 Metrobus from Woodley Park Metrorail Station.

DC9 The upstairs of this two-story club presents up-and-coming local, national, and even international indie rock bands, as well as DJs. The cover charge usually runs from $5 to $15, and sometimes early entry is free. Downstairs, there's never a cover. You can sit at the bar, in a booth, or on a couch and choose from 130,000 songs on the digital jukebox. Happy hour—5 to 8pm every day—features $2.50 Bud and Bud Light in bottles, $3 rail cocktails and beer, and half-price appetizers. The full-price menu has sandwiches and munchies from $5 to $10. (Fried pickles, anyone?) Usually, you have to be 21 to enter here. 1940 9th St. NW (btw. T and U sts.). ✆ **202/483-5000.** www.dcnine.com. Metro: U St.

Habana Village Want to learn salsa? (To dance, not to cook.) From 7:25 to 9pm Wednesday through Saturday, $10 buys you a lesson. Already know and want to get better? The instructors give advanced lessons, too. On the second level of this three-story club, DJs spin salsa, merengue, and other Latin music for dancers. Fridays, a DJ also spins Latin on the third floor. There's live music on Saturdays. Cheapskates focus on Wednesday and Thursday, because those nights bring drink deals. All night Wednesday, $3 buys beer, wine, and rail drinks. Thursday from 6:30 to 11pm, you can get beer and wine for $3, rail drinks for $6, and a mojito, margarita, or *caipirinha* (the national drink of Brazil) for $6. Men pay a $6 cover charge on Friday and Saturday, which is waived if you buy dinner or dance lessons. 1834 Columbia Rd. NW (btw. Mintwood Place and Biltmore St.). ✆ **202/462-6310.** www.habanavillage.com. Metrobus 42, 43, or H1 or Circulator.

HR-57 Only in Washington. This jazz club takes its name from federal legislation: House Resolution 57 which, in 1987, declared jazz to be "a rare and valuable national American treasure." The place actually is home for the nonprofit Center for the Preservation of Jazz & Blues, which encourages aspiring musicians, educates the public about jazz and blues, and offers a stage for up-and-comers and old pros alike. It's the site of exhibits, lectures, workshops, and music lessons. For 8 bucks, you can catch jam sessions here from 8pm to midnight Wednesdays and Thursdays, and 7 to 11pm Sundays. Friday and Saturday concerts can be more expensive and feature nationally known artists. The real treat for cheapskates is you can BYOB, and the corkage fee is $3 per person. 1610 14th St. NW (btw. Q and Corcoran sts.). ⓒ 202/667-3700. www.hr57.org. Metro: Dupont Circle or Metrobus 52, 53, or 54.

★ **Madam's Organ Blues Bar and Soul Food Restaurant**   It's a long name, but it's a big club, with live music every night and countless other things going on: Loud music, sweaty dancing, and some cheap drinks are the main draws to this highly popular night spot. Madam's motto: "Where the beautiful people go to get ugly." But they also can go to cool off on the always-open rooftop deck . . . with tiki bar! Blues are performed every Friday and Saturday, but it isn't the only music presented. Monday is for funky jazz, Wednesday for bluegrass (with local TV news anchor Doug McKelway sometimes playing banjo), and Thursday for Latin. Sunday the tiki bar showcases local songwriters who play and sing a variety of genres. Other times in other parts of the four-level club, you might encounter R&B, smooth jazz, reggae, salsa, merengue, and who knows what other kinds of musicians—both local and nationally known—and DJs. On the second floor is **Big Daddy's Love Lounge & Pick-Up Joint,** with another bar, free pool tables, and soft seating. Thursday, women don't pay a cover charge (which usually runs from $2–$10), and nonprofit organizations get a cut of the take and can stage fundraising events. (Get more info at www.madamsorgan.com/nfp.html.) Tuesday is team trivia night. Sunday, it's "drunkeoke"—Karaoke with a two-drink minimum. Sandwiches and appetizers cost $4 to $9, entrees $10 to $14, and there are specials every night. As the music roams beyond blues, the eats stretch beyond soul food. Beer starts at $3. From 5 to 8pm Monday through Wednesday, drinks are half-price. Same time Thursday and Friday, you get a buck off. In honor of the well-endowed redhead on the mural outside, redheads can buy Rolling Rock half-price all the time. 2461 18th St. NW (btw. Columbia and Belmont rds.). ⓒ 202/667-5370. www.madamsorgan.com. Circulator or 96 Metrobus from Woodley Park Metrorail Station.

Useful Websites for Planning a Night Out

The Washington Post is a great newspaper for many reasons, one of which is its coverage of DC culture and entertainment. Near the top of *The Post*'s home page (**www.washingtonpost.com**), you'll see buttons for "Arts & Living" and "Going out Guide." Slide your cursor over each to find the specific topics you're interested in. Cheapskates will find it especially worthwhile to click on "Going out Guide," then on "Find Bars and Clubs." There you'll find lists of "Best Dirt-Cheap Happy Hours" and "Best Dive Bars," among others. There's a "Best Cheap Eats" listing in the "Find Restaurants" section, which you access with the "Going out Guide" button. You also might find it fun to check out the "Got Plans?" chat, which *The Post*'s nightlife experts conduct each Thursday at 11am. You access it through the "Live Q&As" section near the bottom of the left-hand side of *The Post*'s home page. If you can't make the live discussion, click on "Weekly Schedule" to find archived chats. There's a great deal more on this website than we can tell you about here. You'll just have to explore for yourself.

Washingtonian is the DC area's local magazine. It's aimed at an upscale audience, but cheapskates will find useful information at its website (**www.washingtonian.com**). Click on the "Food & Dining" button at the top of the home page, then on the "Dirt Cheap Eats" button. (Where'd they get that idea?). We don't have to tell you what you'll find there. For those who are merely cheap, try the "Cheap Eats"

Mr. Smith's   A sing-along piano bar provides the evening entertainment at this Georgetown institution, which also contains substantial restaurant facilities. Friday and Saturday, the pianist starts to play at 10pm, the rest of the week at 9. The bar at this comfortable neighborhood hangout has antique mirrors and Tiffany lamps. The garden sports a retractable roof and fireplaces for cold-weather warmth. There's never a cover, and there are lots of bargains. Sandwiches and munchies range from $5 to $10. The beer of the month is $2.95 all the time—and it's not Bud Light; as we write this sentence, it's Leinenkugel's Fireside Nut Brown, an English lager. Almost every night there's at least one additional deal: half-price appetizers Monday after 5pm, half-price

button. Under the home page's "Arts & Events" button are a "Happy Hour Finder" and a sub-button (is there such a concept?) that will take you to "Nightlife Guides." There, you'll find sections for "Bargains," "Happy Food Hours," and other topics. As at *The Post*'s website, the *Washingtonian*'s has much, much more for you to explore.

Washington City Paper, a free alternative weekly, lists, covers, and reviews restaurants, night spots, theater, and other entertainment and nightlife both in hard copy and online (**www.washingtoncitypaper. com**).

The **Cultural Alliance of Greater Washington** provides information on hundreds of DC performances, other events, and cultural venues at its Cultural Capital (**www.culturecapital.com**) website.

The untimely shutdown in late 2009 of the *Washington Blade,* DC's 40-year-old LGBT newspaper, left many voids, including one in covering gay entertainment. Within days, the staff was publishing a new newspaper—in print and online—called *DC Agenda* (**www.dcagenda. com**). Its coverage includes the entertainment front.

Metro Weekly (**www.metroweekly.com**) is Washington's gay news magazine, available free around town every Thursday and online all the time. The "Nightlife" button at the top of the home page leads to information about bars, happy hours, special events, and the like.

burgers all day Tuesday, $2 Corona Wednesday after 7pm, $2 Stella Artois Thursday after 7pm, and discount entrees for college students on Sunday. From 4 to 7pm Monday through Friday, you can get rail drinks for $2, domestic beer for $3, wine for $3, and martinis for $4. 3104 M St. NW (at 31st St.). © **202/333-3104.** www.mrsmiths.com. Circulator; Georgetown Metro Connection bus from Dupont Circle or Rosslyn Metrorail station; or Metrobus 31, 32, 36, 38B, or D5.

★ **9:30 Club**   This club's state-of-the-art sound system makes it perhaps the best place in DC to hear popular music. Tickets run from $5 to more than $50, depending on the act. National acts, like The Roots, They Might Be Giants, Arctic Monkeys, Pink, Cat Power, Sheryl Crow,

Smashing Pumpkins, Shawn Colvin, R.E.M., Red Hot Chili Peppers, Ice-T, Alanis Morissette—and Tony Bennett!—have played here. The 9:30 admits patrons of all ages and is strict about checking IDs for alcoholic drink orders. You can get food—mostly sandwiches—for $5 to $10. The club's open only when someone's playing, and you're wise to get advance tickets for big-name acts. Tickets are available through the club's website and at the box office. FINE PRINT The club has very few seats, and they're first-come, first-seated. If you must sit because of a disability, phone ahead of time. 815 V St. NW (at Vermont Ave.). ⓒ **202/265-0930.** Tickets 800/955-5566. www.930. com. Metro: U St.

Rock and Roll Hotel   The "hotel"—it's not, really—embraces all forms of rock and roll and some other music genres as well. There's a lot of variety here: pool tables, bars, music/dance hall. Over time, local and national musicians and DJs have presented house, disco, classic rock, blues, hip hop, funk, indie, salsa, rap, and what one DJ described as "noise." Sometimes, you'll pay a $10 to $20 cover charge. A lot of times you'll get in free. Snacks and sandwiches go for $5 to $10. From 6 to 10pm Thursdays, rail drinks cost $3. Other happy hours have offered half-off burgers, $3 rail drinks, and Bacardi flavored rums for $4. For most shows, all ages can listen and dance in the main hall, but those younger than 18 must be accompanied by a parent or guardian. You must be 21 to enter the bars. 1353 H St. NE (btw. 13th and 14th sts.). ⓒ **202/388-7625.** www.rockandrollhoteldc. com. H St. NE Shuttle or Metrobus X1, X2, or D8.

The Red & The Black   Contemplating what Stendhal's classic novel has to do with New Orleans, we decided it must be that they're both French. This club is decorated in red and black and calls itself a "New Orleans style tavern." An eclectic mix of local and touring musicians performs here, from loud hardcore to mellow acoustic. The upstairs performance area, with 100 seats, provides an intimate setting for sometimes ear-splitting sounds. Cover charges usually run from $6 to $10. There's no cover downstairs, which has a bar, red leather booths, black walls, and red lighting. From 5 to 8pm Monday through Friday, rail drinks and beer are 3 bucks. The menu includes Zapp's Louisiana potato chips ($1.50), red beans and rice ($6.50), gumbo, muffulettas, and Cuban sandwiches (all $8). You must be 21 to come here. 1212 H St. NE (btw. 12th and 13th sts.). ⓒ **202/399-3201.** www.redand blackbar.com. H St. NE Shuttle or Metrobus X1, X2, or D8.

Solly's U Street Tavern Pabst Blue Ribbon is always $3 at this neighborhood tavern. During happy hour—until 8pm Monday through Friday—Miller Lite, Budweiser, and house liquors also are $3. Upstairs in this two-story spot, patrons watch sporting events on a half-dozen TV screens. The upstairs room also frequently hosts live music and occasionally a trivia contest. Performers offer a variety of folk and rock styles, much of it fairly laid back. Check the website for who's playing what when. 1942 11th St. NW (at U St.). ⓒ **202/232-6590.** www.sollystavern.com. Metro: U St.

Velvet Lounge This small club features punk and indie rock and often gets packed to the extreme. Cover charges usually are $8 or less, and there are occasional free shows. Check the website for cost and whether the show you're interested in is open to those younger than 21. 915 U St. (btw. 9th St. and Vermont Ave.) ⓒ **202/462-3213.** www.velvetloungedc.com. Metro: U St.

7 Bars

⭐ **Capitol Lounge** Throughout this book, you'll run into variations of the phrase "congressional staffer hangout." There are quite a few. But not every drinking emporium on Capitol Hill earns that honorific. It's essential that it be on the Hill, but it's also essential that it be affordable to modest congressional staffer salaries. The Capitol Lounge is fun, with pool tables, television screens tuned to sporting events, and a patio that's covered and heated in cold weather. It's an interesting spot, with exposed brick walls and an arched wooden ceiling abutting a pressed tin ceiling. It also has lots of deals on food and good beer. From 4 to 7pm Monday through Friday, all drinks are a buck off, which brings some beers down to $3. Pizza is half-price on Monday night. Buffalo wings are 25¢ each on Tuesday night. Wednesday night, $4 buys you a margarita or a bottle of Corona, Pacifico, or Negra Modelo. This is "Fiesta Night," so quesadillas and taco trios sell for $5. Thursday, you can buy a pitcher of the following for $12: Bell's, Yuengling, Brooklyn Lager, Bud Light, Dale's Pale Ale, Dogfish Head, or the house Capitol Lounge Amber. Friday, you get 2 bucks off Belgian beers. Bloody Marys and mimosas cost $5 during Saturday and Sunday brunch (10am–3pm). After brunch, bottles of wine are half-price. Check out the bar when you enter. If you see your first name on display, you drink beer and some cocktails for free.

Cheap Restaurant Bars

Several of the cheap eateries described in chapter 3 double as good and cheap bars. Consider the following spots:

- **Bullfeathers** (p. 60), a hangout for House staffers near their Capitol Hill offices, offers a lot of cut-rate specials on food and drink.

- **Garrett's** (p. 78) occupies an 18th-century Federalist building in Georgetown, and it's got that dark, run-down, old-school saloon look about it. But it's up to date with 21st-century technology. All three bars here have Internet jukeboxes with access to more than 100,000 songs. Monday through Friday from 4 to 7pm, 3 bucks buys rail drinks, house wines, Bud, Bud Light, Miller Lite, and Yuengling Lager. Burgers, chicken sandwiches, nachos, and wings are half-price. Various beers sell for $3 from 9pm till closing Sunday through Thursday.

- ★ **Hawk 'n' Dove** (p. 64), another popular Hill spot, draws congressional aides after work and after softball games. Monday through Friday from 4 to 7pm, domestic beer and rail drinks cost $2; the "Pint of the Night" costs $3.50 from 4pm till closing. Sunday, Yuengling costs $2.50 from 1 to 9pm, and you can get a pitcher of domestic beer for $8 when sporting events are on the tube. All night Monday, Stella Artois goes for $3. From 5 to 9pm

231 Pennsylvania Ave. SE. ⓒ **202/547-2098.** www.capitolloungedc. com. Metro: Capitol South.

Chi Cha Lounge   A Latin hookah bar? Well, that's what you find here. Folks sit on comfortable oversized sofas and armchairs, eat tapas, sip Latin drinks, and puff on Middle Eastern water pipes. The lounge is named after the traditional drink from the Andes called *"chicha."* It's made of corn soaked in pineapple juice, with cinnamon, cloves, cane sugar and, one more ingredient that this bartender won't reveal. Here, a chicha costs $7. The chef describes his cooking as "Nuevo Latino Andean-inspired tapas." That turns out to include such dishes as plantain chips with guacamole; a salad of avocado,

Tuesday, Miller Lite draft is $2, which also is the price for a dozen wings. From opening till 9pm Wednesday, Miller Lite draft is $2 and a bucket of Corona or Dos Equis is $10. Thursday and Friday from 5 till 9pm, Miller Lite is $2 by the draft glass and $8 by the pitcher. When games are on the TV on Saturday, you can get a pitcher of domestic beer for $8 and a glass of Hawk Amber Ale draft for $3. Thursday through Saturday after 9pm, college students gather to dance in a separate section of the Hawk that's called The Club ($5 cover charge).

● Having moved from its old digs to Logan Circle, **Stoney's** (p. 80) no longer qualifies as a dive. But it still serves Bud and Bud Light for $3.50 Monday through Friday nights.

● Excellent chips and salsa at **Tortilla Coast** (p. 66) make the perfect accompaniment for $3 Dos Equis on Monday, $3 Bud and Bud Light on Tuesday, $3 Miller Lite and Bud Light on Wednesday, $3.50 Corona on Thursday and $3.25 TC Amber on Friday. These happy hours at this Hill haven for Republicans last from 5pm till last call.

● Cheap beer and cheap food have made the **Tune Inn** (p. 66) a drinking institution for congressional staffers and the occasional member of Congress.

cherry tomatoes, queso fresco cheese, and cilantro vinaigrette; and crab cakes over corn purée. The small plates cost $4 to $10. From 5 to 8pm Monday through Friday, you can get cocktails and sangria for $4 and beer for $3. 1624 U St. NW (btw. 16th and 17 sts.). ⓒ **202/ 234-8400.** www.latinconcepts.com/chicha. Metro: U St.

Chef Geoff's Downtown   Thought mostly a restaurant, Chef Geoff's Downtown (there are other locations) puts on a great happy hour and has good prices on some beers all the time. All day every day, a selection of seasonal beers sells for $2.95 and a 16-ounce can of Pabst Blue Ribbon costs $3.50. Happy hour runs all day Saturday and Sunday, from 3pm till closing Monday and Tuesday, and till 7pm

Happy Shopping Hour

If you venture to the Friendship Heights shopping area, you can find a good happy hour in the bar at **Lia's.** It's a cousin of Chef Geoff's Downtown, and offers similar deals at the same times. Geoff Tracy is the chef behind both of these restaurants. 4435 Willard Ave., Chevy Chase, MD (west of Wisconsin Ave.). ℰ **240/ 223-5427.** www.chefgeoff.com/ lias-home.html. Metro: Friendship Heights.

other days. At those times, the Chef charges $2.95 for bottles of Stella Artois, Shiner Bock, Corona, Michelob Ultra, Labatt Blue, Amstel Lite, Bud Light, Miller Lite, and Budweiser. For $7.95, you can get 33.8-ounce mugs of a variety of good beers. As we write, they include Leinenkugel Sunset Wheat, Peak Organic Nut Brown Ale, Magic Hat #9, Sierra Nevada Pale Ale, Pilsner Urquell, Guinness, Leinenkugel Classic Amber, Sam Adams Octoberfest, Yuengling Lager, and Chef Geoff's house amber, as well as old standby Miller Lite. Wine sells for $5.95 a glass throughout the happy hour times. In addition, all bottles of wine are half-price on Monday. Happy hour food includes burgers for $5.95 and pizza for $8.95. 1301 Pennsylvania Ave. NW (at 13th St.). ℰ: **202/464-4461.** www.chefgeoff.com/chef-geoffs-downtown-home.html. Metro: Metro Center.

Recessions   Everything's cheap all the time at this aptly named dive in a basement in the heart of Washington's pricey Downtown office district. But happy hour is depression cheap. Monday through Friday from 5 to 8pm, Miller Lite costs $2, Corona and rail drinks $3, and "King Kong" drafts—28 ounces!—are $4. At the same time, appetizers—onion rings, crab cakes, buffalo wings, fried calamari, and the like—go for $4. The rest of the time, munchies range from $2 (french fries) to $5.25 (chicken quesadilla). Entrees start at $5.95 for a three-egg omelet and top out at $8.95 for steak or a fisherman's platter. Recessions has pool tables, dart boards, TVs, and an Internet jukebox. You can karaoke from 9pm till midnight on Friday. Bring three friends on your birthday and you'll eat for free. This place is dark and worn, but you can't beat the prices. 1833 L St. NW (btw. 18th and 19th sts.). ℰ **202/296-6686.** www.recessionsdc.com. Metro: Farragut North.

The Reef   The best spots here are not the first room you encounter when walking in from the sidewalk. The best places to sample the

Reef's beers are on the second floor—with televisions and the aquariums that give the place its name—and the roof, with its vistas of Dupont Circle and Downtown DC. The Reef offers a changing selection of draft beers from around the world from its 14 taps. Prices for a pint range from $4 (Pabst Blue Ribbon or Miller High Life) to $8. All are a buck cheaper from 5 to 8pm daily, and either Pabst or High Life is $3 all day Sunday through Thursday. Tuesday is karaoke night starting at 9:30pm. A trivia quiz with prizes starts at 7:30pm every Wednesday. FINE PRINT It can be difficult to get in on weekends and in nice weather when people want seats on the roof, so you're wise to arrive early. 2446 18th St. NW (btw. Columbia and Belmont rds.). ℂ **202/518-3800.** www.thereefdc.com. Circulator or 96 Metrobus from Woodley Park Metrorail Station.

★ **RFD** RFD in the middle of urban Penn Quarter? Well, here it means "Regional Food and Drink." The folks here know their beer. And they've got lots of it: 30 labels on tap and more than 300 in bottles. Regular prices aren't cheap. Drafts—which come from all over the world—cost $6 to $9 (if you don't count Miller Lite, which the menu describes as "Training Beer." However, Monday through Friday from 4 to 7pm, Sam Adams and Miller Lite cost $3, and there's a beer of the day for $3.50. RFD has 11 TVs inside and a patio for sipping outdoors. 810 7th St. NW (btw. H and I sts.). ℂ **202/289-2030.** www.lovethebeer.com/rfd.html. Metro: Gallery Place.

Rocket Bar This interestingly decorated basement bar in ever-growing Penn Quarter offers more to drink than $3 beers. Stars, rockets, and an astronaut are painted on the walls. You can watch the game on HD TV, shoot pool, play table shuffleboard, throw darts, play skee-ball, or pick from the collection of board games—all for a fee. A couple pays $12 an hour for a pool or shuffleboard table Sunday through Wednesday, for example, and $14 Thursday through Saturday. Other amusements are less expensive: a buck to rent a board game, for instance. You also can pick from a variety of seating arrangements: bar stools, couches, banquettes, chairs at cocktail tables, and a Ms. Pac-Man table. The jukebox plays a variety of rock styles at four songs for a buck, 25 for $5. Beer costs $3 to $5, wine and rail drinks $5. Another potential cost saver: You can BYO food, and the bartenders keep carryout menus from the many nearby restaurants. 714 7th St. NW (btw. G and H sts.). ℂ **202/628-7665.** www.rocketbardc.com. Metro: Gallery Place.

Hobnobbing at High-End Bars

These three spots have history and probably will fulfill your fantasies about what Washington insiders' drinking spots should look like. They're not cheap. But you won't spend a *lot* if you savor one drink while contemplating your surroundings. You just might bump into White House aides and other movers and shakers unwinding after a hard day of governing and influencing.

Even before Henry Willard bought it in 1850, the old hotel at Pennsylvania Avenue and 14th Street was housing the rich, the famous, the powerful, and the merely influential—in no small part because of its location just 2 blocks from the White House. The **Round Robin Bar** in the current incarnation of the Willard (built in 1901, expanded and renovated in 2000) traces its heritage back to the earlier hostelry where Sen. Henry Clay of Kentucky supposedly introduced Washington to the mint julep in the early 19th century. Grab a leather-upholstered stool at the round, mahogany bar and order one for $15. (The bar honors Clay with an annual Kentucky Derby party.) Before you return to the outside world, take a stroll through the Willard's palatial lobby and Peacock Alley, the first-floor hallway with columns, chandeliers, and rich red carpeting. Try to peek into the opulent Willard Room restaurant, off that hallway, which now is used mostly for private events. If you're headed to the Metro Center Metrorail Station, continue up the alley, go out the back door, and walk to the right. 1404 Pennsylvania Ave. NW (btw. 14th and 15th sts.). ✆ **202/628-9100.** www.washington.intercontinental. com/washa/dining_03.htm. Metro: Metro Center.

Standing by the Willard, the **Occidental** also claims the heritage of an earlier building, this one constructed in 1906, destroyed by fire in 1971, rebuilt and reopened in 1986, and renovated in 2007. The renovation made the first-floor dining room and bar much lighter than it

Toledo Lounge John Denver once sang that "Saturday night in Toledo, Ohio, is like being nowhere at all. They roll back the sidewalk precisely at 10, and people who live there are not seen again." He knew all this because "I spent a week there one day." Toledo natives Stephanie and Mary Abbajay beg to differ. The sisters opened the

used to be. But its walls are still covered with 1,500 autographed portraits of famous Occidental diners, from Buffalo Bill Cody through Huey Long and various Kennedys, up to Oprah Winfrey and contemporary politicians. See if you can commandeer the table where a back-channel U.S.–U.S.S.R. meeting helped resolve the 1962 Cuban missile crisis, which had put the two nuclear powers on the verge of war. You can get a drink for less than $10. 1475 Pennsylvania Ave. NW (btw. 14th and 15th sts.). ⓒ **202/783-1475.** Metro: Metro Center.

The history of the **Old Ebbitt Grill** is a bit murky, but its owners point to the "legend" of when innkeeper William E. Ebbitt bought a boarding house in 1856. President William McKinley supposedly lived there when he was a member of Congress, and presidents Ulysses Grant, Andrew Johnson, Grover Cleveland, Theodore Roosevelt, and Warren Harding are said to have imbibed at the bar. The Ebbitt moved several times. We first ate and drank in it when it occupied a narrow 19th-century building on F Street, and looked and felt as if Teddy Roosevelt could walk in the door at any minute. The Ebbitt moved to its current location, around the corner from the White House, in 1983 when its F Street building was demolished. The new Old Ebbitt is a large, handsome establishment that evokes older times with antique gas chandeliers and fixtures, mahogany bars with brass and beveled glass, an antique clock from the F Street building, a marble staircase with an iron-spindled rail, as well as displays of antique beer steins, hunting trophies, and decoys. Teddy Roosevelt may have bagged the walrus head. Alexander Hamilton may have collected the wooden bears. Drinks start at $6. 675 15th St. NW (btw. F and G sts.). ⓒ **202/ 347-4800.** www.ebbitt.com. Metro: Metro Center.

Toledo Lounge in 1994. It's become a popular spot, and offers many good deals. Continuing the Ohio theme, the Abbajays—both graduates of Ohio's Kenyon College—offer 20% discounts to Kenyon alumni and students on Friday nights. You must be 21, and show a Kenyon ID or correctly answer Kenyon trivia questions. The bar's specials are many and complex. Whenever it rains, you can buy drafts for 2 bucks. Sunday through Tuesday from 6 to 9pm, drafts cost $2 and rail drinks $3. Thursday through Saturday plus Wednesday, those deals are available till 8pm. Monday brings half-price appetizers, Tuesday and Sunday half-price burgers, Wednesday half-price cheese sandwiches and hotdogs. Tuesday also is Ladies Night, when women get $2 off everything except burgers. Other times, sandwiches and salads range from $6.95 to $8.95, munchies from $4.95 to $8.95. The bar is decorated with Toledo memorabilia and has an outdoor patio. 2435 18th St. NW (btw. Columbia and Belmont rds.). ℭ **202/986-5416.** www.toledoloungedc. com. Circulator or 96 Metrobus from Woodley Park Metrorail Station.

8 Comedy Clubs

SPLURGE

★ **Capitol Steps** Everyone knows the best comedy in Washington is performed unintentionally in the U.S. Capitol. But everyone is only partly right. The best comedy in Washington was born in the Capitol (and the congressional office buildings) and is now performed *intentionally* twice a week downtown. In 1981, congressional staffers with talent contemplated the humor around them and turned it into an enduring musical act. (Motto: We put the "mock" in democracy.) They routinely take familiar tunes, rearrange the language, and produce hilarious new songs. (Former Surgeon General C. Everett Koop really did let the Steps publish this "Surgeon General's Warning: The Capitol Steps will cause your sides to split.") It's amazing how well they keep changing their act to keep up with current events. As we write, the economic crisis and federal bailouts have inspired "Monster Cash," to the tune of "Monster Mash," and "Subprime Mortgage Holders," to the tune of "Sunshine On My Shoulders." Our 44th president and the holiday season are saluted with "Barackin' Around the Christmas Tree." Oldies but still goodies that still make the hit list: "It's a Whole Newt World," "Papa's Got a Brand New Baghdad," "The Wreck of the Walter Fritz Mondale" and "Dutch, the Magic Reagan"). The Steps perform every Friday and Saturday at 7:30pm. Tickets cost $39. Ronald Reagan Building and International Trade Center Amphitheater, 1300 Pennsylvania Ave. NW (btw. 13th and 14th sts.).

© **800/551-7328** or 202/397-7328. www.capsteps.com; tickets www.ticketmaster.com. Metro: Federal Triangle.

The Improv Touring comics perform here. In the past, such superstars as Ellen DeGeneres, Jerry Seinfeld, Robin Williams, David Spade, Chris Rock, and Adam Sandler have been on the bill. If you watch Comedy Central or the late-night talk shows, or follow comedy in other ways, you'll probably be familiar with the performers on the Improv's upcoming calendar as we write this: Christian Finnegan, Joe Recca, Eddie Gossling, Aisha Tyler, Tony Rock, and Jamie Kennedy. Tickets usually cost $15 to $17, but can rise to as much as $75 for a special event. You can avoid the $3 service charge by buying your ticket at the box office. There's also a two-item minimum: any combination of food or drink. Early shows offer light meals (sandwiches, salads, burritos, tacos), appetizers, and desserts, late shows only appetizers. Prices range from $5.95 for french fries to $11 for a taco salad or steak tortilla platter. Wine starts at $6.95 a glass. Minimum age is 18 for all shows. 1140 Connecticut Ave. N.W. (btw. L and M sts.). © **202/296-7008**. www.dcimprov.com. Metro: Farragut North.

9 LGBT in DC

JR's Bar & Grill JR's is highly popular—it could even be called *venerable*—with upscale gay men. The place can be especially packed for Monday's show tune sing-alongs and Sunday, when Skyy vodka highballs sell for $2 all day. The decor includes brick walls, stained glass windows, and a large TV screen. You can shoot pool upstairs. Cheapskates find much to like here besides Sunday's cut-rate vodka drinks. Monday through Thursday, the magic price is $3 and the magic time period is 3pm to closing. That's what pints cost on Monday, rail drinks and domestic beers cost on Tuesday (which is comedy night), rail drinks cost on Wednesday, and rail vodka and drafts cost on Thursday (retro night). Same time on Friday and Saturday, you can get Red Bull and vodka for $5, plus $4 Corona on Friday, $4 Skyy on Saturday, $3 Coors Light on Saturday. 1519 17th St. NW (btw. Q and Church sts.). © **202/328-0090**. www.jrswdc.com. Metro: Dupont Circle.

★ **Halo** This comfortable, laid-back spot is a popular place for gay men of diverse ages and races and also attracts some lesbians and straights. It's a nice spot to relax, chat, and sip cocktails, because the jazzy music doesn't interfere with conversation. Halo features cocktails made with fresh fruit—such as the blueberry mojito, perhaps the best—and 24 kinds of vodka, including one flavored with acai, a palm tree fruit. Beer costs 5 bucks, and wine and cocktails range from $6 to $16. From 5 to 7pm every day, buy one drink and you get the second free. 1435 P St. NW (btw. 14th and 15th sts.). ✆ **202/797-9730.** www.halodc.com. Metro: Dupont Circle or Metrobus 52, 53, 54, or G2.

Remington's Yes, Washington has gay dancing cowboys—and a place for them to strut their stuff. Long before Ennis and Jack rode up Brokeback Mountain, DC's gay country-western fans found compadres on Capitol Hill. This would be at Remington's, a country-western bar that offers dance lessons in case you don't know the Texas Two-Step. It's gay men mostly who mosey into Remington's after a hard day on the Washington range. They're testament to DC's large, active, and diverse gay community which, though centered on Dupont Circle, lives, works, and plays throughout the city and its suburbs. Remington's has swinging saloon doors, fence posts, antlers, saddles, and other Western paraphernalia. It's named for Frederick Remington, the artist known for his paintings and sculpture of the West. Remington's main floor has two bars and a 700-square-foot dance floor. If the dancing doesn't interest you—or if you're just plumb tuckered out—climb to the second floor, where pool tables and karaoke (sometimes) await you. Dance lessons are offered 8:30 to 9:30pm Monday and Wednesday and cost $5. From 4 to 8pm Tuesday through Friday, you can get a buck off top-shelf drinks or pay $3 for rail drinks, $4.50 for imported beer, $2.75 for domestic, and $2 for draft Bud or Bud Light. Monday, those deals continue all night long. Tuesday, 8pm to closing, buy one rail drink or domestic beer and get the second free. Wednesday from 4 to 8pm, it's $2.50 for domestic drafts and $3 for Skyy and Bacardi specials. Same time Thursday, you can get Heineken for $3 and Cosmos specials for $5. Saturday, it's $4.50 domestic beers, $5.50 imports, and $4.75 rail drinks. After midnight Friday and Saturday, Skyy vodka specials are $3. 639 Pennsylvania Ave. SE (btw. 6th and 7th sts.). ✆ **202/543-3113.** www.RemingtonsWDC.com. Metro: Eastern Market.

Nellie's Sports Bar   This place is aimed, first and foremost, at gay men who like sports, and it does a great deal to attract them to its premises. But owner Douglas Schantz says he wants Nellie's—named for two of his great-great-grandmothers—to be straight-friendly as well. There's a lot here to attract all sports fans. Nellie's TV screens can show 11 different sporting events at the same time. The restrooms are furnished with sinks from Griffith Stadium, where the Senators and Redskins played long ago. It completes its decoration with other sports equipment. It's got a rooftop deck and free Wi-Fi. It's got poker night on Monday, drag bingo on Tuesday, trivia on Wednesday, and board games for those who are less into spectator sports or group competitions. One of Schantz's partners is Rocio Anzola-Mendez, a Venezuelan-born restaurateur, so Nellie's empanadas and *arepas* (corn muffins with various toppings) are excellent. Food prices range from $5 for soup to $12 for the arepas. Nellie's "Beat-the-Clock" happy hour works this way Monday through Friday: 5 to 6pm beer and vodka are available for a buck, 6 to 7pm for $2, 7 to 8pm for $3. Additional food and drink deals are offered for the first hour. You can buy beer for $2 Sunday from 3 to 8pm. 900 U St. NW (at 9th St.). © **202/332-6355.** www.nelliessportsbar.com. Metro: U St.

Phase 1   Opened in 1970, Phase 1 is Washington's oldest bar for lesbians and claims to be the oldest in the country. It has a laid-back neighborhood/community feel early in the evening. Later, especially on the weekend, it can really get hoppin' with women eager to party and dance. The decor includes crystal chandeliers, red draperies, dark tables and banquets, and a pool table. Phase 1 puts on varied—sometimes raucous—entertainment. Wednesday is Jell-O-wrestling night. Thursdays are for karaoke. DJs spin Friday and Saturday, and musicians perform live some Sundays. Cover charges usually range from $5 to $8. Regular drink prices are low by DC standards: wine and domestic beer for $4, imported beer for $4.50, spirits $5 to $10. Wednesday, $3 buys Dos Equis and shooters. Thursday, 3 bucks gets Dos Equis, Heineken Light, and Sol. Sunday, Bud Light is $3, Heineken Light and Sol $3.50. All ages frequent Phase 1—all ages older than 21, that is. Bring cash, because credit cards aren't accepted. 525 8th St. SE (south of E St.). © **202/544-6831.** www.phase1dc.com. Metro: Eastern Market.

DC street hockey players take over security-closed Pennsylvania Avenue in front of the White House at noon every Saturday and Sunday, weather permitting. All comers are welcome to BYOS&S. (Bring your own skates and stick.) See p. 213.

FREE & DIRT CHEAP LIVING

As you've seen in earlier chapters, there are lots of things to do for free in Washington. We've also shown you ways to minimize the costs of dining out and renting a room when visiting the city. Living cheaply in DC is a challenge, however, especially if—like us—you want to live within the District to avoid the hassles of a long commute and to have all the wonderful DC resources at your fingertips.

In Exchange for No Representation . . .

Congress never has been willing to grant Washington residents the most basic rights of American citizenship. We have no voting representation in Congress, and Congress can—and routinely does—overturn the actions of our locally elected City Council. The lawmakers from the rest of the country occasionally throw us a sop, however. Recognizing that we don't have a comprehensive higher education system, Congress established a special scholarship program for Washington high school graduates. Congress also established a voucher program to allow some lower-income children to attend private elementary and secondary schools, although that program may be headed to the endangered species list.

● **District of Columbia Tuition Assistance Grants:** Federal taxpayers gave our family $40,000 to help pay for daughter Julie to attend the College of William and Mary, an excellent but expensive Virginia state university. You can tap that financial-aid source, too, if you or your child is a DC resident who graduates from high school and attends a state university. You don't have to graduate from a DC public school or a private school in DC. You simply have to be a Washington resident when you graduate. The grant gives you up to $10,000 a year to pay the out-of-state surcharge at a public higher education institution anywhere in the country. You can get $2,500 to attend a private university in the Washington region, a historically black college anywhere in the United States, or a 2-year institution nationwide. You can't have the grant if your family earns more than a million dollars a year—but, if that's the case, you're probably not reading this book. Applications usually become available at the beginning of the year and must be filed by the end of June. Information: 51 N St. NE, Lower Level,

Luckily, the unique institutions that make Washington such an attractive and inexpensive place for tourists also provide opportunities for us locals to enrich our lives at little cost. First, obviously, those who live here can take advantage of the free and cheap attractions

Washington, DC 20002. ✆ **877/485-6751** or 202/727-2824. www. osse.dc.gov/seo/cwp/view,A,1226,Q,536770,seoNav_GID,1511.asp.

- **District of Columbia Opportunity Scholarship Program:** While "vouchers" for private schools remain a political football in the national discussion on education, this federally funded scholarship program was established in 2003 when Republicans controlled Congress and the White House. It provides financial assistance for low-income students to attend private elementary and secondary schools. As we write this—with Democrats now in control of the federal government—the program is in trouble. The politics of this are interesting, with District Democrats supportive of what Republican federal officials did in 2003 and opposed to what federal Democrats now are attempting to do. In the 2008–09 school year, more than 1,700 DC children received up to $7,500 to put toward tuition payments at 49 private schools located within the city. To find out the program's status, call the DC hotline by dialing ✆ **311** from within the city, or contact the DC Education Department at 441 4th St. NW, Ste. 350 North, Washington, DC 20001. ✆ **202/727-6436.** www.osse.dc.gov.

- **Signature Scholarship Program:** No matter what the fate of the opportunity scholarship, this privately funded program is likely to continue. It provides scholarships for low- and moderate-income DC children to attend any private school in Washington, Maryland, or Virginia. It pays just $3,000, however, which is below the tuition at most—if not all—private schools in the Washington area. For information, write 4201 Connecticut Ave. NW, Ste. 406, Washington, DC 20008. ✆ **202/222-0535.** www.washington scholarshipfund.org.

we've described in the first several chapters and will describe in the ones that follow this one. Take up residence here, and you'll discover many more ways to enrich your mind and body and to manage life's daily needs.

Embassies, think tanks, and many of those U.S. government facilities lay out a daily buffet of free lectures, debates, panel discussions, concerts, films, and other food for the mind. Washingtonians are avid readers—and many are avid writers as well—so you might catch someone like George Will or Bob Woodward talking about his latest book at **Politics and Prose,** Washington's best local bookstore. Or you might bump into them browsing in the aisle.

There's a great deal of free and low-cost recreation around Washington. We have excellent public transportation (all the better to avoid the horrible traffic congestion). Bicycle racks and trails facilitate the cheapest transportation of all (except, of course, for walking). Washington residents, who are definitely U.S. citizens, but without a home state (or representation in Congress, which we find inherently unfair), can take advantage of special support for home buyers, college students, and parents who want to send their children to private elementary and secondary schools (see earlier box).

1 Essential DC Reading

In addition to covering the news and entertaining us with feature stories and going-out guides, *The Washington Post* and *Washingtonian* magazine publish useful guides to local living—some of it available free online. We've also got a local magazine that evaluates local services the way *Consumer Reports* rates products.

Washington Consumers' Checkbook   From acupuncturists to wood-floor refinishers, *Checkbook* evaluates and tracks the prices charged by service-providers in the Washington area. Twice a year, *Checkbook* publishes a magazine with 100 or more pages of reviews, advice, and ratings. A robust collection of reviews, advice, ratings, price surveys, reader surveys, and other information appears on the *Checkbook* website. The organization also operates automobile shopping and leasing services. *Checkbook* is a project of the nonprofit Center for the Study of Services, which was founded in 1974. Like *Consumer Reports, Checkbook* attempts to assure its credibility by not selling advertising and not accepting donations from businesses. It is supported entirely by subscriptions, donations from individuals, and fees for its products. FINE PRINT A 2-year subscription costs $34 and includes occasional newsletters plus access to the website. We've subscribed for most of the time we've lived here.

1625 K St. NW, 8th Floor, Washington, DC 20006. ℭ **800/213-7283.** www. checkbook.org.

Washingtonian   This city magazine is known for its many guides. In other chapters of this book, you meet *Washingtonian*'s guides to dining and entertainment. The magazine also publishes guides to neighborhoods, best places to work, weekend getaways, schools, summer camps, stores, home-repair and -improvement contractors, charities, beauticians, veterinarians, kennels, spas, weddings, lawn services, window washers, housecleaners, and so on. All of this—and more—appears on the magazine's website. And the website lets you search, browse, and access information when you want it, rather than when the magazine happens to drop into your mailbox. The "Homes" button on the *Washingtonian* home page takes you to information on home improvement and repair as well as evaluations of neighborhoods. The "Work and Education" button leads to evaluations of schools and employers; there's also a tool for searching for jobs. Clicking on the "Best of" button gets you access to—among many other topics—"Where to get Great Stuff Cheap." You also can sign up for e-mail newsletters about shopping and other topics. FINE PRINT You must be a magazine subscriber to access much of the most-useful information online. A 1-year subscription for $30 gets you 12 issues of the magazine plus access to all the website's features. Discounted multiyear subscriptions usually are available.

1828 L St., NW, Washington, DC 20036. ℭ **202/296.3600.** www.washingtonian.com.

The Washington Post   As journalists who have written for newspapers for much of our lives and read them since we learned to read, we can't imagine *not* subscribing to the local paper. In DC, the local paper happens to be a great paper, despite the slow erosion that's occurring in all printed journalism these days. In addition to the excellent local, national, and international news stories that *The Post*'s staff produces each day, the newspaper's website carries much useful information for folks who live here. On The *Post*'s home page, hover your curser over "Local," then click on "Local Explorer." Plug in your zip code, and you'll find a tool that enables you to locate groceries, drug stores, hospitals, libraries, places of worship, and other institutions. You also can get neighborhood-specific information about schools, home sales, and crime. Click on "Community Handbook" for information on civic organizations and recreation centers. Clicking on the home page "Jobs" button enables you to search or browse for job listings and to read advice about job-hunting and succeeding in the job you have. You'll also see home-page links to information and advertising about motor vehicles for sale, houses for sale, and houses and apartments for rent. FINE PRINT We've encountered glitches when using some of these online tools. As we write this, you don't have to pay to use The *Post* website, although someday newspapers are going to have to figure out how to charge for their online products. Introductory subscriptions for home delivery of the *Post* can be quite cheap—$1.11 a week for a 26-week subscription, for instance. As long-time subscribers, we pay about $4.50 a week.

1150 15th St. NW, Washington, DC 20071. ☏ **202/334.6000.** www.washpost.com.

2 Exercising the Mind

A key function of many Washington institutions is to try to impress and influence the U.S. government and its constituents. A side effect is to give DC residents many opportunities for attending free lectures, debates, films, concerts, art shows, and tons of other events. **Embassies** want to show off their nations' culture and to promote their points of view. **Interest groups** want to demonstrate why their legislative priorities are best for the country. **Think tanks** want to showcase their scholars' work. **Bookstores** and authors want to promote book sales through readings, talks, and signings. The District's many cultural and educational organizations also want to share their knowledge, and nearly every museum or historical attraction has some kind of public presentation program. It's a rare night in DC when there isn't a lecture, panel, display, or performance for free or a small fee for your edification (or your vote!).

GLOBETROTTING AT THE EMBASSIES

As our nation's capital, Washington attracts representatives of nearly every government in the world, as well as countless private organizations dedicated to various aspects of international affairs. Diplomacy can be a super-secret business, but these organizations also reach out to the general public.

You can look for their lectures, panel discussions, concerts, exhibits, and other events in online calendars maintained by **Cultural Tourism DC** and by local publications. Click the "Calendar of Events" button on the Cultural Tourism home page (**www.culturaltourismdc.org**). On *The Washington Post* home page (www.washingtonpost.com), click "Going out Guide," then "Events." At www.washingtonian.com, click "Arts & Events," then "Where & When Events Calendar." At the *Washington City Paper* home page, hover your cursor over the "Arts & Events" button, then click on "Books & Talks." Or you can go directly to the embassies website. The **U.S. State Department maintains** a list of embassy websites here: **www.state.gov/s/cpr/rls/dpl/32122.htm**. When you find an event that you want to attend, check the embassy's website to find out if you need to make reservations or pay a fee. Note the event's location, because sometimes the embassies sponsor activities in other sites around Washington or beyond. Here are a few embassies that are known for their robust programming:

Canada   The striking Canadian embassy occupies prime diplomatic real estate on Pennsylvania Avenue between the Capitol and the White House. Its open air rotunda makes for spectacular display of its Christmas tree. Its rooftop is a prime spot for viewing Independence Day fireworks and the quadrennial inaugural parade. Unfortunately, only VIPs get invited to up there on those occasions, but the public is welcome to the embassy's many cultural programs in the art gallery and theater, most of which are **free.** The gallery mounts rotating displays of works by Canadian artists. The embassy hosts dance, music, theater, film, and other art-forms that highlight the nation's English, French, and aboriginal heritage. To get to the embassy's schedule of events from the embassy home page, click "Exhibition at the Embassy," then "Canadian arts and culture in Washington, DC."

501 Pennsylvania Ave. NW (at Constitution Ave.). ℂ **202/682-1740.** www.canada
international.gc.ca/washington/index.aspx?lang=eng. Metro: Archives.

Germany   Something is going on almost all the time at the German Embassy. In late 2009 to early 2010, for example, the embassy mounted several art exhibits, including two related to the Berlin Wall. It showed several films. It hosted a Beethoven's Birthday concert, and it sponsored a lecture (in German) about President Kennedy and the Berlin Wall. To find out what's going on, go to the embassy's home page and click "German Embassy," then "Events Calendar."

4645 Reservoir Rd. NW (west of Foxhall Rd.). ℂ **202/298-4000.** www.germany.info/relaunch/index.html. Metrobus D3 or D6.

Japan   The Japanese Embassy carries out its cultural activities at the **Japan Information and Culture Center,** rather than at the embassy itself. The center presents a regular schedule of events throughout the year in its auditorium and gallery. Exhibits include Japanese photography, paintings, and prints. The auditorium hosts musical performances, lectures, and films, including *anime* and a children's film festival. The center sometimes sponsors events elsewhere in Washington, including a 2009 program about baseball, a sport the United States and Japan share a deep interest in. Held at the Freer and Sackler Galleries' auditorium on the Mall, the event featured former Los Angeles Dodgers player and manager Tommy Lasorda, and a film about Bobby Valentine, who managed the New York Mets to the National League championship in the United States and the Chiba Lotte Marines to Japan's championship. Learn about the cultural center's activities by clicking on "Events" at the center's website home page. Most events are **free.**

1155 21st St. NW (btw. L and M sts.). ℂ **202/238-6949.** www.us.emb-japan.go.jp/jicc/index.htm. Metro: Farragut North.

Sweden   Between the opening of Sweden's new embassy in October 2006 and late 2009, about 100,000 people attended events in the **House of Sweden,** a modern structure by the Georgetown Waterfront. The embassy actively entices visitors with exhibits, lectures, music, and other kinds of programs year round. The Nobel prizes, of courses, are held in Stockholm, Sweden, so around the time the prizes are awarded—usually in the beginning of each December—the embassy invites **Nobel laureates** to speak and answer audience questions. December also sees the embassy's annual **gingerbread house competition** and **Swedish Christmas Bazaar.** You can find a schedule of events by clicking "News and Events" on the embassy home page. Most events are free.

2900 K St. NW (btw. 29th and 30th sts.). ℂ **202/467-2600.** www.swedenabroad.com/Start____6989.aspx. Circulator; Georgetown Metro Connection bus from Dupont Circle or Rosslyn Metrorail station; or Metrobus 31, 32, 36, 38B, or D5.

A Note on Dressing Diplomatically

Diplomats tend to dress for business, and so do most of those who make presentations at think tanks. You'll never go wrong wearing business attire yourself. But our friends Henry and Lynne Heilbrunn—who have perfected the art of ferreting out the best of these events—say dressing up isn't always required. Henry has detected an ideological tilt to dress patterns: Most people attending events at the conservative Heritage Foundation or American Enterprise Institute tend to wear their business duds. More people dress business-casual at the more centrist Brookings Institution. The further left you turn, the more blue jeans you see. Evening events at the embassies tend to draw people in business attire. Weekend afternoon events or exhibits in embassy galleries see more informal dress.

WATCHING THINK TANKS THINK

From the conservative American Enterprise Institute to the environmentalist Worldwatch Institute, Harvard University's Kennedy School of Government has compiled a list of think tanks that is too long to count and is heavily based in Washington. That makes sense, of course. If your thinking is designed to influence public policy, then where better to concentrate your brains than in the most powerful city in the world?

The beauty of this for Washingtonians is that many of the think tanks' programs are open to the public and free. Now, if your tastes run to TV reality shows, these programs might not be for you. But if you're interested in public affairs of just about any stripe, you'll find at least some of these events fascinating. Sometimes you can take part in an audience discussion or talkback, and sometimes you'll even get snacks with your food for thought!

We can't list every one here. But we can refer you to the Harvard list at **www.hks.harvard.edu/library/research/guides/think-tanks-directory. htm**, which has links to the organizations' websites. Most or these organizations promote their programs pretty prominently on the home page and tell you if they're open to the public, require reservations, or carry an admission fee. If the deal isn't clear to you, phone and ask. And be sure to note the location. Not only are some events held away from the groups' headquarters, but some also occur outside of Washington. Below are a few of the most prominent think tanks in DC.

American Enterprise Institute   Founded in 1943, AEI is a graybeard among these institutions and for a long time was the country's leading conservative think tank. (The Heritage Foundation now challenges for that title.) While proclaiming itself nonpartisan, AEI declares that its scholars are committed to "expanding liberty, increasing individual opportunity, and strengthening free enterprise"—a Trinity of conservative politics in the United States. Among its well-known fellows are former Republican House Speak Newt Gingrich; Michael Barone, longtime co-author of the *Almanac of American Politics,* a reference Bible for politicians and political journalists; philosopher and theologian Michael Novak; and Paul Wolfowitz, deputy defense secretary and World Bank president during the George W. Bush administration. Hit the "Events" button on the AEI home page and you may find public programs and events about health-care reform, international trade, financial regulation, nuclear arms reduction, and a discussion of the question "Is Capitalism Worth Saving?"

1150 17th St. NW (btw. L and M sts.). Ⓒ **202/862-5800.** www.aei.org. Metro: Farragut North.

Brookings Institution   The quintessential Washington think tank, Brookings was founded in 1916 as the Institute for Government Research and later took the name of one of its founders, Robert S. Brookings. In 2009, *Foreign Policy* magazine named Brookings America's No. 1 think tank, also calling it tops for scholarship, impact on public policy, and research in security, international affairs, international development, and international economic policy—quite a list. Its scholars—who often pop in and out of government—helped design the United Nations and the Marshall Plan. Many conservatives see Brookings as leaning to the left, but an interesting study in *The Quarterly Journal of Economics* placed it in the middle of the political spectrum. The study's authors counted the number of times Brookings was cited by Republicans and Democrats in congressional debates. On a 100-point scale, with 50 being dead-even, Democrats cited Brookings 53.3% of the time. Only The Carnegie Endowment for International Peace and the Institution for International Economics scored closer to 50-50. And when it's time to snack during the proceedings, Brookings also brags about the quality of its cookies. You'll find an events button on its home page. Topics up for discussion during one week in late 2009: climate change, counterterrorism, health services for Iraqi refugees, prospects for economic recovery, European unity, the Internet and diplomacy, and refugees in Afghanistan.

1775 Massachusetts Ave. NW (btw. 17th and 18th sts.). 🕐 **202/797-6000.** www. brookings.edu. Metro: Dupont Circle.

Cato Institute   Named for a series of pre-Revolution pamphlets titled "Cato's Letters," this think tank puts a libertarian perspective on public affairs. Like their conservatives counterparts, Cato's scholars promote limited government, free markets, and individual liberty. Unlike many conservatives, however, these libertarians' opposition to state power tends to extend to regulation of abortion, discrimination against homosexuals, and waging of most wars. The *Journal of Economics* study ranked Cato as the top think tank for innovative ideas. Topics of Cato programs as we write: international trade, the federal deficit, global economic integration, the travel embargo on Cuba, and health-care reform.

1000 Massachusetts Ave. NW (at 10th St.). 🕐 **202/842-0200.** www.cato.org. Metro: Mount Vernon Square.

Heritage Foundation   Since its birth in 1973, Heritage has forthrightly described its mission as promoting conservative public policies that are based on "the principles of free enterprise, limited government, individual freedom, traditional American values, and a strong national defense." The organization grasped for leadership of the conservative movement in 1980 when it published the 1,077-page "Mandate for Leadership: Policy Management in a Conservative Administration." The publication was intended to be a handbook for conservative government, and that's what it became. Newly inaugurated President Ronald Reagan gave copies to all of his Cabinet members at their first meeting in 1981. According to Heritage's count, more than two-thirds of its recommendations were adopted during the Reagan administration. Currently, Heritage has teamed with conservative broadcasters Sean Hannity and Laura Ingraham to create a "What-Would-Reagan-Do?" education campaign. *The Quarterly Journal of Economics* placed Heritage behind only Brookings in its impact on public policy. The think tank's approach to public affairs is illustrated in the titles of its programs: "Leading Evangelical Scholars

Booking a Talk

The following bookstores routinely play host to authors both local and national (though some locals are definitely national figures), who sign and discuss their books. Call or check their websites for info on how to track these events.

- **Barnes & Noble:** 555 12th St. NW (btw. E and F sts.). ✆ **202/347-0176.** Metro: Metro Center.

- **Barnes & Noble:** 3040 M St. NW (at Thomas Jefferson St.). ✆ **202/965-9880.** Circulator; Georgetown Metro Connection bus from Dupont Circle or Rosslyn Metrorail station; or Metrobus 31, 32, 36, 38B, or D5.

- **Borders:** 600 14th St. NW (at F St.). ✆ **202/737-1385.** Metro: Metro Center.

- **Borders:** 1801 K St. NW (at 18th St.). ✆ **202/466-4999.** www.borders. com/online/store/StoreDetailView_50. Farragut West Metrorail Station.

- **Borders:** 5333 Wisconsin Ave. NW (btw. Jenifer St. and Wisconsin Ave.). ✆ **202/686-8270.** Metro: Friendship Heights.

- **Busboys & Poets:** 2021 14th St. NW (btw. U and V sts.). ✆ **202/387-7638.** www.busboysandpoets.com. Metro: U Street.

- **Busboys & Poets:** 1025 5th St. NW (btw. K and L sts.). ✆ **202/7892227.** www.busboysandpoets.com. Metro: Mount Vernon Square.

- **Politics and Prose:** 5015 Connecticut Ave. NW (btw. Fessenden St. and Nebraska Ave.). ✆ **202/364-1919.** www.politics-prose.com. Metrobus L1, L2, or L4 from Cleveland Park Metrorail Station.

- **Potter's House Bookstore:** 1658 Columbia Rd. NW (btw. 17th St. and Quarry Rd.). ✆ **202/232-5483.** www.pottershousedc.org/bookstore. Metrobus 42, 43, or H1.

- **Reiter's Scientific & Professional Books:** 1990 K St. NW (entrance on 20th St.). ✆ **202/223-332.** www.reiters.com. Metro: Farragut West.

Warn that Global Warming Alarmism Will Hurt the Poor"; "The Five Big Lies about American Business: Combating Smears Against the Free Market Economy"; and "Is the Personal Mandate to Buy Health Insurance Unconstitutional?"

214 Massachusetts Ave. NE (btw. 2nd and 3rd sts.). © **202/546-4400.** www.heritage. org. Metro: Union Station.

LIVE PROGRAMMING AT MUSEUMS

Many of the cultural and arts institutions that we covered in chapter 4 host a wide variety of lectures, discussions, concerts, and other programs. Check their websites or local events calendars to find out what's on when.

- **Anderson House** (p. 121).
- **Clara Barton National Historic Site** (p. 132).
- **Dumbarton Oaks** (p. 117).
- **Folger Shakespeare Library** (p. 105).
- **Freer and Sackler Galleries of Art** (p. 113).
- **Hirshhorn Museum and Sculpture Garden** (p. 114).
- **Holocaust Memorial Museum** (p. 105).
- **Library of Congress** (p. 104).
- **National Air and Space Museum** (p. 106).
- **National Air and Space Museum Udvar-Hazy Center** (p. 133).
- **National Arboretum** (p. 134).
- **National Archives** (p. 120).
- **National Building Museum** (p. 126).
- **National Gallery of Art** (p. 102).
- **National Geographic Museum** (p. 107).
- **National Museum of African Art** (p. 115).
- **National Museum of American History** (p. 103).
- **National Museum of the American Indian** (p. 107).

- **National Museum of Natural History** (p. 108).

- **National Museum of Women in the Arts** (p. 117).

- **National Portrait Gallery** (p. 116).

- **National Zoological Park** (p. 128).

- **Phillips Collection** (p. 118).

- **Smithsonian American Art Museum** (p. 117).

- **United States Botanic Garden** (p. 129).

- **Washington National Cathedral** (p. 125).

3 Back To School: Continuing Ed

Many DC residents, in addition to flocking to readings, panels, and discussions, are also interested in expanding their skills, both to enhance their careers, and to acquire new skills, crafts, and general knowledge. You'll find a lot of continuing education available, much of it at an affordable price point (you can also call or visit the institution's website to find out about scholarships or grants).

Community College of the District of Columbia   Washington's new online community college launched an armada of continuing education classes at the beginning of 2010. They include classes to hone job skills and to improve your life. The more than 1,000 online classes offered usually consist of a dozen sessions of each course spread over six to eight weeks. Tuition for most is between $99 and $150. Career-oriented subjects include accounting fundamentals, introduction to Excel, and business law for the small-business owner. There also are arts and humanities classes on music, art, poetry, and photography. Parents can study how to help their children read better, how to understand adolescents, and how to assist their aging parents. Cooking and weight loss are among other topics. The college was planning to begin in-person continuing ed courses in physical classrooms in late 2010. Most are scheduled to last from one to six sessions, and tuition will be between $65 and $300. The college was set to move to new quarters on Capitol Hill around the end of August. Some classes will be offered there, others in various locations around the District.

4200 Connecticut Ave. NW (at Van Ness St.) until late August 2010; Metro: Van Ness. Then 801 N. Capitol St. (at H St.); Metro: Union Station. © **202/274-5536.** www.udc. edu/cc/continuing_education.

First Class Inc. Learning Center This nonprofit has been offering a wide variety of classes generally oriented around increasing individual business skills and career-building since 1984. Offerings range from seminars that last a couple of hours and start at $39 to six-week online courses that cost $129. Sample seminars include: meeting planning, writing grant proposals, creating a successful business plan, starting a gift basket business, yoga, calligraphy, and chocolate tasting.

1726 20th St. NW (btw. R and S sts.). © **202/797-5102.** www.takeaclass.org. Metro: Dupont Circle.

★ **U.S. Department of Agriculture** The Agriculture Department also runs a continuing education program, and the classes stretch *far* beyond farming. The department styles itself as "the government's continuing education provider," and it teaches many courses especially for government employees—government accounting and government acquisition, for example. But it also offers classes in foreign languages, business management, computer software, and other subjects of interest to the general public. Courses—which are taught online and in DC classrooms—range from a few days to a couple of months. Most cost between $295 and $895.

600 Maryland Ave. SW (at 6th St.). © **202/314-3619.** www.graduateschool.edu. Metro: L'Enfant Plaza.

4 Cheap Personal Maintenance

DC doesn't have a barber collage or dental school where you can go for cheap haircuts or tooth care if you're willing to be worked on by students just learning the trade. We've been able to find a few places that will make you look better for less than the going rates, however.

★ **Aveda Institute** This prominent manufacturer of plant-based beauty products and operator of beauty salons and spas also runs beauty schools, like this one in Penn Quarter. The Aveda Institute promises its students "extensive hands-on learning," which they get by performing hair and skin care for far less than Aveda salons charge. A haircut and style costs $18, a shampoo, blow-dry and style $15.

Go to School, Get a Massage!

The **Potomac Massage Training Institute,** 5028 Wisconsin Ave NW (btw. Fessenden and Garrison sts; ✆ **202/686-7046;** www.pmti.org. Metro: Friendship Heights) provides students interested in making a career out of bodywork a chance to take the coursework that leads to a certificate in massage; and for people interested in an inexpensive massage, it's a chance to get rubbed the right way for a fraction of the cost of a treatment at a high-end spa. For over 30 years, PMTI has been training massage therapists, and offering its students a chance for hands-on practice in clinics that are open to the public.

The Student Clinic offers one-hour of supervised Swedish massage by intermediate Level 2 students and advanced Level 3 students for $37; or, if you want to spend a few bucks more, the Graduate Clinic offers massages from its graduates at $55 for an hour. This clinical experience offers a choice of qualified practitioners who have recently completed their training and are offering massages at a fee lower than the usual professional rate (and hoping to acquire a regular clientele).

The Professional Clinic (at $80 an hour, $120 for 90 min., still not a bad rate for an experienced massage therapist) offers practitioners who have many years of experience in massage and therapeutic body-work. Included in this group are faculty members from the Profes-sional Training Program. The times and days for each clinic are posted on PMTI's website, and you must call to schedule an appointment.

Hair coloring starts at $35. Manicures start at $22, waxings at $12, facials at $30.

713 7th St. NW (btw. G and H sts.). ✆ **202/824-1624.** www.avedainstitutes.com. Tues–Thurs 9am–5pm, Fri–Sat 8:30am–5pm. Metro: Gallery Place.

Georgetown Hairstyling All three Prices frequented this family-owned barbershop when we first moved to Washington, and Tom still gets his hair cut here. Rigo, Ed, and their associates do a good job for some of the lowest prices in town. For men and women, a simple haircut is $22. A shampoo, cut, styling and blow-dry costs $27. Ask

Rigo about his latest world travels and Ed about how he installed the stained-glass windows.

1329 35th St. NW (btw. N and O sts.). ℂ **202/338-2250.** Mon–Fri 9am–6pm, Sat 9am–5pm, Sun closed. G2 Metrobus from Dupont Circle.

Haircuttery This may be the cheapest haircut in town for men or women: $18 for shampoo and cut, $26 for shampoo, cut, and blow-dry. Depending on the skills of the stylists on duty, you can get a variety of other hair care services.

DC's Cheap Dry Cleaner

ZIPS Dry Cleaners, a Baltimore-Washington chain of 19 dry-cleaners, will launder your shirt for $1.19 and dry-clean your clothing for prices starting at $1.99 an item. It's at 4418 Connecticut Ave. NW (btw Yuma and Albemarle sts.) ℂ **202/686-8495.** www.321zips.com. Mon–Fri 7am–8pm, Sat 8am–7pm, Sun Closed. Metro: Van Ness.

1645 Connecticut Ave. NW (btw. Q and R streets). ℂ **202/232-9685.** www.hair cuttery.com. Mon–Fri 9am–9pm, Sat 8:30am–7:30pm, Sun 10am–7pm. Metro: Dupont Circle.

5 Healthcare Resources

FINDING INFORMATION

Newcomers to town—and oldsters whose doctors retire (such as us)—can get excellent help locating new caregivers from *Washington Consumers' Checkbook* and *Washingtonian* magazine. Health-related government institutions in the Washington area offer a wealth of information online, and it can be accessed by anyone from anywhere in the world.

Health and Human Services Department `FREE` As its name implies, the nation's health is an important part of this massive agency's mission. HHS administers the Medicare and Medicaid programs for the elderly and the poor. It also provides health-related information to the public. To navigate your way through this information, click on the following buttons on the HHS website's home page: "Families," "Prevention," "Diseases," "Preparedness," and "A–Z Index."

200 Independence Ave. SW, Washington, DC 20201. ℂ **877/696-6775.** www. hhs.gov.

National Institutes of Health `FREE`   The federal government's support of health research is coordinated by this conglomeration of 27 institutes and centers headquartered in the Washington suburb of Bethesda, MD. In addition to conducting and funding research, NIH distributes health and medical information to the general public as well as to scientists and healthcare professionals. The NIH website's "Health Information" page is a portal to an enormous amount of this information. There, you'll find links to such topics as "Healthy Lifestyles," "Child and Teen Health," "Women's Health," "Men's Health," and an index to health topics.

9000 Rockville Pike, Bethesda, MD 20892. ℂ **301/496-4000.** www.nih.gov; health information page: www.health.nih.gov.

Washington Consumers' Checkbook   This nonprofit services-rating publication and website—which we mentioned earlier—pays special attention to health care. Primarily by surveying health-care professionals and their patients, *Checkbook* compiles lists of best caregivers in various categories. It publishes separate lists of doctors rated best by other doctors and those rated best by their patients, for instance. Surveyed physicians were asked to name one or two doctors in various specialties to whom they would refer a loved one. Surveyed patients were asked to evaluate the quality of their doctors. At the *Checkbook* website, you can search both lists by specialty and location. You also can search to see the ratings of specific doctors you're interested in. The lists tell where the doctors went to medical school, which certifications they hold, how many surveyed doctors mentioned them, what percentage of patients graded them "very good" or

More Health Info on the Web

● **Healthfinder** `FREE`   Contains links to health information plus tools for learning how to tend to your and your family's health needs. **www.healthfinder.gov**.

● **MedlinePlus** `FREE`   Provides access to understandable information from the National Library of Medicine and many other sources. **www.medlineplus.gov**.

"excellent," where they practice, and how they can be contacted. *Checkbook* publishes similar reports about dentists, eyeglasses dispensers, contact lens dispensers, hearing aid dispensers, and HMOs. The magazine also evaluates such health-related organizations as gyms and health clubs. FINE PRINT You have to subscribe to the magazine to use the website. A 2-year subscription costs $34 and includes occasional newsletters.

1625 K St. NW, 8th Floor, Washington, DC 20006. ✆ **800/213-7283.** www.check book.org.

Washingtonian This local monthly magazine also asks physicians to whom they would refer an ill family member. When we're looking for a caregiver, we look for doctors who are listed by *Washingtonian* and *Checkbook* and who participate in our insurer's PPO. Then we ask our family doctor what she knows about them. As with the *Checkbook* rating, you can search the *Washingtonian* list online by specialty and location, and you can search for specific practitioners. The list shows the doctors' hospital affiliations, what insurance they take, where they practice, and how they can be contacted. *Washingtonian* conducts similar surveys of dentists and mental health practitioners. The website also contains ratings and a great deal of information about area hospitals. As we write, however, the hospital information dates back to 2005. FINE PRINT You must be a magazine subscriber to access the most recent ratings. A 1-year subscription retails for $30, but discounted multiyear subscriptions usually are available.

1828 L St. NW, Washington, DC 20036. ✆ **202/296-3600.** www.washingtonian.com.

GETTING HEALTH CARE

Mental Health Services The District of Columbia Department of Mental Health operates a round-the-clock telephone hotline for dealing with all kinds of mental health issues. The phone line is staffed by professionals who can connect a customer with immediate emergency help or start the process toward getting ongoing care. The staff is prepared to help young people sort out problems related to death of a friend or relative, school hassles, drugs, gangs, violence, and other difficulties. You can learn about the department's other services at its website.

✆ **888/793-4357.** www.dmh.dc.gov.

Planned Parenthood Although it's often in the news because of America's never-ending battle over abortion, Planned Parenthood actually offers a wide range of health-care services—especially related to reproductive health—to women, men, and teens. Planned Parenthood of Metropolitan Washington operates two clinics within the city. Both provide such services as emergency contraception, teen pregnancy prevention programs, family planning, breast and cervical cancer screening, testing and treatment for sexually transmitted infection, HIV/AIDS testing and counseling, rape crisis counseling, and LGBT services. You don't need an appointment for pregnancy testing, emergency contraception, or HIV testing. Depending on how busy the clinic is, walk-ins also may be able to get screening for sexually transmitted diseases, well-woman exams, and the initial screening required for birth control. It's best to make an appointment, however. The organization distributes publications and conducts educational programs that teach about sex and help parents learn how to communicate with their children about the topic. Fees are based on the patient's income. If you think you qualify for a low-income discount, you should bring proof of your income. Planned Parenthood of Metropolitan Washington accepts Medicaid and participates in major health insurance programs. Payment—by cash, credit card, debit card, or money order—is expected at time of service.

1108 16th St. NW (at L St.). ✆ **202/347-8512.** www.plannedparenthood.org/ppmw. Metro: Farragut North. 3937A Minnesota Ave. NE (south of Benning Rd.). ✆ **202/388-4770.** www.plannedparenthood.org/ppmw. Metro: Minnesota Avenue.

Whitman-Walker Clinic Founded in 1978 to serve Washington's gay, lesbian, bisexual, and transgender community, Whitman-Walker absorbed the Washington Free Clinic in 2007 and began offering comprehensive medical care. The clinic's mission is to care for medically underserved communities with a focus on LGBT and HIV services. Volunteers augment the paid staff at Whitman-Walker's two DC facilities—one near Dupont and Logan circles at the heart of Washington's gay community, the other in the low-income Anacostia neighborhood. The clinic's services include gynecological, prenatal, postpartum, neonatal, pediatric, dental, pharmaceutical, mental health, addiction, counseling, crisis intervention, and chronic disease management. The clinic performs annual physical exams, pregnancy tests, mammography, and screenings for sexually transmitted disease.

Whitman-Walker accepts Medicare, Medicaid, and private insurance and charges the uninsured according to their ability to pay.

1701 14th St. NW (at R St.). ℂ **202/745-7000;** new clients 202/939-7690. www.wwc. org. Metro: U St. 2301 Martin Luther King Jr. Ave. SE (at Morris Rd.). ℂ **202/610-7114;** new clients 202/939-7690. www.wwc.org. Metro: Anacostia.

6 Housing Resources

★ **DC Housing Search** FREE This online tool lets you search for housing that's for rent and for sale. You can specify the number of bedrooms and bathrooms you want, a price range, the location, and proximity to public transportation. You then can sort the results by those criteria plus the date the properties are available, the building type, and if the listing includes photos. When you search for housing for sale, you also can specify proximity to shopping and a hospital, and if you are interested in special seniors housing or a retirement community. Unfortunately, the tool can't perform miracles on Washington's high property values. The cheapest rentals turn out to be single-room-occupancy properties with shared bath, cooking, and laundry facilities. The cheapest places for sale are condominiums in the less-desirable parts of town.

www.dchousingsearch.org.

DISTRICT OF COLUMBIA DEPARTMENT OF HOUSING AND COMMUNITY DEVELOPMENT

The city housing department manages several programs that are designed to make housing more affordable:

- The **Home Purchase Assistance Program** makes interest-free and low-interest loans for purchase of houses, condominiums, and cooperative apartments. Eligibility and the amount of the loan— which is intended for low- and moderate-income residents—depend on the purchaser's income and assets.

- To make public-service employment more attractive, Washington's **Employer Assisted Housing Program** provides aid to city employees who are first-time homebuyers in the District. This takes the form of grants, loans with favorable terms, and tax incentives.

- Homeowners can get assistance in making repairs if their property fails to comply with the housing code, is not safe, has a faulty roof, or needs to be made accessible to a disabled resident. The **Single Family Residential Rehabilitation Program** awards grants and makes low- and no-interest loans. A family of four can qualify with an annual income below about $62,000

The department is located at 1800 Martin Luther King, Jr. Ave. SE (at Good Hope Rd.; ✆ **202/442-7200;** www.dhcd.dc.gov; Metrobus 90, 92, or 93).

First-Time Homebuyer Tax Credit   Here's another only-in-Washing- ton benefit. If you're buying a home in the city for the first time, you can cut up to $5,000 off your federal taxes that year. You qualify as a first-timer as long as you didn't own a home here during the 12 months before the date of purchase. You lose eligibility if you're an individual with income of $90,000 or more, or joint filers with income of $120,000 or more. You simply claim the credit on your tax form. FINE PRINT In 2009, Congress enacted a nationwide credit of $8,000 for homebuyers. But it was scheduled to expire on May 1, 2010, leav- ing the DC credit as the only one available.

PROGRAMS FOR YOUR HOME (ONCE YOU'VE FOUND ONE!)

You may have heard of the U.S. Agriculture Department's Coopera- tive Extension Service and assumed it had something to do with farm- ing. Recently renamed the National Institute of Food and Agriculture, the old Extension Service flowed from the Morrill Acts of 1862 and 1890, which gave federal lands to states for generating income to support public universities and to promote research and education in agriculture and mechanical arts. Working with state and local exten- sion services, the agency disseminates the fruits of that research, and much of its work is indeed providing advice to farmers. But even the District of Columbia now has a land-grant college—the University of the District of Columbia—with a Cooperative Extension Service that provides information to DC residents.

Basic Home Repair and Energy Conservation Program FREE   This program distributes fact sheets and sponsors hands-on workshops to teach DC residents how to make minor home repairs and conserve energy in their homes. You can learn to fix a toilet tank or leaky faucet, repair a wall, or perform basic electrical work.

4200 Connecticut Ave. NW, Washington, DC 20008. ℭ **202/274-7161** or 202/274-7165, 202/274-7162, 202/274-7129. www.udc.edu/ces/hep/programs.htm#basic.

Home Lawn and Gardening Program `FREE` Do you have a brown lawn? Did you find a bizarre insect in your basement? Do your tomatoes look and taste like golf balls? UDC's Home Lawn and Gardening Program may be the solution to your difficulties. The program provides advice to residents and neighborhood associations about growing healthy lawns, trees, shrubs, and other plants. We're talking recommendations for treating plant disease, pruning and transplanting, and suggestions for what you might plant to replace the stuff that's not growing. You can get consultation over the telephone and sometimes even a site visit.

4200 Connecticut Ave. NW, Washington, DC 20008. ℭ **202/274-7166** or 202/274-7115. www.udc.edu/ces/enr/programs.htm#home.

Working Homeowner Program `FREE` This program teaches more advanced home-maintenance skills. Topics include replacing sinks and faucets, installing wallpaper, changing light fixtures, installing a toilet, replacing a garbage disposal, installing door locks, laying ceramic tile, installing vinyl flooring, and painting.

4200 Connecticut Ave. NW, Washington, DC 20008. ℭ **202/274-7161** or 202/274-7165, 202/274-7162, 202/274-7129. www.udc.edu/ces/hep/programs.htm#working.

7 Sports & Recreation

The American College of Sports Medicine reports that Washington, DC, is one of the fittest cities in the U.S. (trailing only San Francisco, Seattle, and Boston). And you can see it all around you. We're a city of parks that you can use for anything from lounging on a bench to playing an energetic game of touch football or ultimate Frisbee. The National Mall and nearby green spaces attract softball, volleyball, and even polo players. The city maintains a large collection of recreation centers and playing fields. You can play a pretty cheap round of golf—as greens fees tend to go—within the city limits.

GOLF

East Potomac Golf Course   Where else can you use the Washington Monument to line up your shot? There actually are four courses here: one 18-hole par 72, one 9-hole par 33, and one 9-hole par-3 course. The fourth is an 18-hole miniature golf course that's listed on the National Register for Historic Places as the oldest continuously operating mini course in the country. East Potomac also has a driving range, three practice holes, a putting green, a pro shop, a golf school, a snack bar, and a restaurant. Fees range from $9 for the par-3 course Monday through Thursday to $30 for the 18-hole course Friday through Sunday and holidays. You can get a discount if you're 60 or older or if you're 18 or younger.

972 Ohio Dr. SW (southwest of Buckeye Dr.). ℂ **202/554-7660.** www2.cybergolf. com/sites/courses/layout11.asp?id=691&page=38684. 20-min. walk from Smithsonian Metrorail Station.

Langston Golf Course   Playing this course by the National Arboretum makes you part of Civil Rights history. Langston opened in 1939, the fruit of a campaign by black golfers for a place to play 18 holes in the then-segregated, Southern Washington area. Blacks could play only on a 9-hole course on the National Mall. Otherwise, they had to travel to Northern cities—as far as Philadelphia, New York, Boston, or Pittsburgh—to find courses that would admit them. Langston has a driving range, putting green, golf school, restaurant, and weekend snack cart. Fees range from $15 for 9 holes Monday through Thursday to $30 for 18 holes Friday through Sunday and holidays. Discounts for those 60 or older and 18 or younger.

2600 Benning Rd. NE (at 26th St.). ℂ **202/397-8638.** www2.cybergolf.com/sites/ courses/layout11.asp?id=693&page=38716. Metrobus X1 or X3.

Rock Creek Golf Course   This 18-hole course, as you might guess, is in Rock Creek Park. It's short (4,886 yd.), but its hilly landscape, small greens, and tight, tree-lined fairways require attention to accuracy. You could spot a deer, wild turkey, raccoon, fox, hawk, or coyote while you play. The course has a putting green, pro shop, golf school, and snack bar. Fees range from $15 for nine holes Monday through Thursday to $25 for 18 holes Friday through Sunday and holidays. Discounts are offered to those 60 or older and 18 or younger. The course offers a bunch of deals to women on Wednesdays, including two-for-one greens fees between 10am and 3pm and various discounts on food and golf equipment.

6100 16th St. NW (at Rittenhouse St.). ℂ **202/882-7332.** www2.cybergolf.com/sites/courses/layout11.asp?id=694&page=38723. Metrobus S2, S4, or S9.

HOCKEY

★ **White House Street Hockey** FREE When security hysteria closed Pennsylvania Avenue in front of the White House, some enterprising athletes created the world's most prestigious address for a street-hockey rink: 1600 Pennsylvania Ave. With no motor vehicles allowed on the flat and wide roadway, street-hockey players commandeer the spot for their sport every Saturday and Sunday at noon. Anybody can show up to play. All you need are skates and a stick. Other protective equipment—helmets, padding— is optional, although the veteran players recommend wearing at least hockey gloves. They play five-on-a-side pickup games. If more than 10 want to play, players rotate every 10 minutes. Check out the White House Hockey website, and sign up for the players' Google group to be informed about schedules and weather-related cancellations.

Pennsylvania Ave. (btw. 15th and 17th sts.). http://sites.google.com/site/whitehousehockey; groups.google.com/group/WhiteHouseHockey. Metro: McPherson Square.

ICE SKATING

You can't play ice hockey in front of the White House. (Just roller hockey). But you can ice skate nearby.

Pershing Park A place for picnics and park-bench relaxation in spring, summer, and fall, this little park near the White House freezes ice for skating in winter. Admission for a 2-hour skate costs $6 for students with ID, children age 12 and younger, and adults age 50 and older. Others pay $7.

Pennsylvania Ave. (btw. 14th and 15th sts.). ℂ **202/737-6938.** www.pershingpark icerink.com. Metro: Metro Center.

Sculpture Garden Ice Rink To the many activities in the National Gallery of Art's Sculpture Garden (jazz concerts, cafe, sculpture) you can add winter ice skating. The garden's pond and fountains freeze over, and skaters glide, slide, and fall. Admission for a 2-hour skate costs $6 for students with ID, children 12 or younger, and adults 50 or older. Others pay $7. If you're a really avid skater, you can buy a season pass for $195. Skates rent for $3, lockers for half a buck.

Constitution Ave. (btw. 7th and 9th sts.). ℂ **202/289-3360.** www.pavilioncafe.com/ ice_rink.html. Metro: Archives.

TENNIS
Rock Creek Tennis Center   Here, you can play where the pros do every year at the Legg Mason Tennis Classic. The 2009 tournament drew 72,000 fans and paid $1.4 million in prizes. Since the tournament began in 1969, winners have included such superstars as Andy Roddick, Andre Agassi, Michael Chang, Jimmy Connors, and Arthur Ashe. The rest of the year, anybody can play. Outdoor hard courts cost $10 an hour weekdays until 6pm, and $12 on weekends and evenings. Clay courts are $18. Indoor play in the winter starts at $28.50. The center offers lessons, rents equipment, and has a pro shop and snack bar.

16th St. NW (at Kennedy S. and Morrow Dr.). ℂ **202/722-5959;** reservations 202/722-5949. www.rockcreektennis.com; reservations https://online.spectrumng.net/RCPTC. Metrobus S1, S2, S4, or S9.

SWIMMING
FREE The Washington city government maintains 33 swimming pools, including eight that are inside and open year-round. DC residents swim for free. Nonresidents pay $3 if they're 6 to 17 years old or 55 or older. Children younger than 6 are free. Everyone else pays $4. Season passes (for non-residents) cost youths and seniors $46, other adults $130. You can get a complete list of swimming facilities at **www.dpr.dc.gov/dpr/cwp/view,a,1239,q,550518.asp**. Below are some of our favorites:

INDOOR POOLS
- **Marie Reed Aquatic Facility:** 2200 Champlain St. NW (at Kalarama Rd.), in Adams Morgan. ℂ **202/ 673-7771.** Metrobus L2.

- **William H. Rumsey Aquatic Center:** 635 North Carolina Ave. SE (btw. 6th and 7th sts.), on Capitol Hill. ℂ **202/724-4495.** Metro: Eastern Market.

- **Wilson Aquatic Center:** 4551 Fort Dr. NW (btw. Albemarle and Brandywine sts.), in Upper Northwest. ℂ **202/730-0583.** www.dpr.dc. gov/dpr/cwp/view,a,1239,q,643975.asp. Metro: Tenleytown.

FREE The District's Free Tennis Racket

Free tennis courts can be grabbed on a first-come, first-served basis all over town. For a complete list of city-owned courts, visit www.dpr.dc. gov/dpr/cwp/view,a,1239,q,643982.asp. Here are a few of them:

- **Fort Reno Tennis Courts:** Chesapeake St. NW (btw. 40th and 41st sts.), in Upper Northwest. Metro: Tenleytown.

- **Francis Tennis Courts:** 24th and N streets NW, in West End. Metro: Foggy Bottom.

- **Garfield Park:** 3rd St. SE (at G St.), on Capitol Hill. Metro: Capitol South.

- **Montrose Park:** R St. NW (btw. 30th and 31st sts.), in Georgetown. Metrobus 31, 32, 36, D1, D2, D3, or D6; Circulator.

- **Marie-Reed Recreation Center:** 18th St. NW (at California St.), in Adams Morgan. Circulator Green Line or Metrobus 96 from Woodley Park Metrorail Station.

- **Rose Park:** 26th and O streets, in Georgetown. Metrobus G2.

- **Volta Park Recreation Center:** 1555 34th St. NW (btw. Volta and Q sts.), in Georgetown. Circulator or Metrobus 31, 32, or 36.

OUTDOOR POOLS

- **East Potomac Pool:** 972 Ohio Dr. SW (south of Buckeye Dr.), in East Potomac Park. ✆ **202/727-6523.** 20-minute walk from Smithsonian Metrorail Station.

- **Francis Pool:** 2435 N St. NW (btw. 24th and 25th sts.), in West End. ✆ **202/727-3285.** Metro: Foggy Bottom.

- **Randall Pool:** S. Capitol St. SW (at I St.), on Capitol Hill. ✆ **202/727-1420.** Metro: Navy Yard.

- **Volta Park Pool:** 1555 34th St. NW (btw. Volta and Q sts.), in Georgetown. ✆ **202/282-0381.** Circulator or Metrobus 31, 32, or 36.

TRAILS (FOR RUNNING & BIKING)

FREE Biking, running, and walking—like butterflies—are free. And they're good for you, too. Here are some great places to engage in whichever of these exercises appeals to you.

You can run in a circle—or at least in ellipses (not to be confused with ellipsis)—on **The Ellipse,** the elliptical roadway just south of the White House. An added benefit: In December, you can run around the White House Christmas tree, menorah, Yule log, and carolers. At other times, other festivals are held here as well. One lap is a bit more than half a mile. It's between the White House and Constitution Avenue NW. Metro: Federal Triangle.

Run or walk around the **Tidal Basin,** and you'll put 1.8 miles on your pedometer. You also can tip your cap to Thomas Jefferson at his memorial, and pass close by Franklin Roosevelt's. In the spring, the cherry blossoms are spectacular. But then—given the enormous crowds—you'd probably have trouble moving faster than a crawl. You'll find the Tidal Basin just south of Independence Avenue, between East Basin and West Basin drives. (Where do they come up with these names?) Metro: Smithsonian or Metrobus 13A, 13B, 13G, 13F, or 11Y.

Walkers, runners, and cyclists share the often-crowded path/sidewalk that parallels **Rock Creek Parkway** and **Beach Drive** from the Potomac River north into Maryland.

Enjoy breathing the fumes from passing cars as you get your aerobic exercise; **Rock Creek Park's** less-beaten paths are more pleasant. From 7am Saturday till 7pm Sunday, and on holidays, Beach Drive is closed to motor vehicles between Military and Broad Branch roads. The rush-hour auto traffic jam is replaced by a walker-runner-bicycle jam.

There are parking lots along Beach Drive. You'll find a map at the website (*©* **202/895-6070** or 202/895-6000; www.nps.gov/rocr).

If you want to take a really long hike or bicycle ride, the **C&O Canal Towpath** is what you're looking for. It begins near the C&O Canal National Historical Park's Georgetown visitor center and travels northwest for 184.5 miles to Cumberland, MD. Most of the route is relatively flat, wide, and composed of hard-packed dirt or gravel, making it ideal for bicycle and foot traffic. There are many access points from roads along the route. It's at 1057 Thomas Jefferson St. NW (south of M St.; *©* **202/653-5190;** www.nps.gov/choh).

The **Mount Vernon Trail** runs 18.5 miles along the Virginia bank of the Potomac River from Theodore Roosevelt Island to George Washington's estate at Mount Vernon. Like the Rock Creek Parkway trail, this one parallels a busy road, the George Washington Memorial Parkway. But it doesn't always run right along the road, the views across the river to the Washington skyline are terrific, and the riverside becomes ever-more idyllic as you move farther south of Alexandria. The trail has many access points. Parking at Roosevelt Island is limited. There are many parking spaces at Lyndon Baines Johnson Memorial Grove, Gravelly Point, Dangerfield Island, Fort Hunt Park, and Mount Vernon. But even they get crowded on beautiful weekend days. There's a map at the website. Information: ✆ **703/289-2500;** www.nps.gov/gwmp/mtvernontrail.htm.

OTHER PUBLIC RECREATION FACILITIES

Washington has a large number of other recreation facilities. Recreation and community centers host many activities: baseball, softball, basketball, soccer, roller hockey, weight training, other sports and fitness activities. They also provide picnic areas and playgrounds as well. There are even three **dog parks** where residents can take their pets to run. For a complete listing of all the public facilities in the District, as well as rules for using them and to see if a particular center or program charges a fee, visit **http://dpr.dc.gov/dpr/cwp/ view,a,1239,q,642750.asp**.

Eastern Market flea market operates every weekend throughout the year. Farmers, florists, artists, butchers, grocers, and other vendors display their products every weekend at the historic Eastern Market on Capitol Hill (p. 228).

SHOPPING

The nation's capital has some of the most unusual shopping of any major U.S. city—everything from politically themed souvenirs to imported goods that appeal to the many nationalities of the people who live and work here.

Washingtonians generally don't manufacture things—we mostly make laws and regulations—so, you won't find one particular area that's the best place for bargains. Instead, there are deals to be found all over town. Luckily, the District is a relatively small place to get around, with excellent public transportation, so it's worth it to try several neighborhoods to unearth the best bargains. Because each area

10 Souvenirs Under $15 (Some under $10!)

Washington is steeped in politics and history. Many souvenirs are tied to elections (campaign buttons and clothing with elephants or donkeys), the federal government (CIA or FBI hats and hoodies), or reproductions (fake Hope Diamond, anyone?). So many choices, how to pick? Here are some "best of" selections.

- **Flag Flown Over the Capitol.** Mark a special occasion such as a birthday or anniversary with one of these. (Yes, there really are staffers who run flags up and down the Capitol's flagpole all day!) These can be ordered for as little as $13 depending on size (plus shipping and handling), and can be obtained only through the office of a member of Congress. Each flag comes with an authentication certificate indicating the flag was flown on the date you requested. Most lawmakers have ordering information on their websites.

- **Stuffed Baby Panda,** $14, or reusable panda conservation bag, $3, National Zoo (p. 128).

- **Astronaut Ice Cream,** $5. This freeze-dried treat, like what astronauts take into space, is a top seller at the National Air and Space Museum (p. 106) and also in some of the other Smithsonian shops.

- **Inaugural celebration chocolate bar,** $6. Apres Peau (p. 237).

- Set of three **golf balls,** $9.95, with presidential and White House emblems, Decatur House (p. 238).

- **"Preamble" mouse pad,** $8.50, depicting the famous painting by Mike Wilkins using license plates to form the words of the

has a character all its own, from preppy Georgetown to hip Dupont Circle to funky U Street, you'll enjoy the journey even if all you do is window shop.

The plethora of enticing shops in the city's museums and historic attractions offer unique items in a wide range of prices. Washington shoppers don't just hit the malls, they hit *the* Mall—the National Mall, that is—where the numerous Smithsonian museums, the National

Preamble to the Constitution, Smithsonian American Art Museum (p. 117). See the original painting while you're there.

- **Alexander Calder mobile coffee mug,** $11, with the image of the famous Calder that dominates the atrium of the National Gallery of Art (p. 102).

- **National Building Museum Calendar,** $13. The Building Museum (p. 125) has one of the most interesting museum shops in Washington, with an emphasis on architecture and design.

- **White House hand towel** or **Presidential baseball,** with images of all 44 presidents, $8 each, America! (p. 236), at Union Station. If you are flying home, you can visit America! shops at Dulles or National airports for a last-minute souvenir fix.

- Metal **bookmark** depicting cherry blossoms seen through a White House window, $9.95, White House Visitors Center (p. 98).

For that extra-special (cheap) gift: Although it doesn't make the $15 cutoff, each year's official **White House Christmas Tree Ornament,** produced by the White House Historical Association, is a popular collectible for locals and visitors alike. The current year's version costs $17 at the White House Visitors Center shop (p. 98; ✆ **202/208-7031**) and also is sold at a few other authorized outlets. You can buy previous years' ornaments, as well, if you want to start a collection. Don't be fooled. Lots of shops sell "White House" ornaments, but with different images. These are not the official version. Look for the WHHA logo to make sure you are getting the real collectible.

Gallery of Art, the National Archives, and other public venues offer items not found elsewhere. Most have markdown tables, often populated with items tied to temporary exhibitions that are over and have been replaced by new ones. Choices include unusual scarves, clothing, ties, art, toys, books, glassware, china, textiles, jewelry, and reproductions of art and artifacts, just to name a few. But don't just stick to the Mall. Other interesting shops can be found at the National

Building Museum, the Capitol, the National Zoo, and many other landmarks. You'll also save money in the museum shops because, as nonprofits, they don't charge DC sales tax (currently 6%). And every dollar you spend helps these institutions stay admission free.

1 Dirt Cheap Shopping Zones

ADAMS MORGAN

Washington's most culturally diverse neighborhood, Adams Morgan is home to some of the city's most lively nightlife, widest variety of international cuisine, and a cluster of unique stores selling goods from all over the world, some at bargain prices. Radiating from the intersection of 18th Street and Columbia Road NW, the neighborhood is the hub of the city's Hispanic immigrant community, but with African, Asian, and other ethnicities also represented. Visit on the first Tuesday of each month and enjoy **"Shop and Dine"** discounts, with a selection of stores offering 10% to 30% off, and many restaurants providing deals on drinks and dinner. Parking is challenging (and really terrible on Fri and Sat nights). From Woodley Park–Zoo Metrorail Station, take the Circulator Green Line bus or Metrobus 96.

CAPITOL HILL

Shopping in the Capitol Hill area is more spread out geographically and is split by the grounds of the complex that includes the Capitol and the Congressional office buildings. North of the Capitol is **Union Station** (p. 124), at 50 Massachusetts Ave. (Metro: Union Station). This historic building not only serves as a busy train station, but it also houses a large complex of stores and eateries. Southeast of the Capitol, along Pennsylvania Avenue, are more stores and the historic **Eastern Market** (p. 228; Metro: Eastern Market).

Save on All Things Smithsonian

For the bargain price of $19, you can join the Smithsonian, receive the award winning *Smithsonian Magazine* each month, and get a 10% discount on all purchases made from museum shops, dining facilities, and catalogs.

FRIENDSHIP HEIGHTS

Don't be put off by the limos waiting in front of Neiman Marcus or the occasional picketers from PETA protesting the sale of

Bargain Shopper Equipment

Parking can be scarce and expensive, but the city is very walkable so bring your comfy shoes. Buy a **Metro Farecard**—everything we recommend here can be reached by subway or bus. And BYOB (bring your own bag). In this environmentally conscious town, some merchants will ask if you need a bag before automatically giving you one. A law that took effect January 1, 2010, *requires* stores selling food or alcohol to charge you a nickel for each paper or plastic bag you need.

furs. While this neighborhood has some of Washington's priciest venues (it's sometimes called DC's Rodeo Dr.), there are several **discount stores** mixed in. Saks Fifth Avenue, Jimmy Choo, Tiffany's, and Barney's Co-op are among the luxury lines rubbing shoulders with Loehmann's, Filene's Basement, T.J. Maxx, Stein Mart, and World Market. Some of these popular chain discounters are located in one of two enclosed, multi-story malls flanking both sides of Wisconsin Avenue at Western Avenue—**Mazza Gallerie** and **Chevy Chase Pavilion.** There also are plenty of restaurants and a multi-screen movie theater, making this an ideal neighborhood for a full-day bargain-shopping excursion. Eat at a Washington institution, the **Booeymonger** (p. 77), at the corner of Jenifer Street and Wisconsin Avenue, which offers an array of sandwiches, salads, and a frozen yogurt bar, as well as wine and beer (Metro: Friendship Heights).

DUPONT CIRCLE

Dupont Circle is home to dozens of art **galleries** and **boutiques,** many tucked into historic town houses and flanked by hip nightspots. It's home to young singles and couples as well as baby boomers fleeing suburbia for urban life. It's also the center of Washington's gay community. Here's where you'll find one of only three stores in the country run by the Human Rights Campaign; you can shop for merchandise and also send a message to Congress on the store's dedicated computers. The several hotels in the area add tourists to the mix, and the result is an eclectic neighborhood for shopping and eating. (There are restaurants on nearly every block.) Interesting shops abound. Among

DC SHOPPING

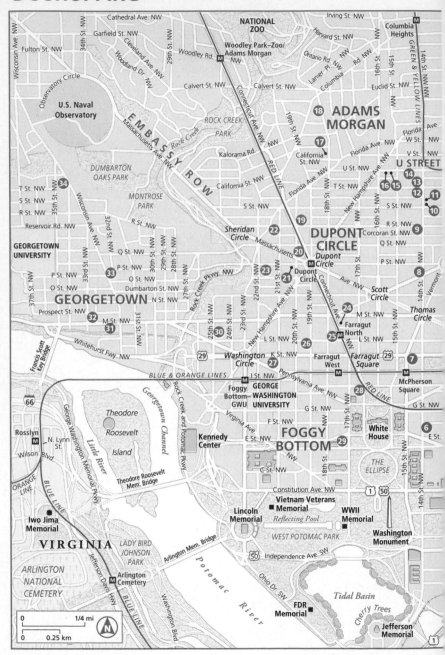

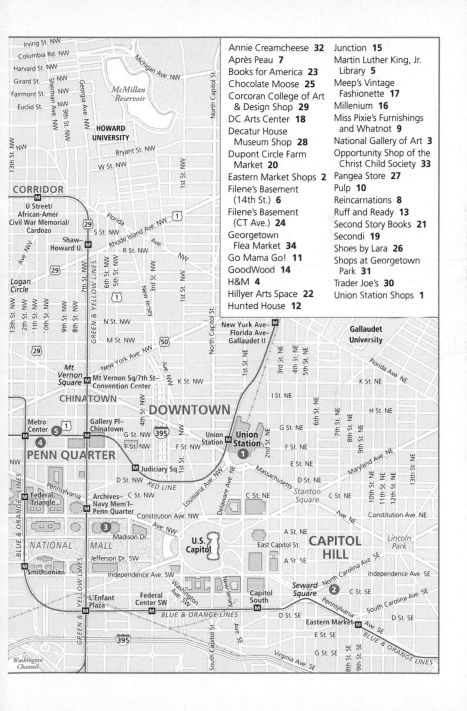

the boutiques lining Connecticut Avenue are several that sell unusual gifts, edibles, and other items at reasonable prices.

The Sunday **farmers' market** is a popular destination for organic food, fresh cheese, meats, and homemade soap. Buy a snack here for a mid-shopping pick-me-up (p. 235; Metro: Dupont Circle).

GEORGETOWN

Although it's one of the most expensive DC neighborhoods to live in—and home to members of Congress, diplomats, and wealthy professionals and business executives—Georgetown also is populated by Georgetown University students and is a major tourist magnet. You'll find designer **vintage clothing** and consignment **antiques** at prices below retail but not exactly dirt cheap. Still, it's worth a visit because of the high concentration of all kinds of stores, including major chains. The multi-level, Victorian-style **Georgetown Park shopping mall** includes H & M, the European clothing store where chic is cheap. Most Georgetown stores are on Wisconsin Avenue or M Street NW, but a few can be found on side streets off those two main thoroughfares. Walk from Foggy Bottom Metro or take the Georgetown Connection bus from the Dupont Circle Metrorail Station or the Circulator Bus Yellow Route.

U STREET CORRIDOR

Described as the Harlem of Washington decades ago, the U Street Corridor was the home of middle class black families and such luminaries as Duke Ellington. The neighborhood fell on hard times after suffering serious damage in the riots following the assassination of Martin Luther King, Jr., in 1968. In recent years, it's undergone major gentrification. Bargain hunters are drawn especially to the many **used furniture stores** that are outfitting all the new condos being built and town house rehabs underway. This also is where to come for the best selection of **vintage clothing** and accessories. Every third Thursday, stores stay open until 9pm and offer special deals. The main shopping and dining area runs a bit north and south from U Street NW, roughly between 9th and 16th streets (Metro: U St.).

FANTASTIC FLEA MARKETS

Georgetown Flea Market   Every Sunday year round, bargain hunters converge on a junior high school parking lot in posh Georgetown

How to Snag Free—or Almost Free—Stuff

Washington is a town of transients. Election years inevitably result in major staff turnover. The large student populations at several major universities add to the movement in and out of town. So do the people who work in embassies and other international institutions who are in the country for defined periods. When they get transferred back to their home countries, they shed a lot of their belongings.

All this coming and going translates into a bonanza for dirt-cheap and free shoppers. One popular spot to find freebies is the DC section of **Freecycle** (www.groups.yahoo.com/group/freecycleDC). Freecycle is like a dating service for junk. Its goal is to reduce consumption and waste by connecting people who have something to get rid of with someone who wants it. You'll find computers, furniture, clothing, magazines, sports equipment . . . you name it. We know one young grad-student couple who furnished most of their apartment for free this way. You don't even have to take potluck. You can "shop" by posting something you need, such as a television or desk chair, and chances are someone will fulfill your wish.

In addition, many city neighborhoods have active online discussion groups through which you'll often find used items offered cheap or for free. These groups also are good places to find yard sales. One way to find groups: Go to **www.groups.yahoo.com** and type "Washington, DC" into the search box.

You can do some selective scavenging by hitting a neighborhood before its weekly trash collection. Lots of useful items are put out in alleys and along sidewalks. To find **trash collection dates,** go to **http://www.collectionday.dcgis.dc.gov**.

Every morning, News Channel 4 features several free deals or bargains. Go to **www.NBC4.com** and enter Bargain Blast in the search box.

to unearth all manner of treasure from this favorite haunt of decorators, collectors, tourists, and an occasional celebrity. Started in 1972, this Washington favorite was depicted in Larry McMurtry's novel *Cadillac Jack*. More than 100 vendors are happy to bargain with you over their varied wares, including furniture, china, silver, antiques, garden accessories, art, books, chandeliers, jewelry, vintage clothing, posters, antique tools, lamps, linens, and political memorabilia. We've spent many hours here unearthing old magazine covers to frame as art, urns for our patio, glass serving pieces, and all manner of unusual gifts. Bargaining gets easier later in the day or when rain threatens. The less the vendors have to pack and take home the better—for them and you. 1819 35th St. NW (at Hardy Middle School with an entrance on Wisconsin Ave.). ✆ 202/775-3532. www.george townfleamarket.com. Circulator or Metrobus 31, 32, or 36.

Eastern Market Completed in 1873, Eastern Market is the oldest market in the city. After a 2-year renovation which followed a devastating fire in 2007, the Capitol Hill market's newly restored historic architecture serves as the backdrop for stalls selling meats, produce, seafood, pasta, poultry, baked goods, and cheese. But it's the weekends when the bargain hunters gather for the combination art fair and flea market, with dozens of vendors selling handmade pottery, jewelry, ceramics, crafts, furniture, and flea market goodies. For a quick bite before you shop, get in line at Market Lunch for its famous blueberry pancakes. 225 7th St. SE (btw. C St. and Independence Ave.). Flea Market Sat–Sun only. Food market Tues–Sun. ✆ **202/698-5253.** www.easternmarketDC.com. Metro: Eastern Market.

2 Bargain Shopping A to Z

ART

District of Columbia Arts Center This nonprofit supports emerging artists who display their work in a 750-square-foot gallery in Adams Morgan. This lively space also includes a small theater for performing artists and has a regular schedule of events. 2438 18th St. NW (btw. Belmont and Columbia rds.). ✆ **202/462-7833.** www.DCartscenter. org. Wed–Sun. Circulator or Metrobus 96 from Woodley Park Metro.

Corcoran College of Art + Design Students' works are offered for sale in revolving exhibits throughout the year. The best time to come for a big selection is at "Off the Walls," an annual art sale held for a few days in December featuring gifts for the holiday season. You'll find jewelry, ceramics, wearable art, painting, and sculpture in all sizes and prices, hand-crafted by Corcoran students, alumni, faculty, and staff. 500 17th St. NW (btw. New York Ave. and E St.). ✆ **202/639-1789.** www.corcoran.org. Metro: Farragut West.

Hillyer Arts Space   This Dupont Circle gallery's unassuming entrance off an alley (a renovated historic carriage house) hides a surprisingly large space displaying works by emerging and established artists living in DC and the mid-Atlantic alongside those by international artists. On **First Fridays,** there's a crowd dancing to the music, either by a DJ or live musicians. 9 Hillyer Court NW (west of 21st St.). ✆ **202/338-0680.** www.artsandartists.org/hillyer.html. Metro: Dupont Circle.

> ★ **First Fridays at the Galleries**
>
> On the first Friday of each month, galleries in Dupont Circle are open late for the monthly gallery walk with wine and snacks. You'll find most of the galleries along R Street and Connecticut Avenue NW.

National Gallery of Art   If your taste runs to Old Masters but your budget doesn't, the National Gallery (full review on p. 102) offers "Art on Demand." Reproductions from the gallery's collection can be ordered in three sizes, framed or unframed, on paper or canvas for prices ranging from $25 to $375 plus shipping. The pictures can be ordered only through a touch-screen kiosk at the gallery's gift shop for home delivery. Constitution Avenue NW (btw. 3rd and 7th sts.). ✆ **202/737-4215.** www.nga.gov. Metro: Archives.

ANTIQUES/USED FURNITURE

GoodWood   Specializing in American furniture and decorative arts, this attractive U Street Corridor store makes antique seem hip. The affordable prices, friendly staff and frequent rotation of inventory make repeat visits a must. 1428 U St. NW (btw. 14th and 15th sts.). ✆ **202/986-3640.** www.goodwoodDC.com. Metro: U Street.

Hunted House   Walk through the unrestored second-floor rooms in this U St. Corridor town house, and you might feel like you're in someone's apartment . . . someone who likes to decorate with mid-century modern furnishings from the 1950s to the 1970s. The modestly priced pieces are displayed in settings reminiscent of the TV hit "Mad Men." 1830 14th St. NW, 2nd Floor (btw. T and Swann sts.). ✆ **202/549-7493.** www.huntedhouseDC.org. Metro: U Street.

★ Artomatic, a Traveling Art Show

Once a year, for about a month, 1,000 artists come together in a borrowed building for this truly remarkable art extravaganza. The quality of the art is uneven, because any artist can participate as long as he or she pays the entrance fee and agrees to volunteer for a certain number of hours. But there's bound to be something that appeals to you and fits your budget. The volunteer-run event is scheduled in summer or fall depending on the availability of a donated space, usually an unoccupied commercial building. The free event features paintings, sculpture, photography, music, theater, poetry, dance, workshops, and a film screening theater. You can get to know the artists and then buy from them directly year round. Check the website to see whether the next dates and location have been announced. **www.artomatic.org**.

Millennium   This subterranean gem in the U Street Corridor is a place to buy, sell, and consign mid-century modern furnishings. From Danish teak side tables to bright green vinyl wingback chairs, the attractive shop serves up its more straightforward pieces with what is described as "a small but healthy bit of kitsch." 1528 U St. NW (btw. 15th and 16th sts.). ⓒ **202/483-1218.** www.millenniumdecorative arts.com. Metro: U Street.

Miss Pixie's Furnishings and Whatnot   The owner of Miss Pixie's handpicks a wide assortment of home furnishings at auctions for her customers to peruse in this popular shop in the U Street Corridor. Shabby chic furniture, artwork, old photographs, used books, old quilts, mirrors, wicker, and more are available in the storefront and in Miss Pixie's back room. New things typically arrive on Thursday. 1626 14th St. NW (btw. Corcoran and R sts.). ⓒ **202/232-8171.** www. misspixies.com. Wed–Sun. Metro: U Street or Metrobus 52, 53, or 54.

Opportunity Shop of the Christ Child Society   A long-time fixture in Georgetown, this nonprofit consignment shop offers fine antiques, jewelry, sterling silver, and crystal. Proceeds from the volunteer-run shop support the many projects of the DC chapter of the Christ Child Society serving the needs of children. This is where to go for a deal on Steuben glass, Meissen china, Tiffany brooches, pocket watches, or unusual figurines. 1427 Wisconsin Ave. NW (btw. O and P sts.). © **202/333/6635.** christchildDC.org. Circulator or Metrobus 31, 32, or 36.

Reincarnations This sumptuous store near Logan Circle excels at displaying its eclectic mix of "reincarnated" vintage furnishings sold alongside new furniture and accessories. You can find everything here from mirrored dressers to delicate chandeliers to one-of-a-kind sculptures and vases. There also are seasonal decorative items, especially for Christmas. 1401 14th St. NW (at Rhode Island Ave.). © **202/ 319-1606.** www.reincarnationsfurnishings.com. Metro: Dupont Circle or Metrobus 52, 53, or 54.

Ruff and Ready Wander through this rabbit warren of used furniture, vintage appliances, antique art, and plain old junk, and you're bound to find a treasure. But picking your way through these aisles of furniture stacked to the ceiling can prove daunting. There's also a basement, an outdoor area in back with lots more junk leading to a second leaky building. Ah, but the scrounging is worth it when you find that perfect chair (just needs some paint) for your living room, or the classic lunch box just like the one you had as a kid. Don't overlook the shelf where every item costs a dollar. 1908 14th St. NW (btw. U and T sts.). © **202/667-7833.** Metro: U Street.

BOOKS (NEW & USED)

Books for America This Dupont Circle shop's tagline is "a bookstore with a purpose." Run as a nonprofit, Books for America takes donated books, re-sells them at very low prices, and uses the proceeds to support literacy programs in the community. You can also find movies and CDs cheap. 1417 22nd St. NW (south of P St.). © **202/835-2665.** www.booksforamerica.org. Metro: Dupont Circle.

★ **Politics and Prose** Washington is reputed to have the highest number of readers per capita of any city in the country. As Washington's premier independent bookstore, Politics and Prose does a lot to feed that habit. (Real estate ads sometimes note as a selling point that a house is "within walking distance of P&P.") The store's almost daily book talks feature leading authors who consider this store a must stop on their U.S. tours. A $20 annual membership fee is good for 20% discounts on best sellers and periodic storewide sales. The downstairs has a large selection of bargain books plus a coffeehouse with reasonably priced pastries and sandwiches. 5015 Connecticut Ave. NW

Don't Just Borrow Books at the Library

Many DC public library branches have racks of used books—and sometimes CDs and DVDs—for sale for a dollar or less apiece. The main branch, the **Martin Luther King Jr. Memorial Library,** even has a small enclosed shop for used books on the main floor. It's at 901 G St. NW between 9th and 10th streets NW. ℭ **202/727-1111.** www.dc library.org. Metro: Gallery Place.

Some library friends groups also hold large sales on specific dates. To find out about periodic sales, check **www.DClibrary.org/node/556** to locate the friends group at a branch near you and learn about its upcoming events. Also, several nonprofit organizations have huge annual book sales to raise funds. To find out when and where, check the books section of *The Washington Post* website for each week's literary calendar of book talks and special events. At www.Washington Post.com, hover your cursor over "Arts & Living," then click on " Books."

(btw. Fessenden St. and Nebraska Ave.). ℭ **202/364-1919.** www. politics-prose.com. Metrobus L1, L2, or L4.

Second Story Books   This longtime Dupont Circle establishment is a cut above your average used book store. The dozens of categories are neatly shelved, the inventory is mostly in good condition, and there are sections for posters and rare books. The best deals are the discount tables placed each day on the sidewalk adjacent to the store. 2000 P St. NW (at 20th St.). ℭ **202/659-8884.** www.secondstory books.com. Metro: Dupont Circle.

CLOTHING: VINTAGE AND CONSIGNMENT

Annie Creamcheese   Visit this high-end, designer/couture vintage boutique in Georgetown, and you might spot a celebrity (who probably isn't looking to save money but rather to find a new way to make a rare or unusual fashion statement). Hollywood stars and tourists have rubbed elbows here in search of some of the biggest labels in fashion from the 1940s to the 1990s. Although primarily for women, it has a small selection of vintage men's fashions, too. 3279 M St. NW (btw. Potomac and 33rd sts.). ✆ **202/298-5555.** www.anniecream cheese.com. Georgetown Metro Connection bus from Dupont Circle or Rosslyn Metrorail station, or Metrobus D5 or 38B.

Junction   One of the city's best vintage stores, Junction resides in a smallish basement space in the U Street Corridor, where the artful displays of both vintage and new fashions feature stylish and unique items at affordable prices. Beaded handbags and formal gowns live next to men's shirts and ties. 1510 U St. NW (btw. 15th and 16th sts.). ✆ **202/483-0261.** www.junctionwDC.com. Metro: U Street.

Meeps Vintage Fashionette   One of DC's most popular venues for vintage clothing, this Adams Morgan store also showcases work by local designers. The focus is on men's and women's clothing from the 1940s to the 1980s that can mesh with today's wardrobe. New items, including accessories, are stocked each week. It's also a good place to look for a costume. Call ahead and ask to peruse vintage bridal gowns that are usually kept in storage. 2104 18th St. NW (at California St.). ✆ **202/265-6546.** www.meepsDC.com. Metrobus L2.

Secondi   Invited to an embassy party or state dinner? You can pull an entire designer outfit together at the upscale vintage Secondi, while you imagine what exclusive DC event these party duds went to with the original owner. Choose from Chanel, Manolo Blahnik, Mark Jacobs, Prada, Donna Karan, and other famous designers. In February and August, the Dupont Circle store advertises "designer labels at rock bottom prices." Secondi also carries shoes, bags, sunglasses, and jewelry. 1702 Connecticut Ave. NW (at R St.), 2nd floor. ✆ **202/667-1122.** www.secondi.com. Metro: Dupont Circle.

CLOTHING: DISCOUNT

Filene's Basement   This chain really did begin in a basement, as the discount section of the Boston-based Filene's department store. Washington is blessed with three of the chain's 20 stores nationwide. Filene's Basement is like a mini-department store, offering discounted designer and brand-name clothing and accessories for women, men, and children, as well as shoes, luggage, home furnishings, and fragrances. The store may be best known for its famous bridal sale. (See "Running of the Brides," p. 239). Farragut North location: 1133 Connecticut Ave. NW (btw. L and M sts.). ✆ **202/872-8430.** Metro: Farragut North. Friendship Heights location: 5300 Wisconsin Ave. NW (at Jenifer St.). ℭ **202/966-0208.** Metro: Friendship Heights. Metro Center location: 529 14th St. NW (at F St. in the National Press Building). ℭ **202/638-4110.** www.filenesbasement.com. Metro: Metro Center.

H & M This Swedish company offers inexpensive contemporary clothing and accessories for the whole family. It's a great place to go if you're looking to update your wardrobe with some trendy items without breaking the bank. Just don't plan on having them forever. These duds aren't made to last much longer than the popular trends they represent. Washington has two locations. Downtown: 1025 F St. NW (btw. 10th and 11th sts.). ℭ **202/347-3306.** www.hm.com. Metro: Metro Center. Georgetown: 3222 M St. NW (btw. Wisconsin Ave. and Potomac St. in the Shops at Georgetown Park). ℭ **202/298-6792.** Georgetown Metro Connection bus from Dupont Circle or Rosslyn Metrorail station, or Metrobus D5 or 38B.

Loehmann's The offspring of a discount apparel store that was born in Brooklyn nearly nine decades ago, the DC Loehmann's resides in the upscale Friendship Heights neighborhood. With name-brand fashions for both men and women, it's known especially for designer evening wear and has higher-end offerings than most of its discount peers. Merchandise changes regularly and is discounted 30% to 65%. 5333 Wisconsin Ave. NW (btw. Jenifer St. and Western Ave.). ℭ **202/362-4733.** www.loehmanns.com. Metro: Friendship Heights.

Stein Mart You might overlook this discount department store since it's on an upper floor of the Chevy Chase Pavilion retail complex in Friendship Heights. But it's worth a look for bargains on clothing, linens, dishes, seasonal home decor, and even a small selection of furniture. 5345 Wisconsin Ave. NW (btw. Western Ave. and Jenifer St. in the Chevy Chase Pavilion). ℭ **202/363-7075.** www.steinmart. com. Metro: Friendship Heights.

T.J. Maxx T.J. Maxx at Friendship Heights is packed with a jumbled assortment of discounted clothing and accessories for the whole family, along with housewares, toys, bath and body products, and seasonal items. Its basement level space may not be glamorous, but you can find some great deals if you don't mind searching. 4350 Jenifer St. NW (btw. Wisconsin Ave. and 44th St.). ℭ **202/237-7616.** www. tjmaxx.com. Metro: Friendship Heights.

EDIBLES

★ **Rodman's Discount Gourmet**   We are lucky enough to live two blocks from one of the weirdest and most wonderful discount stores in Washington. This family-owned business in the Friendship Heights neighborhood carries a variety of wine and beer, with weekly specials, plus a wide range of international foods, snacks, chocolate, cheese, olive oil, and produce on the first floor. Head down the escalator to the basement to have a prescription filled or shop for kitchen items, small appliances, hardware, European soaps, candles, linens and holiday decor, much of it at discount prices. We buy our Christmas stocking stuffers and hostess gifts here. There's also a reasonably priced watch- and jewelry-repair shop tucked into one niche of the basement. 5100 Wisconsin Ave. NW (btw. Harrison and Garrison sts.). ✆ **202/ 363-3466.** www.rodmans.com. Metro: Friendship Heights.

Trader Joe's   In uptight Washington, it's a nice change of pace to visit the DC outpost of this laid-back grocery chain, featuring foods from all over the world at low prices. This place has a cultlike following. For proof, go to Amazon.com to see how many authors have published cookbooks devoted to recipes using Trader Joe's foods. The friendly clerks wear Hawaiian shirts to further the image of world traders, and they ring a maritime bell to communicate (no irritating intercoms here). You'll find the basics like milk and eggs, but mostly shoppers come here for the store's own-label fresh and frozen foods, sauces, nuts, snacks, and international foods. There's also a large selection of wines and fresh flowers. There are no coupons or special sales at Trader Joe's, because the goal is to keep prices reasonable throughout the store's varied (and frequently changing) offerings. 1101 25th St. NW (btw. L and M sts.). ✆ **202/296-1921.** www.trader joes.com. Metro: Foggy Bottom.

Dupont Circle Fresh Farm Market   Considered one of the top farmers markets on the East Coast, this market started in 1997 and has spawned several in other sites around the city. Local chefs, residents, and tourists all shop at the stands set up in a bank parking lot. During the peak season, there are more than 30 farmers offering fresh-off-the-farm fruits and vegetables, meat, poultry, fish, cheeses, fruit pies, breads, fresh pasta, cut flowers, potted plants, soaps, and herbal products. Although sometimes pricier than the produce in supermarkets, it's

Road Trip: Discount Malls Outside DC

Potomac Mills　This Virginia discount mecca, 30 miles south of Washington, is so huge it has hotels nearby for the shoppers who come from far away or who can't manage the 200 stores in 1 day. One big draw is Ikea, the huge Swedish home furnishings store where people on a budget can buy modern furnishings and housewares at dirt cheap prices—some assembly required. Even DC decorators find good basic pieces to mix in with furnishings from more high-end stores. Popular outlets in this mega-mall are Neiman Marcus Last Call, Saks Fifth Avenue Outlet, OFF 5TH, Nordstrom Rack, COSTCO, Off Broadway Shoe Warehouse, Modell's Sporting Goods, and the factory stores of Ralph Lauren, Brooks Brothers, and Banana Republic, just to name a few. One standout is the Smithsonian Catalog outlet. **To drive** to Potomac Mills from central DC, go south on 14th Street NW and watch for signs to I-395, which will take you across the Potomac River into Virginia. Take I-395 South, then I 95 South to the Dale City exit. Then follow the signs to Potomac Mills. **By public transit,** take the Metrorail Yellow or Blue Line to the Pentagon station, then board an OmniRide bus toward Dale City, which will take you to the Potomac Mills commuter lot. *Worth Ave. (at Potomac Mills Circle), Dale City, VA. ℂ 703/496-9330. www.PotomacMills.com.*

a good value because the quality is superior and you can buy just the quantity you need—two carrots instead of a whole bag, for instance. 1560 20th St. NW (btw. Massachusetts Ave. and Q St.). ℂ **202/ 362-8889.** www.freshfarmmarket.org. Sun. Metro: Dupont Circle.

GIFTS/SOUVENIRS

America!　This is the best spot on Capitol Hill to find a wide variety of better-quality Washington souvenirs and politically themed clothing and gifts. Think military apparel, First Lady aprons, campaign buttons, Air Force One Flight Crew hats, Commander in Chief mouse pads, Rose Garden Soap, and items featuring Michele and Barack Obama. 50 Massachusetts Ave. NE (in Union Station's West Hall, plus a small kiosk in the Main Hall). ℂ **202/842-0540.** www.america store.com. Metro: Union Station.

Leesburg Corner Premium Outlets   While its total of 110 stores is only half the number at Potomac Mills, Leesburg Corner still has enough name-brand outlets to make a trip worthwhile. Dress for the weather, because this is an outdoor shopping center. Among the outlets: Crate & Barrel, Pottery Barn, Williams-Sonoma, Benetton, Seiko, Gap, J Crew, Kate Spade, Coach, Reebok, and Cole Hahn. Reston Limousine runs a **round-trip shuttle** on weekends between Leesburg Corner and the Metro Center Metrorail Station in Downtown DC. The shuttle leaves DC at 8:30am, leaves the outlet mall at 3pm, and arrives back Downtown at about 4:30pm. Cost is $40. Advance reservations are required. To drive from central Washington, go west on Constitution Avenue to westbound I-66. Follow I-66 to Virginia 267 West (the Dulles Toll Road/ Dulles Greenway). At exit 1B, go north on U.S. 15 (Leesburg Bypass). Use the far right lane and follow signs to the Fort Evans Road exit. *241 Fort Evans Rd. NE, Leesburg, VA (at Leesburg Bypass).* ✆ *703/737-3071; shuttle* ✆ *800/546-6141 or 703/478-0500 (hit Option 1 for reservations). www.premiumoutlets.com; shuttle www.restonlimo. com/tours-trips.*

Aprés Peau   This downtown shop carries an array of exclusive, Washington-related items, more sophisticated than typical souvenirs. You'll find a coaster set featuring an old map of DC, silk ties with the handwritten Constitution, and chocolate bars honoring Washington landmarks such as the Kennedy Center and White House Rose Garden. The dermatologist-owner also stocks a variety of skin lotions and perfumes. 1430 K St. NW (btw. 14th and 15th sts.). ✆ **202/783-0022.** www.aprespeau.com Metro: McPherson Square.

Chocolate Moose   You'll hear chuckling the minute you walk into this downtown store. There's always some crazy item that strike people as funny. Novelty socks and ties, toys, greeting cards, kitchen gadgets, games, holiday decorations, and gifts for pets are mingled with handcrafted jewelry, scarves, and bags in bright colors. If you can't find the perfect gift in the rest of the store, there's a front counter selling a large selection of European chocolates. 1743 L St. NW (btw. Connecticut Ave. and 18th St.). ℭ **202/463-0992.** www.chocolate moosedc.com. Metro: Farragut North.

Decatur House Museum Shop   Once the home of Naval hero Stephen Decatur, this historic house and museum is within steps of the White House. The former carriage house has been converted to a cozy shop with a unique selection of history-related gifts. You'll find replicas of White House china, Salisbury pewter, books, historical prints of Washington, scarves, purses, decorative items, toiletries, note cards, candles, toys, games, food items, and nautically themed gifts. 1610 H. St. NW (btw. 17th St. and Jackson Place). ℭ **202/842-1858.** www.decaturhouse.org. Metro: Farragut West.

Pangea Market   Supported by the International Finance Corp.—a unit of the World Bank—Pangea brings high quality handicrafts, made by artisans in developing countries, to a sleek wood-and-glass showroom. The word *pangea* means "all lands," and these fair-trade crafts come from countries across Asia, Africa, and Latin America. The unique creations, priced very reasonably, include beautiful bags, jewelry, toys, baskets, pillows, unusual coasters, scarves, journals, stationery, and art. By scanning the bar code at a special computer kiosk, you can watch a video of the craftspeople who made a particular item. There's also a small cafe where you can have a sandwich or buy a bag of fair-trade coffee. Enjoy your purchase and know that you're helping create a sustainable livelihood for the people who made it. 2121 Pennsylvania Ave. NW (at 21st St.). ℭ **202/872-6432.** www.pangeamarket.com. Metro: Farragut West.

Pulp   This is *the* place for funky, funny—and sometimes slightly outrageous—gifts and greeting cards. You won't want to leave before you've browsed through all the wrapping paper, toys (and not just for kids), stationery, books, and items with political statements to wear or hang on the wall. The U Street Corridor store's slogan is "Come Feel the Love," and the welcoming staff lives up to it. 1803 14th St. NW (btw. Swann and S sts.). ℭ **202/467-7857.** www.pulpdc.com. Metro: U Street.

HOME FURNISHINGS

Go Mama Go!   Almost like an international bazaar, Go Mama Go! features colorful, affordable and fun home furnishings and gifts from

Timing Is Everything—
Tips on Seasonal Sales

In August, the DC City Council typically declares a "Sales-Tax-Free Week," to encourage back-to-school shoppers to buy in the city. In 2009, the practice was suspended due to the economic downturn's impact on the city budget, but keep an eye out for announcements in the news media about this savings opportunity being revived.

Running of the Brides: The **Filene's Basement** location in Friendship Heights hosts a sale of designer bridal gowns every summer. Future brides, their bridesmaids, and their moms assault the store in a manner that's likened to the running of the bulls in Pamplona, Spain. The dresses—originally priced from $900 to $9,000—sell for $249 to $699. *Here's a tip:* In the first frenzied minutes after the store opens, all the racks are stripped bare as brides grab as many gowns as they can carry to try on. By mid-morning, the lines are gone, the racks replenished, and less frenetic shoppers still can find plenty of bargains. *5300 Wisconsin Ave. NW (at Jenifer St.).* ① *202/966-0208. www.filenesbasement.com/bridal.php. Metro: Friendship Heights.*

DailyCandy.com consolidates some of the most interesting offerings in Washington and other cities. Click on "Deals" to find specials on food, drink, and merchandise. The "Weekend Guide" has information about restaurants, shows, and nightlife.

The *Washington Post'*s **Thursday Home Section** runs a weekly listing of sales and liquidations at local home-furnishing and antique stores. At The *Post'*s website (www.WashingtonPost.com), click on "Arts and Living" to find the "Home and Garden" section. Also under "Arts and Living," click on "Fashion and Beauty," then on "DC Scout" for info on shopping deals.

Holiday Shopping: Each December, the **Downtown Holiday Market** gathers more than 150 local artisans and exhibitors in an outdoor showcase of clothing, jewelry, crafts, fine art, and pottery at reasonable prices. The 20-day event also features live local music and homemade snacks. *7th and F sts. NW.* ① *202/638-3232. www.downtownDC.org. Metro: Gallery Place.*

around the globe. This shop in the U Street Corridor is frequently singled out for its unique offerings, fun atmosphere, and friendly staff. The wide price-range means there's lots here for people on tight budgets. Asian ceramics, Murano glassware, woven placemats, and unique candlesticks make distinctive table settings. Decorative pieces, journals, jewelry, and myriad other items put this store on the not-to-be-missed list. 1809 14th St. NW (btw. S and T sts.). ℭ **202/ 299-0850.** www.gomamago.com. Metro: U Street.

World Market The only DC outlet of this national chain, World Market anchors the basement level of Chevy Chase Pavilion, directly above the Friendship Heights Metrorail Station. Although other discount stores near this one—such as Filene's Basement, Stein Mart, and T.J. Maxx—also sell home furnishings, they primarily are clothing stores. World Market stands out in focusing mainly on furnishing the home, and doing so as cheaply as possible. You'll find furniture for every room, curtains, mirrors, rugs, pillows, glassware, dishes, kitchenware, and bath products. There also is a large selection of food items, wine, and beer. 5335 Wisconsin Ave. NW (at Western Ave.). ℭ **202/244-8720.** www.worldmarket.com. Metro: Friendship Heights.

SHOES

Shoes by Lara These tiny shops carry designer and brand-name shoes at discount prices. The "final sales" rack in the back has particularly good buys. You'll find shoes by Anne Klein, Joan & David, Via Spiga, Franco Sarto, Nine West, Aerosole, Naturalizer, and Rockport. On the half-price rack, you might find a bargain in a designer shoe by Versani, Andre Assous, Calvin Klein, Joan & David, Stuart Wietzman, Zanotti, or Calvin Klein. The three DC stores also carry a few handbags. 1030 19th St. NW (btw. K and L sts.). ℭ **202/659- 9420.** www.shoesbylara.com. Metro: Farragut North. 707 14th St. NW (btw. G St. and New York Ave.). ℭ **202-637-9787.** Metro: Metro Center. 1139 18th St. NW (btw. L and M sts.). ℭ **202/331-5002.** Metro: Farragut North.

WINE & SPIRITS

Calvert Woodley Wine and Spirits A huge selection of wine, beer, and liquor awaits you here, along with knowledgeable staff who are happy to help, even when your price range is limited. There's also an excellent selection of cheese, crackers, and other party food—and frequent wine tastings. For the best prices, check out each week's sales in the store's weekly *Washington Post* ad and at CW's highly useful website. The site lets you check the price of wines by specific brand, and enables you to browse by country of origin, varietals, or vintage. 4339 Connecticut Ave. NW (btw. Veazey Terrace and Windom Place). (*) **202/966-0445.** www.calvertwoodley.com. Free parking. Metro: Van Ness.

Rodman's Discount Gourmet   Our neighborhood general store has excellent specials on popular wines and beers and a knowledgeable staff to boot. There's a wine tasting every Saturday afternoon. (See full review on p. 235.)

Joel Bernger adds character to his giant "Afro-Colombian Mural Project" at 1350 U St. NW. You'll encounter several murals as you walk the Adams Morgan and U Street itineraries (p. 265).

ITINERARIES FOR THE INDIGENT (OR MERELY THRIFTY)

Washington is a wonderfully walkable town, especially in the spring or fall when the weather's nice. The nation's capital also is a lot more diverse than many people realize, and walking the neighborhoods gives you the opportunity to learn about our diversity up close.

In this chapter, we've given you four interesting walks that are easy for anyone in average shape, that will show you some completely different parts of the city for not a whole lot of cash (there are a lot of free things to look at, and we direct you to cheap, good eateries). As for the terrain, Washington does have hills, but we won't send you on any killer climbs. All big cities have crime, of course. But if you follow these routes during daylight hours and stay aware of your surroundings, you shouldn't run into any unpleasant experiences. And you'll always be a short stroll from places where you can refresh yourself with food and/or drink.

What follows are our suggestions for exploring four of DC's most fascinating neighborhoods. In addition to seeing interesting sights and getting some healthful exercise, you'll learn history about the capital we bet you never knew before.

Capitol Hill: More than the Government

Start:	Union Station Metrorail Station.
Finish:	Eastern Market Metrorail Station.
Time:	Three hours to walk. A day or more if you tour the sights you pass.
Best Times:	9am to 4pm Monday through Friday for the best chance to see the federal government in action.
Worst Times:	Spring days when students on field trips clog the sidewalks near the Capitol, Library of Congress, and Supreme Court. (But spring, alas, also boasts some of Washington's nicest weather.)
Remember to Bring:	A government-issued photo ID (like a driver's license or passport) to get into government buildings.

Everyone knows that Capitol Hill is home to Congress and the Supreme Court. But it's also a charming residential neighborhood with Mom & Pop shops and restaurants frequented by the lawmakers, congressional staffers, lobbyists, and journalists who work—and sometimes live—here. The neighborhood originally was called Jenkins Hill, and Washingtonians now usually refer to it simply as "the Hill." This stroll will take you past government edifices, such as the Library of Congress and the Marine Barracks. It also will introduce you to the homes of contemporary Washingtonians and the houses of DC dwellers of historical note, such as the great abolitionist Frederick Douglass and march music master John Philip Sousa. You won't spend any money on this itinerary—even if you tour all but one of the sights—unless you purchase food or drink or succumb to buying a souvenir. Only one place we pass asks you to pay for admission, and that's a suggested $5 donation.

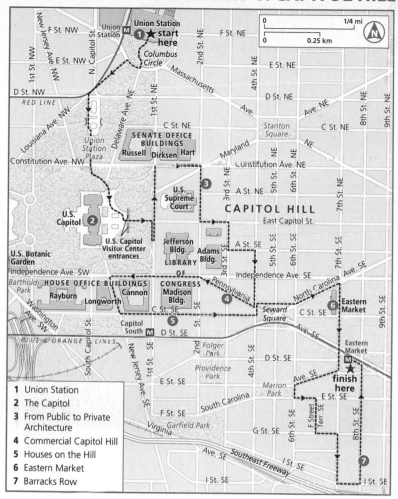

1 Union Station
2 The Capitol
3 From Public to Private Architecture
4 Commercial Capitol Hill
5 Houses on the Hill
6 Eastern Market
7 Barracks Row

❶ Union Station

Beyond being a transportation hub, **Union Station** (p. 124) merits a visit for its own attributes. If you arrive hungry, you can visit the large food court on the ground floor and find other food establishments on the main level. There are shops throughout the station—including the My Obama Shop—and window-shopping is free.

A fountain and a statue of Christopher Columbus stand outside, along with a replica of the Liberty Bell called the **Freedom Bell.** You can sit out here and eat if you have a snack—joining other tourists and perhaps some of the area's homeless. Or, if you'd like a more leafy setting for your picnic, walk away from Union Station toward the Capitol grounds, cross Massachusetts Avenue, and find benches scattered under shady trees.

As you face Union Station, look to left at the **Old Main City Post Office** which now houses the **National Postal Museum** (p. 108) and **Capitol City Brewing Company,** a brew pub that offers reasonably priced beer and food.

② The Capitol

For an attractive approach to the **Capitol** (p. 97) from Union Station, cross Massachusetts Avenue, then bear right on Louisiana Avenue to D Street, where on your right stand modern buildings that house offices for lobbyists and news media. To the left, you can see the Capitol dome rising beyond a park with pools, fountains, shrubbery, and flowers.

As you walk through the park, enjoy the views of the Capitol framed by the flowers, fountains, and trees. At the end of the park, turn left on Constitution Avenue and walk toward the Senate office buildings. Nearest to you is the **Russell Building.** The Beaux Arts structure, the oldest Senate building, was completed in 1908.

It's named for Georgia Democrat Richard B. Russell, Jr., a senator from 1933 until his death in 1971, who was best known for chairing the Senate Armed Services Committee. Of the three Senate buildings, Russell best fits the stereotyped vision of what senators' offices should look like, with its fireplaces, marble hallways, high ceilings, and dark woodwork. It was used as a set for the classic Frank Capra film, *Mr. Smith Goes to Washington*. If you want to take a look, use the visitors' entrance at Constitution and Delaware. Of note are the columned and domed **rotunda** near that entrance, the marble **staircases,** and the ornate **Senate Caucus Room,** the site of hearings into such dramatic events as the sinking of the *Titanic* in 1912 and the Watergate burglary in 1973. Some doors are likely to be ajar, allowing you to glance into some of the offices themselves.

At Delaware Avenue, cross Constitution to the Capitol grounds. Walking straight, you'll end up in the plaza at the Capitol's East Front. Be thankful that the interminable construction of the Capitol Visitors Center is complete and you again can stroll across the plaza, where presidential inaugurations were staged until they were moved to the West Front for Ronald Reagan's swearing-in in 1980. **Capitol tours** begin from the **Capitol Visitors Center,** starting at 8:45am through 3:30pm Monday through Saturday. (See p. 98 for how to get tickets.) You can view exhibits in the center without taking a tour. The center can be entered by elevator from the plaza or by ramps from First Street at the east end of the plaza.

Leave the Capitol grounds to the east, cross First Street, then walk to the right to the Library of Congress's (p. 104) **Jefferson Building.** Note the **Neptune Fountain** beneath the grand stairs to the main entrance of this, the library's oldest and still main facility. You can enter beneath the stairs, and view exhibits or take a guided tour Monday through Saturday.

When you leave the library, turn right and walk along First Street to the **Supreme Court** (p. 99). Lines form on the steps for entrance to hear the court arguments. You also can enter around the corner, on Maryland Avenue, to see exhibits and watch a film about the court.

When you're finished at the court, continue north on First to Constitution. Across Constitution to your right is the **Dirksen Senate Building,** opened in 1958 and named for Everett McKinley Dirksen of Illinois. Dirksen served in the House from 1933 to 1949 and in the Senate from 1951 until his death in 1969. For the last decade of his life, he was the Senate Republican leader, known for saying (approximately) "a billion dollars here, a billion dollars there, and pretty soon you're talking about real money." Adjacent to Dirksen is the **Hart Building,** opened in 1982 and named for Michigan Democrat Philip A. Hart, a senator from 1959 until his death in 1976. I've never liked Hart (Tom says). The soaring marble atrium, surrounded by balconies at the building's center, seems more appropriate for a dictatorship than a democracy. It's easy to imagine a Supreme Leader standing on a high balcony and exhorting the masses below. As you pass by Hart, note that its southeast corner is cut out to allow the **Sewall-Belmont House** to remain standing. Sewall-Belmont was the home of Alice Paul (1885-1977), founder of the National Woman's Party and author of the never-ratified Equal Rights Amendment. The building now houses the party's headquarters and a museum of the campaigns for women's rights. It's open noon to 4pm Wednesday through Sunday. Visitors are asked to make a $5 donation.

③ Government Meets Residences

Turn right on Second Street and see where governmental Capitol Hill meets residential Capitol Hill. To your right is the rear of the Supreme Court, to your left apartment buildings and town houses. Watch for the occasional plaque that identifies a house's place in history.

Turn left on East Capitol Street, and walk along the front of the **Folger Shakespeare Library** (p. 105) toward the library's main entrance at Third Street. Note the inscriptions along the top of the facade. They're not Shakespeare's words, but words of praise from others.

Turn right at Third. Once again you'll find residences to your left and, this time, the library's Adams Building to your right. After you turn left on A Street, you'll come to 320 A, the Washington home of famed abolitionist Frederick Douglass, who lived here in the 1870s. The building now houses the **Frederick Douglass Museum** and the Caring Hall of Fame which honors those who have served others. Tours are by appointment (📞 **202/547-4273;** www.nahc.org/fd/index.html).

④ Commercial Capitol Hill

Walk right on Fourth Street, cross Independence and Pennsylvania avenues, then walk right on Pennsylvania to check out some popular Capitol Hill hangouts. **The Tune Inn** (p. 66), at 331½ Pennsylvania, 📞 **202/543-2725,** is a dive that attracts congressional staffers and the occasional member of Congress. The **Hawk 'n' Dove** (p. 64), at 329, 📞 **202/543-3300,** picked up its name from the Vietnam era battle between "hawks," who supported the war, and "doves," who wanted to end it. This place wanted to serve food and drink to everybody, and it's achieved that goal. Hill staffers and journalists come here after work and after softball games when the losers buy the pitchers.

Across Third Street, at 231 Pennsylvania, is the **Capitol Lounge** (p. 177), 📞 **202/547-2098,** another Hill staffer hangout, known for happy hours and walls covered with political memorabilia. The house beer, Capitol Amber, is $2.50 at happy hour. Farther along Pennsylvania at 205, the **Burrito Brothers** (p. 60), 📞 **202/543-6835,** happily whip up fast and inexpensive burritos.

⑤ Houses on the Hill

Cross Second Street, bear left on Independence Avenue, and you're back in governmentland, this time on the House side of the

Eating with Uncle Sam

Most major government buildings on Capitol Hill open their dining facilities to the public. The food, while not making DC's top-restaurants lists, tends to be palatable and reasonably priced. These eateries can get quite crowded at lunchtime, and some give priority to serving government workers at that time. You can eat in the Hart and Dirksen Senate buildings, the Rayburn and Longworth House buildings, the Supreme Court, and the Library of Congress Madison and Adams buildings. See p. 62 for details.

Hill. The Jefferson Building of the Library of Congress, stands to your right, the library's Madison Building to your left.

Across First Street is the **Cannon House Office Building,** completed a few months before the Senate's nearly identical Russell Building in 1908. It's named for Illinois Republican Joseph G. Cannon, a House member for 46 years in three separate stints. He held the House's highest office, Speaker, from 1903 to 1911. Across New Jersey Avenue stands the House's **Longworth Building,** completed in 1933 and named for Ohio Republican Nicholas Longworth, a House member from 1903 to 1913 and again from 1915 till his death in 1931. He was speaker from 1925 until he died. If you want to visit the **Rayburn Building,** you'll need to walk on to South Capitol Street. Completed in 1965, this modern structure is named for Texas Democrat Samuel T. Rayburn. He served in the House from 1913 until his death in 1961 and was speaker for 19 years.

Otherwise, turn left on New Jersey, walk to C Street, and turn left again. Look to the right down 1st Street, and you'll see the Capitol South Metrorail Station on the right side and two more popular Hill eating and drinking establishments. **Tortilla Coast** (p. 66), at 400 1st St., ✆ **202/546-6768,** serves decent Tex-Mex. Most folks come to **Bullfeathers** (p. 60), at 410 1st Street, ✆ **202/543-5005,** for burgers and other sandwiches, but the restaurant offers more ambitious dishes as well. The name springs from what supposedly was Teddy Roosevelt's favorite euphemism, something which is hurled frequently around Capitol Hill.

Some members of Congress like to live in this neighborhood because of its proximity to the

Capitol. To save expenses, some lawmakers share DC homes. They don't need elaborate accommodations because many return to their districts as often as possible to keep up their perpetual re-election campaigns. Much House business is conducted Tuesday through Thursday, so representatives often fly into DC Monday night or Tuesday morning, then fly out Thursday night or early Friday.

As you continue along C across 1st, note the redbrick **town house** on the right at 133 C St. This classic Capitol Hill residence earned much unwanted notoriety in 2009 when three Republicans associated with it confessed to extramarital affairs. The scandal achieved extreme levels of juiciness when it was reported that the house is owned by a religious group that organizes the annual National Prayer Breakfast and that the philandering politicians had campaigned as "family-values" conservatives. Sen. John Ensign of Nevada was living at 133 C St. when he confessed to an affair with a campaign aide who was married to his Senate staff chief. Former Rep. Chip Pickering of Mississippi was living there when he began an affair with a woman he had dated earlier while in college. South Carolina Gov. Mark Sanford, a former representative, didn't live at the house but said he went there for counseling. Sanford disappeared for five days in 2009, then acknowledged he was visiting his mistress in Argentina.

⑥ Eastern Market

Continue on C Street, across 3rd Street, turn left on 4th, cross Pennsylvania Avenue, then turn right on Seward Street. As you cross 6th Street, bear left on North Carolina Avenue. Large town houses with real front yards line both sides of this wide avenue with wide sidewalks. After you turn right on 7th Street, you'll see **Eastern Market** (p. 228), the large redbrick building on the right at 306 7th St. This place really bustles on weekends when farmers peddle their produce under the market's canopies and 100 or so exhibitors set up shop in the large flea market across the street. The market is crowded inside on weekdays, especially around mealtimes when people buy carryout food or compete for seats at **Market Lunch** (p. 64), ⓒ **202/544-0083.** Here you'll find counters of produce, flowers, deli selections, and baked goods.

Just south of the Eastern Market, **Marvelous Market** (p. 65) serves good and inexpensive food and drink at 303 7th St.,

☏ **202/544-7127.** Born as a bread bakery in Upper Northwest, MM now operates 11 shops in DC and Virginia. Sandwiches on very good bread start at about $6. This Capitol Hill spot sports a few seats inside as well as a pleasant, shady sidewalk cafe where you can sit and watch the Capitol Hill traffic stroll by. The many baby carriages testify to the residential aspect of the neighborhood.

⑦ Barracks Row

Continue down 7th Street, cross Pennsylvania Avenue, then turn right onto South Carolina Avenue, another broad avenue with wide brick sidewalks, and large town houses with front yards. Turn left at 6th Street and left again onto E Street, which has modest frame row houses on its left side. Halfway down the block, turn right into the alley named **F Street Terrace,** then turn left again into the alley called **Archibald Walk.** These are some of the handful of alley residences remaining in Washington.

Continue down F Street Terrace to G Street (there is no F St. here), then turn left. John Philip Sousa—composer of many popular marches and best-known leader of the Marine Corps Band—was born in the yellow-painted brick house on the left at

636 G St. He grew up around the corner at 502 7th St. From G Street, turn right on 7th Street, turn left on I Street where I-295 traffic roars overhead (there's no H St. here), then turn left on a stretch of 8th Street known as **Barracks Row.**

As you walk up 8th Street, the **Marine Barracks** are on the right side of the street. The brick barracks show their backs to 8th Street and front on a parade ground. Here, at 8:45pm on summer Fridays, the **Marine Band** performs a concert and the Marines conduct an impressive precision drill. Free tickets—which disappear fast—can be reserved online at www.mbw.usmc.mil/parades. asp. (See **Marine Corps Parades,** p. 157.) **Barracks tours** are conducted Wednesdays at 10am. Call ☏ **202/433-4073** for information.

The barracks comprise the oldest active U.S. Marine post. The location was selected by President Thomas Jefferson and Marine Commandant William Ward Burrows because it's near the Washington Navy Yard and the Capitol. Congress established the Marine Band, which is headquartered here, in 1798. It has played for every president since John Adams, who succeeded George Washington and was the first president to live in the White

Capitol Hill Costs

Free	
Looking at all the cool buildings and houses	$0
Dirt Cheap	
A happy-hour beer at the Capitol Lounge	$2.50
Add-On for Spendthrift Millionaires	
Sandwich at Marvelous Market	$6

House. Jefferson called the band "the President's Own," and the name stuck. Sousa led the bank from 1880 to 1892.

The left side of 8th Street here is lined with shops, bars, and restaurants. The **Shakespeare Theatre Company**'s (p. 152) studios—costume shop, rehearsal facilities, and administrative offices—are at 516 8th St. Turn left on Pennsylvania Avenue to the Eastern Market Metrorail Station, where this tour ends.

Georgetown: A Tale of Three Villages

Start:	M and Thomas Jefferson streets NW. From downtown, take Metrobus 31, 32, 36, 38B, or D5. From the Dupont Circle or Rosslyn Metrorail station, take the Georgetown Metro Connection. From Union Station or Downtown, take the Circulator.
Finish:	27th and Q streets NW. Take the D1, D2, D3, or D6 Metrobus to Dupont Circle.
Time:	Three and a half hours to walk. More if you visit sights or stop for meals, snacks, or drinks.
Best Times:	During daylight when the weather's nice.
Worst Times:	July and August afternoons when the weather's hot and humid.

For some Washingtonians, Georgetown is a place to shop or partake of the vibrant nightlife. For others, it's where they go to college or where they go to root for the Georgetown University basketball team. For yet others—many of them with a great deal of money—Georgetown is home. This itinerary partakes of all three Georgetowns. We'll peek at parts of M Street and Wisconsin Avenue—the main drags lined with shops, restaurants, and bars. We'll pay a quick visit to Georgetown University's lovely and historic campus and glimpse the student housing nearby. Our emphasis will be on the quiet residential streets

ITINERARY 2: GEORGETOWN

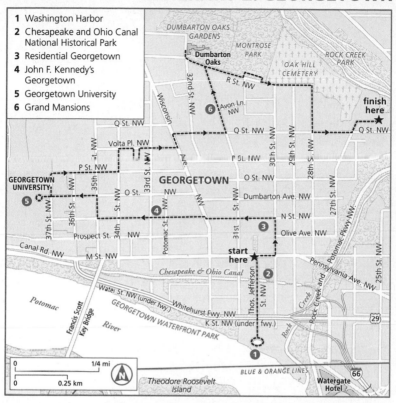

1 Washington Harbor
2 Chesapeake and Ohio Canal National Historical Park
3 Residential Georgetown
4 John F. Kennedy's Georgetown
5 Georgetown University
6 Grand Mansions

and their places in Georgetown's very rich history. Established by Maryland's colonial legislature in 1751, Georgetown became a thriving tobacco and slave port. The wealthy built their mansions on Georgetown's hills, where the climate was considered cooler and more healthful. Freed slaves flocked here during and after the Civil War, and African Americans became a significant portion of the area's population. Georgetown flourished as an industrial town, with flourmills, a textile mill and paper factory in addition to port facilities. The area declined after World War I, and many homes were neglected and deteriorated. The New Deal's growing government workforce increased the demand for housing and helped to reverse Georgetown's decline. By the 1950s, it was becoming home to some of the most influential and wealthy residents of the capital—which it still is. You can make this trek for free if you pass on the few sights that charge admission. Of course, it can be tough to resist the shopping, eating, and nightlife along Wisconsin and M.

① Washington Harbour

To start, walk down Thomas Jefferson Street to the Washington Harbour complex, where you'll see a large pool with dancing fountains. Walk around the pool to the boardwalk at the Potomac River. In the distance to your left, you can see the **Watergate** complex—site of the burglary that precipitated President Richard Nixon's resignation in the 1970s—with the **Kennedy Center** (p. 158) just beyond. To your right is the **Key Bridge,** named for U.S. National Anthem composer Francis Scott Key, which connects Georgetown and Arlington, Virginia. Ahead of you across the water is **Roosevelt Island** (p. 135), which contains a memorial to President Theodore Roosevelt and some pleasant walking paths. The Harbour complex contains several eating and drinking establishments, including outdoor cafes that let you imbibe while you watch people and boats pass by. At night, this place becomes a major meet market for Washington singles.

Before leaving the Harbour, note its post-modern architecture, which stands in stark contrast to the 19th-century houses that populate most of Georgetown. Then start back up Thomas Jefferson Street. At first, you will pass through a canyon of new redbrick buildings. Then, at the bridge over the Chesapeake and Ohio Canal, the 18th century meets the 21st. This is the southern terminus of the canal and of the national historical park of the same name.

② Chesapeake and Ohio Canal National Historical Park

President John Quincy Adams turned the first shovel of dirt for the canal's construction on July 4, 1828, about five miles west of here. The link to Cumberland, Maryland, 184 miles to the west, wasn't completed until 1850, and the plan to continue on to the Ohio River at Pittsburgh was abandoned. Traveling no more than four miles an hour, mules took a week to pull boats carrying goods and passengers the canal's length. Its operations continued until 1924.

Information about the contemporary park and historic canal is available at the **visitors center** (✆ **202/653-5190;** www.nps. gov/choh/planyourvisit/georgetown visitorcenter.htm), on the north bank of the canal to the right. Hour-long **boat rides** leave here Wednesday through Sunday at 11am, 1:30 and 3pm May through October. In April, the rides are offered on Wednesday and Sunday. Park personnel in

19th-century costumes drive the mules, guide the boat, relate the history, and answer questions. These schedules can change. Phone the visitors center or check the website for the latest info. Cost is $5, free for children 3 and younger.

Good coffee, tea, pastries, lunch fare, and Wi-Fi are available at **Baked and Wired,** just south of the bridge at 1052 Thomas Jefferson St., ⓒ **202/333-2500.** You can order a snack to go here, carry it up Thomas Jefferson, and cross M Street to the **Old Stone House,** built in 1765, another Park Service site. The benches and lawn in the house's restful rear garden provide a great place to picnic. When you return to M Street, take a moment to look around at the shops, restaurants, and bars. You may want to check them out at greater length later. Now, walk left on M Street to 30th Street, where you'll turn left again. **Garrett's** (p. 78), near the corner at 3003 M, ⓒ **202/333-1033,** offers reasonably priced meals from lunch into the wee hours. Above the street-level saloon, there's a pleasant dining room on the second floor.

③ Residential Georgetown
You've now entered old, historic, residential Georgetown, with 19th-century brick town houses

and sidewalks on both sides of the street. Throughout this walk, you can spy markers that tell when certain buildings were constructed and what role they played in history. Note how homeowners employ paint to distinguish their houses from their similar or identical neighbors. On this block alone, houses sport their natural red brick as well as yellow, green, gray, tan, blue, and brown paint.

Turn left on N Street to 3014 N St. on the left. **Robert Todd Lincoln,** the president's son, split his time between here and Vermont from the early 1900s till his death in 1926. The large redbrick house, with portico and fan window over the door, was built around 1800. An interesting variety of homes lines both sides of N Street as you make your way toward Wisconsin Avenue. Note the large turret at 3032 on the left.

A Washington drinking and dining institution, **Martin's Tavern,** stands on the southwest corner of N Street and Wisconsin Avenue, ⓒ **202/333-7370.** The yellow building with green shutters and awnings has served every president from Harry Truman to George W. Bush. At this writing, Barack Obama hadn't eaten here yet. But he gets out around town a lot, so we wouldn't be surprised if he stops here at some point. Harry Truman, John Kennedy, Lyndon Johnson, and Richard Nixon were Martin's regulars when they served in Congress before moving into the White House. Take a gander up and down Wisconsin, Georgetown's other main entertainment and shopping strip, before entering another residential area to the west.

④ John F. Kennedy's Georgetown Just west of Wisconsin Avenue, some houses are set back from street and have lawns or gardens. Some acquire an extra sense of privacy from having their yards stand six to eight feet above street level. Across Potomac Street, on the left side of N Street, houses' front doors open directly onto the sidewalk. A **plaque** at the southwest corner of N and 33rd streets announces that journalists hung out at 3302 N St. to obtain information about the incoming Kennedy administration in late 1960 and early 1961. Kennedy lived at **3307 N St.,** and his aides could walk across the street to deliver announcements to the waiting reporters, who were staking out the President-elect's house. He frequently conducted press conferences at his front door. The journalists had the plaque made for Charles Montgomery and his

daughter Helen in thanks for the shelter the Montgomerys provided from the winter weather. Kennedy bought 3307 N St. as a gift for his wife Jacqueline after she gave birth to their daughter Caroline in 1957. Jackie moved to 3038 N St. after the president's assassination on November 22, 1963.

A bit beyond the Kennedys' house, at 3327 to 3339 N, stands **Cox's Row,** five town houses that the American Institute of Architects cites as excellent examples of 19th-century Federal architecture. At 34th Street, look to the right and across 34th at an unusual house for this neighborhood—a stone cottage with twin dormers and metal roof. The 3400 block of N Street shows off extremes of Georgetown living accommodations. Two enormous, impressive redbrick houses with tile mansard roofs stand at 3405 and 3407. At 3421 N St., a small brick-and-frame house has *"hoya saxa"* painted on the windows (or at least it did while we were writing this book). That's the Georgetown University cheer. (Translation to follow!) You can bet students live here.

After crossing 35th on N Street, look high up to your right at the **Chapel of Saint Ignatius Loyola,** built in 1792 as Holy Trinity

Catholic Church. At that time, the parish served all of Washington plus adjacent Montgomery and Prince George's counties in Maryland. Turn right at 36th Street, and you'll come to the present **Holy Trinity Church,** the Greco-Roman building on the right which was opened in 1851. Holy Trinity has a rich history. In its early years, it counted slaves among its parishioners. During the Civil War, the Union Army laid planks across the tops of the pews and turned the sanctuary into a surgical hospital. In the mid–20th century, John Kennedy and his family worshipped here.

⑤ Georgetown University

Continue north on 35th Street, turn left on O Street, and you'll come to the main gate of the Georgetown University Campus across 37th Street. Ahead is the statue of **John Carroll,** who founded the university in 1789, just as the first U.S. Congress and president were taking office. The spire behind him marks **Healy Hall,** a landmark that can be seen from great distances. It's named for Patrick F. Healy, the first African American to earn a doctorate and the first to be president of a predominantly white American university—Georgetown, from 1874 to 1882. Adjacent to Healy Hall on your right is Gaston Hall.

Walk along the right side of Gaston, and you'll come to **Old North** on the left, the oldest building on campus, completed in 1795. Behind Old North is the **Dahlgren Quadrangle,** where many presidents—from George Washington to Bill Clinton (a 1968 Georgetown graduate)—have delivered speeches. Interestingly, Clinton was elected president of his freshman and sophomore classes here, but failed in his race for student body president. Oh, and about *"hoya saxa"*: According to the university, its athletic teams once were nicknamed the Stonewalls. A student used Greek and Latin terms to create the cheer, "hoya saxa," which translates into "what stones" or "what rocks." Eventually, the teams took the nickname "Hoyas." Oddly, *saxa* is Latin for stones or rocks, so the nickname literally translates as "the Whats!" The teams play in blue-and-gray uniforms, colors adopted following the Civil War to symbolize unity between North and South.

After you've soaked up enough higher education, exit the main gate and turn left on 37th where you'll encounter more of those brightly painted houses on the right. Turn right on P Street. When P crosses 35th Street, you'll see the old cobblestone paving and the rails that used to carry streetcars throughout the city. Watch your step. The cobblestones are treacherous, and the brick sidewalks are very uneven. Walk left on 34th Street, turn right on Volta Street, then right into narrow Pomander Walk. Note the tiny pastel houses, built in 1885. Return to Volta Street and turn right.

Returning to Wisconsin Avenue presents you with another opportunity to get something to eat or drink. To the right and across Wisconsin Avenue, **Marvelous Market** (p. 65), ℂ **202/333-2591,** offers pastries and sandwiches on very good bread. Sandwiches start under $7. The $9 combo includes a sandwich, chips, and a beverage. You can sit on a stool at a windowsill and watch the street scene as you eat. If you're tired when you get here, you can flop down on an overstuffed chair or sofa. Or you can eat at picnic tables outside. Across the street, at Wisconsin Avenue and P Street, **Thomas Sweet,** ℂ **202/337-0616,** serves homemade ice cream, yogurt, and fudge. At Wisconsin Avenue and Q Street, **Dolcezza,** ℂ **202/333-4646,** sells Argentine gelato and sorbet.

⑥ Grand Mansions

Otherwise, walk up (north) on Wisconsin Avenue, then right (east) on Q Street, and you're back in residential Georgetown. As you cross 32nd Street on Q Street, the grounds of Tudor Place lie behind the fence on your left. (More about that shortly.) The extreme wealth in this neighborhood is only hinted at by the large houses on the right. At the corner of 31st Street, ahead on the left, are larger brick and stone houses with turrets. Turn left on 31st Street, and you'll come to the entrance of **Tudor Place** at 1644, ℂ **202/965-0400;** www.tudorplace.org. The property upon which the mansion stands was purchased in 1805 by Martha Washington's granddaughter, Martha Custis Peter, and her husband, Thomas Peter. Construction was completed in 1816, and the estate remained in the family until 1983. The Marquis de Lafayette, Daniel Webster, and Henry Clay were among notables who visited here. Collections on display at the estate include more than 100 objects once owned by George and Martha Washington. Tudor Place is open Monday through Saturday from 10am to 4pm, and Sunday from noon to 4. Tours costs $8 for adults, $6 for seniors 62 and older and for military personnel with ID, and $3 for children 7 to 18. Younger children are free but may not enjoy the experience. You can visit the garden for $3.

Continue up 31st Street. The enormous value of houses in this part of Georgetown stems not just from the size and grandeur of the buildings, but also the large grounds that surround some of them. At the top of hill, turn left on R Street. Turn right at 32nd Street. On the right, at **1703 32nd St.,** is a mansion where John C. Calhoun lived while he was a senator in the second quarter of the 19th century. Today it houses the **Dumbarton Oaks Research Library and Collection** (p. 118). This branch of Harvard University supports scholarship in Byzantine and Pre-Columbian studies as well as into garden and landscape. The museum of Byzantine, Pre-Columbian, and European art is open Tuesday through Sunday from 2 to 5pm. Admission is free. Return to R Street and turn left. At 31st and R streets is the entrance to the Dumbarton Oaks Gardens, which are open Tuesday through Sunday in the afternoon. If you want free admission, come between 2 and 5pm November 1 through March 14. The rest of the year, on the same days but until 6pm, general admission is $8. Seniors 60 and older, children 2 to 12, and students get in for $5.

Continue on R Street, then turn left into **Montrose Park.** At the entrance are a rose garden, some benches, a large lawn, and tennis courts. Continue east in the park and you'll find picnic tables and a playground. At the east edge of park are well-maintained public restrooms. Return to R Street and turn left. At 30th street, enter **Oak Hill Cemetery** on the left. Walk right after entering the grounds, and you'll come to a stone chapel built in 1849 when the cemetery was founded. It was designed by James Renwick, Jr., architect of the Smithsonian Castle (p. 123) and the Renwick Gallery (p. 116) downtown. It's modeled on old Gothic chapels in England. Notable Americans—from Revolutionary War generals to contemporary leaders—are buried here. You can get a map for locating notable graves at the cemetery's website, **www.oak hillcemeterydc.org/map.html**.

Katharine Graham, the legendary publisher who led *The Washington Post* through Watergate, is buried near the chapel along with her husband Philip, who ran the paper before her. So are members of the Peter family of Tudor place. A sign of life being lived amidst death: To the left of the entrance, graves lie just outside the windows of the caretaker's house which sports a two-car garage and a basketball hoop.

Across the street from the cemetery, at 2920 R St., is the mansion where the Grahams lived. Part constructed in 1784, it sits far back from the street behind a long circular drive and iron fencing. From the cemetery, walk left to where R Street ends at 28th Street and you must turn right. Just down from R Street on the left is an entrance to **Evermay,** a private 3.6-acre estate on the market (as we write) for a mere $39.5 million—neither free nor dirt cheap. You can barely glimpse a portion of the redbrick, 13,000-square-foot, Federalist mansion behind the heavy iron fence. (There's also a 2,300-sq. ft. gatekeeper's house.) From the inside, the property's high elevation allows occupants and visitors to see the **Washington Monument** (p. 113). The mansion was built from 1792 to '94 by Samuel Davidson with proceeds from the sale of land he owned that now makes up part of the White House grounds and Lafayette Park. Presidents, diplomats, and other dignitaries visited here over the centuries.

Continue down 28th Street and turn left on Q Street. On the left, at 2715 Q St., is **Dumbarton House** (© **202/337-2288;** www. dumbartonhouse.org), another large, redbrick, Federalist mansion behind a redbrick wall and iron fence. (If you're wondering about the many Dumbartons around here, they stand on land that once was part of a 795-acre tract called the Rock of Dumbarton.) Samuel Jackson began to build this mansion in 1799 but work was stopped when he went bankrupt. An auction turned the property over to Joseph Nourse, a Revolutionary War general's aide who held numerous federal government positions beginning before the Constitution was written. Nourse finished construction by 1804 and lived here with his family until 1813. Dolley Madison sought shelter here in 1814 when she fled the British burning of the White House.

The National Society of The Colonial Dames of America purchased the property in 1928, located their national headquarters here, and opened Dumbarton House as a museum. The museum displays furniture, paintings, textiles, silver, and ceramics from the Federal Period, 1790 to 1830. There's also a manuscript collection that includes an original copy of the Articles of Confederation, which organized the first U.S. government in 1777. Docents lead tours on the hour from 10am to 1pm Tuesday through Saturday. Admission is $5, children and students with ID free.

Georgetown Costs

Free	
Walking the streets of Historic Georgetown	$0
Dirt Cheap	
A mule-powered boat ride on the C&O Canal	$5
Cheap Add-on	
Tour Tudor Place	$8
Big Splurge	
Buy the Evermay estate	$39.5 million

When you leave Dumbarton House, turn left on Q Street, then left again at 27th Street. On your left is the Dumbarton House parking lot and another entrance. Ahead is the **Mount Zion Cemetery,** which comprises the Old Methodist Burial Ground and the Female Union Band Society Graveyard. The Dumbarton Street Methodist Episcopal Church—which had black and white members—bought land for the Old Methodist Burial Ground in 1808. Chafing under the segregation enforced within the church, African-American members left to form the Mount Zion Methodist Church in 1816. Mt. Zion acquired the burial ground from the Dumbarton Street church in 1879. In 1842, a group of free black women organized the Female Union Band Society as a cooperative whose members pledged to assist each other in sickness and death. They bought land for their burial ground the same year. Collectively, the two burial grounds became known as the Mount Zion Cemetery. Internments ceased in 1950.

Adams Morgan: Washington's Latin Quarter & More

Start:	Woodley Park Metrorail Station.
Finish:	16th and W streets NW.
Time:	Three hours to walk. More if you visit sights or stop for meals, snacks, or drinks.
Best Times:	During daylight when the weather's nice.
Worst Times:	After dark, when you should stick to the busy commercial streets.

Adams Morgan is best known today as the hub of Washington's Hispanic community and as a burgeoning nightlife district that's still sketchy off the main drags after dark. Like many DC neighborhoods, however, it's much more than that. In the late 19th and early 20th centuries, wealthy families moved into newly built grand apartments and elegant houses.

This was one of the higher elevation areas of Washington, coveted in the days before air-conditioning as a cooler and more healthful place to live, especially in summer. Embassies—particularly of Spanish-speaking governments—were established on 16th Street and their employees moved into the neighborhood, some becoming permanent residents. In the 1930s, many wealthier residents began to relocate to other, newly fashionable parts of the Washington region. Large town houses were subdivided into rental properties. By the 1950s, a number of liberals had taken up residence in the neighborhood, so the Supreme Court's 1954 desegregation ruling was implemented more easily here than in many other places.

Residents organized the Adams Morgan Better Neighborhood Conference in 1955, taking its title from two formerly segregated public schools—the Morgan School for "colored" children, named for DC Commissioner Thomas P. Morgan, and the Adams school for whites, named for President John Quincy Adams. The name eventually stuck to the entire neighborhood. In the '60s and '70s, Adams Morgan vibrated with antiwar and radical activists, as well as young artists and musicians. Some of those folks still prowl the streets. See if you can spot their Earth Mother dresses and still-long but graying, hair. In fact, all of the neighborhood's history has left indelible marks—from the imposing residences of the wealthy to the diplomatic establishments and Spanish culture. Oh, and John F. Kennedy lived here briefly.

① The Heart of Adams Morgan
From the Woodley Park Metrorail Station, you can walk or take a bus to the heart of Adams Morgan near the intersection of 18th Street and Columbia Road. Either way, from the Metro station, walk south on Connecticut Avenue to Calvert Street. To catch the Circulator or 96 Metrobus, cross Calvert to the southwest corner. To make the 10-to-15-minute walk, cross Connecticut Avenue, and stroll along Calvert Street. The bridge that carries you above Rock Creek Park is named for Duke Ellington, the famed musician who got his start in the U Street neighborhood, the subject of our next itinerary. Note the bus turnaround. It's the terminus for some of the buses you can take back from the end of this itinerary.

Calvert Street is a busy four-lane boulevard here, but it's also a residential area with town houses lining both sides. A sign at the Exxon station at Calvert Street and Adams Mill Road

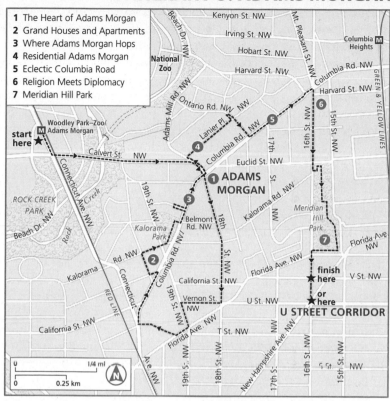

1 The Heart of Adams Morgan
2 Grand Houses and Apartments
3 Where Adams Morgan Hops
4 Residential Adams Morgan
5 Eclectic Columbia Road
6 Religion Meets Diplomacy
7 Meridian Hill Park

highlights the never-ending conflict between commercial and residential Adams Morgan: "Please be quiet for residents and neighbors. Turn off engine and radio." Bear right on Adams Mill Road, which becomes 18th Street. This is where the neighborhood begins to reveal its multi-ethnic nature and its stature as a popular purveyor of food, drink, and music.

The glass-and-steel facade at **2477 18th St.** now fronts a sushi bar with a popular nightclub downstairs. In an earlier incarnation, it was the Show Boat Lounge, where the great jazz guitarist Charlie Byrd played regularly in the '50s and '60s. Along with tenor saxophonist Stan Getz and bassist Keter Betts, Byrd introduced America to what became known as the bossa nova with the 1962 album "Jazz Samba." It was recorded at All Souls Unitarian Church (a later stop on this itinerary) because the musicians liked the acoustics. If you like sushi, **Saki** (p. 58),

📞 **202/518-9820,** is a good—if cramped—place to eat it. Other Japanese dishes are available as well. The club downstairs has a dance floor and often good DJs. The decor is unusual for a nightclub, with white covering most surfaces and color-changing panels hanging on the walls. The small plates start at $4, and some are half-price between 5 and 7:30pm daily.

Several Adams Morgan buildings sport colorful murals. The most famous adorns 2461 18th St., home of the popular **Madam's Organ Blues Bar and Soul Food Restaurant** (p. 174), which presents live music every night. The mural is a red-headed, buxom broad who was painted (with 13-ft. breasts) by Charlie Habababananda in 1998. In her honor, the club offers redheads half-price on Rolling Rock beer all the time.

This also is the birthplace of the Toys 'R' Us chain. Charles Lazarus grew up at this address, where his fathered also operated a bicycle shop on the first floor. In 1948, Charles took over the shop and turned it into a store for children's furniture and, later, toys. He opened a second store in 1957, which he called a "toy supermarket" and named Toys 'R' Us.

Down the street, at 2431, you'll find a crude copy of a Toulouse-Lautrec portrait of a cabaret singer. It was painted in 1980 by Andre Neveux, who owned a bar in the building at the time. Nothing says multicultural like the **Amsterdam Falafelshop** (p. 56), at 2425 18th St. This small, inexpensive restaurant serves the Middle Eastern croquets in pita bread along with twice-cooked Dutch-style fried potatoes. In nice weather, this is a great place to take a break. Try to score a table inside the small restaurant or on the patio. The street is pretty barren south of Kalorama, where the rear of the Reed school and recreation center occupy 2 blocks on the left. The tennis courts are on the site

---

Have Fun, but Keep Your Eyes Open!

For added safety, leave well before the bars close if you're out partying in Adams Morgan or the U Street Corridor. The biggest danger in these neighborhoods seems to be posed when you become an innocent victim of someone else's drunken brawl.

of the Morgan School, which was demolished in the early '70s. Glance up most side streets to the right and you'll see residential blocks that stand in stark contrast to this sketchy, bustling, commercial strip.

2 Grand Houses and Apartments Pass Wyoming and California streets, then turn right on Vernon Street, which is lined with apartment buildings and town houses. Take a close look at the apartment building on the right of Vernon at 19th Street. It served as the **Imperial Chinese Embassy** from 1902 to 1944. Across 19th Street to the right, the large redbrick building with columns at the main entrance is the **Adams School,** which was built in 1930 and helped to give the neighborhood its name. Now part of the two-campus Oyster-Adams Bilingual School, it hosts classes taught in English and Spanish. (The Oyster campus is about 3 blocks west of the Woodley Park Metrorail Station at 2801 Calvert St. NW.) From Vernon, head down the hill to the left on 19th Street. The massive curved concrete structure on the right which looms over everything is the back of the **Hilton Washington.** It contains DC's largest ballroom and hosts large events such as the annual White House Correspondents Association dinner.

Turn right on Florida, then right on T Street. The hotel entrance on T Street is where John Hinckley, Jr., shot President Ronald Reagan on March 30, 1981, leading some irreverent Washingtonians to start calling this the "Killer Hilton."

Turn right on Connecticut Avenue and continue walking around the Hilton to Columbia Road. You're now entering a neighborhood of grand apartment buildings. On the right at 2022 Columbia Road is **The Wyoming,** a brick structure with an ornate metal awning over the entrance and old-fashioned globe lights. Built around 1905, the Wyoming once was home to President Dwight D. Eisenhower.

Turn left on Wyoming Avenue. The building on the right at 1901 Wyoming Ave. is **The Altamont,** built in 1915 as one of Washington's premier addresses. Turn right on 20th Street. **The Mendota,** at 2220, was built in 1901 and is the city's oldest luxury apartment house that hasn't been subdivided into smaller units, according to the Cultural Tourism DC publication, *Roads to Diversity: Adams Morgan Heritage Trail.* (To get a copy of this publication and to check out the organization's publications about other neighborhoods, go to **www. culturaltourismdc.org** and click on "Featured Neighborhoods.")

The luxury buildings in this area typically sported "elaborate facades, elegant lobbies, and spacious units of more than 2,000 square feet." Many had swimming pools, beauty parlors, and servants' quarters, as well as elevators, dishwashers, and air-conditioners, which were rare at the time.

Turn right on Kalorama Road. Take a detour through the park to your left between 19th Street and Columbia Road. The tiny **Kalorama Community Garden** occupies the southeast corner of the park, and there are several small playgrounds. After you exit the park on Columbia Road, turn left. Turn left again on Mintwood Street. Beyond a few apartment buildings, the street becomes lined on both sides by tall row houses, many now broken up into multiple apartments. As Tom walked by while researching this chapter, the redbrick Romanesque Revival house at 1853 was advertising a 1,000-square-foot apartment with a gas fireplace for $2,450 a month. Across the street, 1850 is an inviting Tudor Revival house with a deck in back.

❸ Where Adams Morgan Hops
Return to Columbia Road, which here is lined with apartment buildings, shops, and restaurants, and walk to the left. Across the street at 1834 Columbia is **Habana Village** (p. 172), ⓒ **202/462-6310,** a Cuban restaurant and popular dance club with live Latin music on Saturday, and DJs and $10 salsa lessons Wednesday through Saturday. Best deals are found on Wednesday, when $3 buys beer, wine, and rail drinks all night, and Thursday until 11pm, when you can get beer and wine for $3, rail drinks for $6, and a mojito, margarita, or caipirinha (the national drink of Brazil) for $6. **Perry's** (p. 58), ⓒ **202/234-6218,** on left at the corner of Biltmore and Columbia, has become an Adams Morgan institution over the last quarter century. It's got rooftop seating, a Sunday brunch with performing drag queens, and an affordable eclectic menu with sushi and tapas.

❹ Where Adams Morgan is Quiet and Residential
Turn left on Biltmore Street for a quick look at another residential street of apartments and houses. On your left, at 1848, is an interesting redbrick Colonial Revival house with a fan window over the door. There's Spanish Revival at 1852. Return to Columbia Road and walk to the left. Turn left on Adams Mill Road, then

right at the Exxon station onto Lanier Place, another street lined with trees, apartment buildings, and large row houses. Rabbi Moses Yoelson, father of entertainer Al Jolson, once lived at 1787, on the left. During the 1960s, members of the radical Students for a Democratic Society lived at 1779. The firehouse at 1763, built in 1908, is notable for more than its Mission style. How often do you see a fire station sharing a wall with a house in a quiet residential neighborhood? The Mayday Tribe, an anti–Vietnam War group, bedded down at 1747 during the '60s. Turn left on Ontario Road.

At the corner of 18th Street, you come face-to-face with the enormous **Ontario** apartment building. The Beaux Arts structure opened in stages in 1903 and 1906. Its architect was James G. Hill, who was supervising architect of the Treasury Department from 1876 to 1883, a position that at the time had responsibility for designing post offices. Initially offered as rental units, the Ontario was converted to a co-operative in 1953. Apartments range in size from 557 to 2,195 square feet. They all have 10-ft. ceilings, large windows, and gas fireplaces. When it opened, the Ontario had gas lights. Take a moment to study the exterior. The rambling building stands behind low stone walls and is attractively landscaped. The lower facade is buff brick. Above is stucco with brick arches over the windows. Some apartments have iron balconies.

⑤ Columbia Road's Eclectic Mix

Walk back on Ontario Road to Columbia Road and turn left. Across Columbia you can see the **Three Macaws Mural** on the side of the building that houses one of Washington's ubiquitous CVS drugstores. On the left, at 1725, is **Chief Ike's Mambo Room** (p. 171), ⓒ **202/332-2211,** a neighborhood hangout with a small dance floor, sidewalk seating, an upstairs lounge, and a shot at being called cheap. **Christ House,** at 1717, offers healthcare and temporary housing to the homeless and poor. On the right in the next block, at 1656 Columbia, is the **Potter's House,** ⓒ **202/232-5483,** a coffeehouse and bookstore. Both are projects of the Church of the Saviour, an ecumenical Christian church with a social service mission. Next door is the **Shawarma King,** ⓒ **202/ 462-8355,** which specializes in the Middle Eastern gyro.

6 Religion Meets Diplomacy

As you walk along the 1600 block of Columbia Road, you'll notice church spires rising ahead. The intersection where Columbia meets 16th and Harvard streets could be called God's Corner, because of the three impressive churches that stand there. The first you encounter, on the right at 1610 Columbia, is a **Unification Church,** the controversial denomination founded and led by the Rev. Sun Myung Moon. If the tall spire reminds you of a Mormon temple (minus the statue of the angel Moroni on top), it's because that's what this church was from its opening in 1933 until 1975. Its marble blocks came from Utah. Directly across 16th Street is **All Souls Unitarian Church,** the Neo-Georgian redbrick structure with the tower and columns at the top of its main steps. It was dedicated in 1924. Among its notable members were President William Howard Taft and Democratic Sen. Adlai Stevenson of Illinois, who lost presidential elections to Dwight Eisenhower in 1952 and 1956. The Neo-Baroque **National Baptist Memorial Church** stands on the third corner at 1501 Columbia.

Turn right on 16th Street and look to the left side of the street at the **Mexican Consulate** at 2829. The building next door at 2801— with boarded-up windows when Tom last walked past—used to be the Spanish Embassy. The **Polish Embassy** stands on the right side of 16th Street, just past Fuller Street at 2640. The castlelike structure on the left at 2633 16th St. was once the home of noted Washington architect George O. Totten, Jr. Later, it housed the Antioch Law School, which was dedicated to educating students from groups that were underrepresented at the bar and to encouraging public service. After Antioch University decided to close the school in 1986, the DC government took over the institution as the District of Columbia School of Law, which now is part of the University of the District of Columbia.

The **Cuban Interests Section** of the **Swiss Embassy** is at 2630 16th St. Here, Cuban diplomats conduct their truncated diplomatic relationship with the United States. Switzerland maintains a similar facility for the United States in Havana. **Lithuania's Embassy** is the stone building at 2622. Totten designed the stone and stucco structure at 2600, which houses the **Inter-American Defense Board.** Comprised of military officials from the Americas, it plans for the defense of the region. Across Euclid Street at 2480 16th St. is the **Dorchester House,** a yellow brick Art Deco apartment building that briefly was home for John Kennedy and his sister Kathleen in 1941. Continue down 16th Street to Kalorama Road, where the ornate stone building on the right once housed the French Embassy.

7 Meridian Hill: Rebirth of a Park
Now return to Euclid and cross 16th Street to **Meridian Hill Park.** As you do, you can look down 16th Street all the way to the Washington Monument and the dome of the Jefferson Memorial. The park was constructed between 1912 and 1936. It began to decline in the 1950s and fell victim to vandalism, drug-dealing, and other crime until the early 1990s. Then, neighbors organized the Friends of Meridian Hill and worked with the National Park Service to drive out the criminals and restore the park's facilities—a project that wasn't completed until 2008.

At its top, the park is a long green lawn flanked by walkways that are lined with wooden benches. Along the right side of the park you'll encounter a marble sculpture called *Serenity.* Its twin is located in Luxembourg.

Continue on to a bronze **statue of Joan of Arc,** Washington's only statue of a woman on horseback. It's a copy of a statue by Paul Dubois that stands at Reims Cathedral in France. The original has been called a masterpiece.

Ahead and below is a wall beyond which stretch pools of cascading water. As they descend, the pools get wider, creating an optical illusion. Viewed from the bottom, the cascade appears longer than it actually is. Walk down the steps to the left and along the left-hand path to the bronze statue of Dante, the author of the *Divine Comedy.* Interesting, is it not, that this medieval poet, who wrote in Italian, is holding a book whose title is in English? While pondering that mystery, walk down to the southeast corner of the park and the memorial to James Buchanan who's remembered—if he's remembered at all—as our only bachelor president, the only president from Pennsylvania, and the president who handed Lincoln the Civil War.

Walk across the bottom of the park and note the brownstone walls across 16th Street. They used to surround a castlelike mansion. The mansion was torn down and replaced by the Beekman Place town houses, but the

Adams Morgan Costs

Free	
Walk Adams Morgan's residential streets and nightlife districts	$0
Dirt Cheap	
Sip a drink and salsa the night away Wednesdays at Habana Village	$3
Cheap Add-on	
Savor a falafel with Dutch fries at the Amsterdam Falafel Shop	$6.75

walls were allowed to survive. Continue down the hill on 16th Street. On the right side of 16th at V Street, you can catch the S1, S2, S4, or S9 bus to downtown. Or you can continue to the north side of U Street and board the 96 bus to Calvert Street and Connecticut Avenue near the Woodley Park–Zoo Metro, or take the 90, 92, 93, or 98 bus to the turnaround east of the Ellington Bridge.

U Street Corridor: Washington's Black Broadway Reborn

Start:	U Street Metrorail Station 10th Street exit .
Finish:	U Street Metrorail Station 13th Street entrance
Time:	90 minutes. More if you visit sights or stop to eat or drink.
Best Times:	During daylight when the weather's nice.
Worst Times:	After dark, except on busy commercial streets.

The circle of life is turning again for this neighborhood, which once housed Washington's elite African-American residents and the city's best black entertainment venues. Duke Ellington grew up—and later performed—here. Every other great black musician of the first half of the 20th century performed here, too. Whites were never excluded from U Street venues, but blacks weren't welcomed at many white-oriented venues during segregation. So blacks came to the U Street area to entertain and to be entertained, and the neighborhood became known as Washington's Black Broadway. It was the center of African-American business, shopping, and intellectual life, as well. Thurgood Marshall, the first black Supreme Court Justice; Charles Drew, who developed improved techniques for blood storage; and poet Langston Hughes all spent time here. Black architects designed buildings for black developers who then sold or rented space in them to black businesses and residents. African Americans from

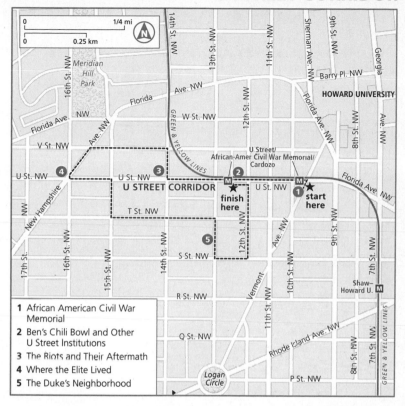

0   1/4 mi

0   0.25 km

Meridian Hill Park

Florida Ave. NW

Meridian Hill Park

16th St. NW

14th St. NW

13th St. NW

11th St. NW

Sherman Ave. NW

9th St. NW

Georgia

Barry Pl. NW

HOWARD UNIVERSITY

Florida Ave. NW

NW

Florida

W St. NW

12th St. NW

8th St. NW

Ave. NW

V St. NW

Ave. NW

GREEN & YELLOW LINES

U Street/
African-Amer Civil War Memorial/
Cardozo

U St. NW

4

U St. NW

3

U STREET CORRIDOR

2

U St. NW

1

Florida Ave. NW

NW

New Hampshire

finish here

start here

T St. NW

NW

17th St.

16th St. NW

15th St. NW

14th St. NW

5

S St. NW

12th St. NW

Ave. NW

11th St. NW

9th St. NW

7th St. NW

R St. NW

Vermont

1th St. NW

Shaw–
Howard U.

GREEN & YELLOW LINES

Q St. NW

Rhode Island Ave. NW

8th St. NW

7th St. NW

Logan
Circle

P St. NW

1 African American Civil War
   Memorial
2 Ben's Chili Bowl and Other
   U Street Institutions
3 The Riots and Their Aftermath
4 Where the Elite Lived
5 The Duke's Neighborhood

across the economic spectrum called the U Street area home. The end of legal segregation in the 1950s broadened opportunities for African Americans, and many began moving their homes and businesses to greener pastures away from U Street. The neighborhood declined, then suffered a divesting blow in riots following the assassination of Martin Luther King, Jr., in 1968.

The DC government gave a boost to U Street renewal by opening the Reeves Municipal Center at 14th and U streets in 1986. Opening the U Street Metrorail Station in 1991 made the neighborhood more attractive as a residential, shopping, and entertainment area. The growing number of restaurants and night spots recalls the wonderful days of Black Broadway—this time with people of all races and nationalities participating. U Street is on the move, but it's far from recovered. Abandoned buildings share blocks with hopping clubs and good restaurants. You'll run into some down-and-out people on your walk, and you should not wander away from the busy commercial area after dark.

① African-American Civil War Memorial

This itinerary begins with a little dramatic flair. As the escalator carries you out of the Metrorail Station's 10th Street exit, the sculpture at the **African-American Civil War Memorial** comes into view. The memorial is dedicated to the 209,145 soldiers known to have served in the units of the Union States Colored Troops during the war. Their names are displayed on the crescent walls that rise behind the sculpture. As you face the statue, look left across Vermont Avenue to the former Grimke Elementary School, which is scheduled to become the site of the **African-American Civil War Museum** (© **202/667-2667;** www.afroam civilwar.org) by mid-September in 2010. Until then, the museum is located 2 blocks west at 1200 U St. It's open Monday through Friday from 10am till 5pm and Saturday till 2pm. Adjacent to the memorial is the **Most Worshipful Prince Hall Grand Lodge** of the District of Columbia, a Masonic hall at 1000 U St. Its windows contain displays of Civil War history. From the memorial, walk to U Street and turn left. At 11th and U streets on the right is the **Bohemian Caverns** (© **202/299-0800;** www.bohemiancaverns. com), a jazz club advertised by a neon saxophone. The Bohemian Caverns traces its history to Club Caverns, which opened here in 1926. The name was changed to Crystal Caverns in the 1950s and to its current name shortly thereafter. Ramsey Lewis recorded his 1962 hit, "The In Crowd," here. Over its many years, the club has hosted such jazz superstars as Ellington, Billie Holiday, Louis Armstrong, Miles Davis, John Coltrane, Wynton Marsalis, and many, many more. The renovated club reopened in 1998 after a 30-year closure. Cover charges often are $15 to $20 or more. Open-mic nights can be free, or run from $5 or $7, depending on the night and the time you arrive. Check the website for the schedule.

Directly across 11th Street is the black-owned **Industrial Bank,** which grew from a building-and-loan association, organized in 1913 by John Whitelaw Lewis. Lewis rose from carrying bricks in 1896 to becoming a successful developer and financier. He built the bank building in 1919 and the building across the street, at 1001 11th St., in 1922. Both were designed by black architect

Isaiah T. Hatton. *Black Enterprise* magazine named Industrial Bank the fourth-largest minority-owned financial institution in the country in 2005. **Dukem, ℂ 202/667-8735,** one of Washington's best Ethiopian restaurants, stands on the left side of U street at 12th Street. Most main courses cost between $10 and $15. Across 12th is the **True Reformers Hall,** an Italianate building completed in 1903. John A. Lankford, Washington's first registered black architect, designed it. It also was financed and built by African Americans. Founded by ex-slaves after the Civil War and based in Richmond, Virginia, the United Order of True Reformers was a mutual beneficial organization that provided various financial and other services to African Americans. The building has a large auditorium that hosted debutante balls, fraternity and sorority dances, basketball games, and other social activities. Ellington played his first paid gig here.

Today it houses the Public Welfare Foundation, which purchased it in 1999. Until its new home opens, the African-American Civil War Museum's exhibits are displayed here 10am to 5pm Monday through Friday and till 2pm Saturday. Admission is free.

② Ben's Chili Bowl and Other U Street Institutions

Ben's Chili Bowl (p. 87), **ℂ 202/667-0909,** the brightly painted red-and-white storefront on the right at 1213 U St., is one of Washington's best-known and most-loved eating spots. Ben and Virginia Ali opened it in 1956, managed to nurse it through the destruction of the riots and the disruption of Metro construction, then turned it over to their children, who run it now. Local politicians frequent the place. Bill Cosby stops in when he's in town. President Barack Obama made his first pilgrimage here— with DC Mayor Adrian Fenty— while he was president-elect in January 2009. Ben's half-smoke sausage with chili may be the closest thing DC has to an official city food. (Half-smoke, by the way, means half beef and half pork.) Except when it's super crowded—especially at lunch time—this is a good place to take a break. And, yes, this place is cheap.

Not so cheap is **Next Door,** **ℂ 202-667-8880,** the full-service restaurant the Alis opened, well, next door. At Next Door's bar, you can have the famous half-smoke, but it'll cost you $7 instead of the $5.20 at Ben's.

Next door the other way, **The Lincoln Theatre** (© **202/328-6000;** www.thelincolntheatre.org) once again presents top-notch entertainment, as it had beginning in the 1920s. When the Lincoln opened, *The Washington Bee,* an African-American newspaper, lauded it as "perhaps the finest and largest theater for Colored people in the world." It was a first-run movie theater with a stage for music and other entertainment. The Lincoln welcomed the same jazz stars who performed at the Bohemian Caverns. Paul Robeson, the great actor and singer, also strode this stage. After years of neglect, major renovations were completed in 2008.

Recently, Maya Angelou, Bill Cosby, Martin Lawrence, Dave Chappelle, Roberta Flack, and the Preservation Hall Jazz Band have been among those featured here. Ticket prices vary widely depending on the event. Check the website for details, including the occasional free show featuring local talent. After you pass the theater, look back at the **Duke Ellington mural** painted in the side of the True Reformer building. Across 13th on the right at 1301 U St. is **Alero,** © **202/462-2322,** a decent Mexican restaurant with many dinner entrees

under $15 and many lunch dishes under $10. Next door, **Sala Thai,** © **202/462-1333,** offers—what else?—inexpensive Thai food. Next up: **U Street Café** (p. 88), © **202/332-1066,** also on the right. The sign—"Waffles All Day"—drew Tom inside for a waffle with a high pile of blueberries, not-too-sweet whipped cream, powdered sugar, a drizzle of blueberry syrup, and maple syrup on the side. Yum! Breakfast items cost $3 to $7, sandwiches $5 to $7.

Across the street, at 1322, **Crème Café,** © **202/234-1885,** dishes up moderately priced comfort and soul food—chicken soup, shrimp and grits, pork and beans, braised-and-roasted chicken. Just beyond Crème, a large colorful mural covers the alley-side wall of the **DC Ink** tattoo and piercing parlor. Tom happened on Joel Bergner when he was painting the mural. Bergner calls it the "Afro-Colombian Mural Project," and it's based on the lives of five of his friends.

❸ The Riots and Their Aftermath The riots, which destroyed or damaged many buildings in this neighborhood and beyond, began at 14th and U streets, after the assassination of Martin Luther King, Jr., on April 4, 1968. Mobs broke windows, looted stores, and set fires. Here you'll find evidence of both the riot's destruction and the area's subsequent rebirth. The large, modern **Reeves Center,** on the northwest corner, replaced damaged buildings. Turn right on 14th Street and walk to V Street.

Three of the four corners here are occupied by modern highrises that replaced riot destruction. Walk to the left along V Street, where you'll pass **St. Augustine Catholic Church and School** on your right. The predominantly black congregation was founded by free African Americans in 1858. In 1961, the St. Augustine Parish merged with predominantly white St. Paul Parish. In 1979, the congregations began sharing St. Paul's 1883 Gothic Revival church, which you see here. The merged parishes went by the name St. Paul and Augustine (note the sign at the school) until 1982, when the name reverted to just St. Augustine. More riot effects can be seen at the southeast corner of V and 15th streets. A modern high-rise building replaces some of the destroyed properties. But adjacent vacant land testifies to the fact that some of the four-decade-old damage remains unrepaired.

4 Where the Elite Lived
Continue ahead on V Street, then turn left on New Hampshire Avenue to an area dominated by large apartment buildings. The structure on the left is the **Northumberland Apartments,** built in 1909 by Harry Wardman, who developed many prominent Washington buildings. The architect was George O. Totten, Jr., whom you also can meet on the Adams Morgan itinerary.

Where New Hampshire Avenue intersects 16th and U streets, look up 16th Street at a row of houses and apartment buildings which, at least once upon a time, were pretty grand. The Beaux Arts building at 2001 New Hampshire houses the **Congressional Club,** originally an organization of congressional spouses but now welcoming spouses of Supreme Court justices and Cabinet members as well. It was built in 1914, 6 years after the club was formed. The white brick structure on the northwest corner of 16th and U streets is **The Balfour** apartment building, erected in 1900. The Spanish Style building on the southwest corner of U Street and New Hampshire Avenue was an automobile dealership in the 1920s. Now it houses a Starbucks, a Subway, Jin's Cleaners, and Local 16, a bar and restaurant with a rooftop deck.

Walk east on U Street, along another block of restaurants and shops. At 1506 on the right, former lawyer Warren Brown bakes and sells controversial cupcakes at his bakery, **Cakelove,** ✆ 202/ 588-7100. We say controversial because DC is polarized over their quality. Many Washingtonians (Susan included) have fallen madly in love with them, and Brown has gained a national following. Others complain that they're overrated—too sweet and often too dry. At $3.25 each, they aren't exactly cheap. But you probably can afford to buy one to find out which pole you stand at.

Brown also runs **Love Café,** ✆ **202/265-9800,** across the street at 1501 U. There you will find sandwiches, soups, salads and breakfast fare along with the cupcakes and other baked deserts. Walk down 15th Street to the right to see another area of three-story row houses and grand old apartment buildings.

⑤ The Duke's Neighborhood
Turn left on T Street. This block features modest row houses on the right, mostly apartments on the left. Look to the right down 14th Street to **Source Theater,** (✆ **202/204-7800;** www.source dc.org) at 1835, which hosts a wide variety of performances. Check the website for schedules

and the occasional pay-what-you-can event. At the southeast corner of T and 14th streets is **Café Saint-Ex,** ✆ **202/265-7839.** In name and decor, the moderately priced restaurant and popular bar honor French aviator Antoine-Marie-Roger de Saint-Exupéry, who wrote the popular children's book *The Little Prince* in 1943, the year before his death in a plane crash. The building on the northeast corner once housed Club Bali, another big-time-jazz joint. Continue along T to 13th Street. **The Whitelaw Hotel,** which opened in 1919 as DC's first luxury hotel for African Americans, stands on the southeast corner. It was built by John Whitelaw Lewis and designed by Isaiah T. Hatton, whose you saw earlier at Industrial Bank. With a dining room and ballroom, the hotel was a dining and social spot for black Washington and the favored place to stay for the musicians and other entertainers who performed on Black Broadway. Ellington—who grew up nearby, then moved to New York—sometimes stayed here. It's now affordable apartments.

Walk down 13th Street to the right. From age 11 to 18, Ellington lived in two redbrick town houses on this block—1805 on the left, from 1910 through 1914, and 1816 on the right from 1915 to 1917.

U Street Costs

Free	
Tour the African-American Civil War Museum	$0
Dirt Cheap	
Chili half-smoke sausage at Ben's Chili Bowl	$5.20
Cheap Add-On	
Breakfast at Dukem, one of DC's best Ethiopian restaurants	$8

Walk left on S Street and note the modest row houses set back from the street on the left. Turn left on 12th Street. The Italian Renaissance building at 1816, on the left, housed America's first YMCA for African Americans. The Y was organized by Anthony Bowen, a former slave, in 1853. President Theodore Roosevelt laid the cornerstone for this building in 1908, and it was completed in 1912. The African-American architect was W. Sidney Pittman, Booker T. Washington's son-in-law. Langston Hughes lived here in the 1920s. Charles Drew was also a member. In addition to offering typical YMCA services, this Y served as the meeting place for many civil rights activists. Here, Thurgood Marshall and colleagues plotted their strategy for the *Brown v Board of Education* case that outlawed school segregation. The building now houses the Thurgood Marshall Center for Service and Heritage. Continue up 12th Street, pass T Street, then turn left on U Street. Metrorail access is on the left, just before you come to 13th Street.

With a SmarTrip card, you get a 10¢ discount on your bus fare, and can ride any other Metrobus for the next three hours at no additional charge. See p. 284.

DC BASICS FROM A TO Z

1 Information Central

Visitor Information Centers   The **District of Columbia Chamber of Commerce** operates a visitor center at 1213 K St. NW (btw. 12th and 13th sts., at McPherson Square Metrorail Station). Staff members can offer advice and answer questions. You can pick up maps, guides, and information about restaurants and lodging. When the center's open, Monday through Friday 9am to 4:30pm, chamber staff members provide information by phone at © **866/324-7386** or 202/638-3222. Or go to the website at **www.dcchamber.org**, and click on "Visiting DC" near the top of the page.

   Destination DC also offers visitor information online (**www.washington.org**) and by phone (© **800/422-8644** or 202/789-7000). Ask for a copy of the organization's 100-plus-page visitors guide, which is updated twice a year.

Free and Cheap Internet Access

Internet access has become pretty ubiquitous in Washington. The vast majority of **hotels** we recommend have free Wi-Fi. Many **coffeehouses** and **bars** do, as well. Every **DC public library** has free Wi-Fi and computers with Internet connections. You can connect to free Wi-Fi in the **Smithsonian Castle,** 1000 Jefferson Dr. SW (at 10th St. on the Mall), and even outdoors at such locations as the Smithsonian's **Enid A. Haupt Garden,** behind the Castle; **Freedom Plaza,** 1445 Pennsylvania Ave. NW (btw. 14th and 15th sts.), near the White House; near the **U.S. Botanic Garden** at 120 Maryland Ave. SW (btw. 1st and 3rd sts.); and around the **Supreme Court,** 1 1st St. NE (at Maryland Ave.). You can get a list of library branches at **www.dclibrary.org**. More than 400 Washington-area Wi-Fi spots are listed at **http://v4.jiwire.com/search-hotspot-locations.htm**. That site has a cool interactive map that's color-coded to let you quickly distinguish between free and for-fee hookups.

The Smithsonian Institution's first building, the Castle, houses the **Smithsonian Information Center,** which is open daily except December 25 from 8:30am till 5:30pm (100 Jefferson Dr. SW, at 10th St. on the Mall; ✆ **202/633-1000;** www.si.edu/visit. Metro: Smithsonian). Volunteer information specialists answer questions. You can watch an orientation video and search for information on Smithsonian computers. If you're carrying your computer, you can access free Wi-Fi in the Castle and the Enid A. Haupt Garden outside.

2 Getting to and Around Washington

GETTING HERE

BY AIR

If you're flying into town, you'll arrive at BWI, Dulles, or Ronald Reagan National Airports. (And when you're looking for flights to DC, make sure you consider flights to all three airports.) Below, we outline the cheapest ways into town from each.

Baltimore–Washington International Thurgood Marshall Airport Named for the native son who became the first black Supreme Court justice, BWI is the farthest airport from DC but you might be arriving here if you got a super-cheap fare from wherever you're coming from. A **taxi** to downtown Washington will cost you about $90 (ouch!), the **Supershuttle** $37 for the first rider and $12 for each add-on. **Maryland Area Regional Commuter (MARC)** trains run from the BWI train station to Washington's Union Station on Capitol Hill for $6. You can take a free shuttle between airport terminals and the train station. When MARC doesn't operate (late night, weekends, and holidays), you can catch an **Amtrak** train, usually for around $9 to Union Station. The **Express Metrobus B30** runs from BWI to the Greenbelt Metro Station. Bus fare is $3 with a SmarTrip card or $3.10 cash. The Metro ride will cost you $3.70 during rush hour, $2.35 at other times. FINE PRINT You need the SmarTrip card or exact change on the bus. Contact BWI at: ☎ **410/859-7111.** www.bwiairport.com.

Dulles International Airport This airport was named for former Secretary of State John Foster Dulles, but he never gets his full name mentioned. Dulles is a *long* way from Downtown. Sometimes it offers cheaper airfares than National, and most international flights take off and land here. A **taxi** to DC costs about $60, the **Supershuttle** $29 for the first passenger and $10 for each additional rider. **Metrorail** doesn't come here . . . yet. You can hook up with Metrorail by taking a $10 **Washington Flyer** bus to the West Falls Church station, then paying $1.85 or $3.20 for the train ride to Metro Center. The cheapest ride is the **Express Metrobus 5A,** which runs to the Rosslyn and L'Enfant Plaza Metrorail stations for $3 or $3.10, depending on whether you're using a SmarTrip card or paying cash. FINE PRINT If you're riding the bus or Metro, you need the card or exact change. Contact: ☎ **703/417-8600.** ww.metwashairports.com/dulles.

Ronald Reagan Washington National Airport The name's a mouthful, but National offers the quickest and cheapest trip into town. The **Metro** ride to Metro Center takes 18 minutes and costs $2 during rush hour and $1.35 the rest of the time. The same trip in a **cab** will cost about $13.50, plus $1.50 for each additional passenger and 50¢ for the second and each subsequent bag if handled by the driver. The **Supershuttle**—a safe bet going away from the airport but sometimes undependable when picking you up at your hotel—costs $14 for the first passenger and $10 for each additional rider older than 3. Contact: ☎ **703/417-8600.** www.metwashairports.com/national.

DC's Subway: More About the Metro

The quickest and most comfortable way to get around the region is on the Metrorail trains. Five lines carry passengers from far-flung suburbs to the heart of the city. Fares are based on distances traveled and time of day. They range between $1.65 and $4.50 weekdays from opening till 9:30am and between 3 and 7pm. Those fares also are charged from 2am to closing Friday and Saturday. The morning and evening rush-hour trains can be packed. Other times, fares start at $1.35 and peak at $2.35. A host of information is available at the Metrorail website, including system maps and timetables and information about stations. A separate organization—**Stationmasters**—publishes an interactive online map that links to maps and information about what's on the surface near each station.

Metro Discounts:

- One or two **children,** 4 or younger, ride **free** when accompanied by a paying adult.

- You can ride for **half-price** if you've reached **age 65.** You pay just **60¢** on **Metrobuses** and get discounts on other participating bus systems. To get the senior discounts, seniors must purchase a **Senior SmarTrip Card** for $5 at the Metro Center Metrorail Station sales office or at other Metrorail locations or retail stores. You must show a government-issued ID that displays your photo and age to prove your eligibility. You can load value onto the card at a Passes/Farecards machine in any Metrorail station or at any bus farebox that accepts SmarTrip cards. When paying cash on a bus, you can get the discount by showing the driver your Medicare card and a government-issued ID that displays your photo.

By Train

Union Station   We think **Amtrak** is the best way to travel from New York to Washington and from points in between. It's not necessarily the cheapest, especially when you check out the below-dirt-cheap bus fares available. But it's comfortable and less susceptible to

- **Visiting senior discount:** You can ride Metrobuses for 60¢ by showing the driver a Medicare card and a photo ID. You can buy a weekly Metrobus Senior Pass or a $10 Senior Metrorail Farecard by showing a government-issued ID that displays your photo and age.

- **Disability discount:** Half-price discounts are available to people with disabilities who require accessibility features to use public transportation. Details on obtaining the card are available at this website: www.wmata.com/accessibility/disability_id.cfm. Or you can phone © **202/962-1245,** 202/962-1558, TTY 202/962-2033 or TTY 202/628-8973.

- **Discount for People with Disabilities:** If you have a transportation ID card from another transit agency and a government-issued ID that displays your photo and age, you can get a temporary Metro Disability ID. Take the documents to the Metro ID Card Office, 600 5th St. NW (at F St.).

- **Student discount:** Elementary and secondary school students who live and go to public or private school in DC can get discounted bus and rail fares. The student must obtain an application at school, then buy the student pass at a Metro sales office.

- **Free transfers:** Paper transfers are history in the Metrorail and Metrobus system. But, if you use a SmarTrip card to pay your fare, you will automatically get discounts while transferring, plus you'll get a Metrobus discount even if you don't transfer.

weather-related disruptions. The New York–Washington trip starts at $49, with AAA, senior, and other discounts available. Between Philadelphia and DC, tickets start at $33 before discounts. Contact: Amtrak © **800/872-7245;** www.amtrak.com. MARC © **800/325-7245;** www. mtamaryland.com/services/marc.

BY BUS

★ **Discount Buses**   Recent years have spawned fierce competition among discount bus lines, some offering a handful of seats for a buck. Getting the idea from the supercheap Chinatown buses (which run from downtown to downtown of all the major cities in the East), the higher-end upstart lines (like Bolt and Megabus) offer new, roomy coaches, with extras like Wi-Fi and movies. Most New York–DC **Bolt Bus** tickets start at $10 (✆ 877/265-8287; www.boltbus.com). We've found **Megabus** tickets on that route for between $3 and $9 (✆ 877/462-6342; www.megabus.com/us). New York–Washington tickets for as little as $20 can be purchased online from **Peter Pan Bus Line** (✆ 800/343-9999; www.peterpanbus.com) and **Greyhound** (✆ 800/231-2222; www.greyhound.com), both of whom are playing catch-up with the cheaper lines. If you're traveling by Bolt, Mega, or a Chinatown bus, chances are you'll get on (at one of many cities and towns from the Mid-Atlantic to New England) on a street corner or parking lot, and debark on a busy downtown street.

GETTING AROUND DC

Washington can be an expensive place to live. But you don't have to spend a lot of money to get yourself around town. The Metrorail system—though suffering aging pains—remains one of the best subways in the world. Metrobuses run throughout the region. DC is a walkable city. Many Washingtonians get to work on their bicycles, thanks to our bike trails and the cyclists' bravery in entering our traffic. The city is facilitating cycling by painting bike-only lanes on city streets and requiring parking garages and lots to include bike parking facilities. Metrorail has placed bike racks and shelters at many stations.

BY BUS AND METRO

Washington Metropolitan Area Transit Authority   Getting around Washington by mass transit is cheap and fairly easy, thanks to the transit authority's **Metrorail** and **Metrobus** systems. Metrorail (aka the Metro) trains start running at 5am weekdays and 7am weekends. They stop at midnight Sunday through Thursday and at 3am Friday and Saturday. The Metro runs underground through most of the District, and aboveground as it heads toward the suburbs. Some buses run round the clock. Metrorail fares—based on the time of day you travel and the distance of your trip—run from $1.35 to $4.50. Almost all bus fares are

It's Smart to Get a SmarTrip Card

Travel by Metrorail and Metrobus with a SmarTrip card, available at any Metro station, or on line (**www.wmata.com/fares/purchase/store**) with a Visa, MasterCard or Discover Card. It costs $30 to $5 for the card plus $25 in value loaded on the card. You also can buy a card for $5 at the **sales office** in the Metro Center Metrorail Station or at locations listed on the website. You use the card by swiping it at Metrorail turnstiles or Metrobus fareboxes. You can replenish the value in a station or at a bus farebox. When you pay your bus fare with a SmarTrip card, you get a 10¢ discount on that fare and you can ride any Metrobus for the following three hours at no additional charge. If you transfer to Metrorail within three hours, you get a 50¢ discount. When you pay a Metrorail fare with a SmarTrip card, you get a 50¢ discount if transferring to a Metrobus within the next 3 hours. FINE PRINT If you use a Metro parking garage, be aware that you can pay *only* with a SmarTrip card at most locations. You can buy one in a vending machine at all Metrorail stations that have parking. Cost is $10: $5 for the card and $5 worth of value loaded onto it.

$1.35. There are discounts available for students, senior citizens, and people with disabilities. Contact: ✆ **202/637-7000;** www.wmata.com. FINE PRINT At press time, the transit authority's staff and board of directors were debating fare increases. Betting among transit experts was that most fares probably would rise by about 15 percent.

DC Circulator The red-and-gray Circulator buses connect main tourist and night-life areas with Metrorail stations and central Washington every 10 minutes during operating hours. Two lines—Georgetown to Union Station and Convention Center to Southwest Waterfront—operate from 7am to 9pm daily. In addition, the Georgetown line runs from Whitehaven Parkway in Upper Georgetown to 17th and K streets, near the Farragut North and Farragut West Metrorail stations, until midnight Sunday through Thursday and 2am weekends. The Woodley Park-Adams Morgan-McPherson Square line operates from 7am till midnight Sunday through Thursday and until 3:30am on weekends. The Union Station to Navy Yard line runs weekdays from 6am to 7pm, with extended service when the Washington Nationals baseball team is playing at its field near the Navy Yard, including on weekends. From 10am till 6pm on weekends, a fifth line runs a loop around the National Mall, from the Capitol to the Washington Monument. The regular fare is $1. Seniors and people with disabilities ride for half-price. Children younger than 5 and students with a DC Student Travel Card ride free. If you pay with a SmarTrip card, you get a free transfer from Metrobus and 50¢ off when transferring from Metrorail. Contact: ℂ **202/962-1423;** www. dccirculator.com.

Georgetown Metro Connection   This bus links Georgetown with the Dupont Circle and Rosslyn Metrorail stations. Every 10 minutes, the bus makes several stops along M Street. It runs Monday through Thursday from 7am to midnight, Friday from 7am to 2am, Saturday from 8am to 2am and Sunday from 8am to midnight. Regular fare is a dollar. People with disabilities and seniors 65 and older ride for a quarter. Children ride free. Regular fare drops to 50¢ when you pay by SmarTrip card at a Metrorail Station. Contact: **www.georgetowndc. com/getting-here/shuttle**.

Metrobus   The Washington Metropolitan Area Transit Authority operates buses throughout Washington and into the suburbs, including routes that function round the clock. Most fares are just $1.35, and many discounts are available. A few express routes charge $3.10. You need exact change or a farecard. Metrobuses link to other transit systems that carry passengers around the region. Great interactive maps of the system and maps/timetables for individual routes are available online. Contact: ℂ **202/637-7000** or 202/962-1234. www. wmata.com/bus; maps www.wmata.com/bus/maps; timetables www. wmata.com/bus/timetables.

BY TAXI

Washington licenses an unusually large number of **cabs,** so taxis are pretty easy to hail most of the time you want one. They tend to disappear late at night, however. The best place to look when cabs are scarce is outside a large hotel. DC finally joined the rest of the civilized world in 2008 by ordering cabbies to put meters in their vehicles. Before then, DC cab fares were based on a geographical zone system that tourists in particular found horribly confusing. Now the rates are $3 for the first ⅙ mile and 25¢ for each additional ⅙ mile.

Driving in DC (NOT!)

One word of advice: *Don't!* Because of the Washington area's comprehensive mass transit system, you don't need a car when you visit. We have friends who live here without owning automobiles. They take Metrorail and/or Metrobus. They take a cab when they have to. They use **Zipcar** (below) when they absolutely, positively have to drive around town. They rent a car when they need to drive out of town. And they spend less than the cost of buying and maintaining a car. Traffic is horrendous in rush hours and throughout much of the workday. When it snows, our roadways become nearly impassable. If you must drive when you visit, be aware of what you'll pay to park at your hotel (which can take a room from "cheap" to "splurge"). Then try to leave your car there during your visit. Parking spaces are hard to find near tourist and entertainment areas. Street parking often is restricted to one or a few hours. Parking meters charge as much as $2 an hour. Washington is full of traffic circles where several streets converge, and you have to watch the signs carefully to stay on your route. Dupont Circle, for instance, has concentric circles, and if you get in the wrong one you won't be able to turn where you want to. *Note:* Traffic already in the circle has the right of way. Some streets change direction during rush hour. Parts of Connecticut Avenue are four lanes south in the morning and four lanes north in the evening. You'll know you're in the wrong lane when you notice rush-hour traffic rushing directly at you! So, really: Don't drive here.

You're charged a pro-rated $15 an hour for waiting when the cab is stopped in traffic or driving below 10 mph. Additional passengers aged 6 or older are $1.50 each. Luggage handled by the driver is 50¢ a bag. You pay an extra $2 when ordering a cab by phone. Fares go up 25% when the city declares a snow emergency. We usually order **Diamond Cab** (© **202/387-6200** or, if busy, 202/797-5916 or 202/797-5915). Another large taxi firm is **Yellow Cab** (© **202/544-1212**).

BY RENTAL CAR

Zipcar Owning a car can be an expensive proposition. If you live in a city and use mass transit, you may be tempted to save a lot of bucks

Finding an Address

Navigating Washington can be maddening—with the traffic circles, avenues running on angles, streets ending then starting again, and the city quadrants which give us four versions of major street names in four different parts of town. But there is a logical grid underneath all this stuff. If you grasp it, you can find addresses with ease—well, most addresses. The Capitol dome is the center of DC geography. Three streets—North Capitol, East Capitol, and South Capitol—run in those directions from the Capitol grounds. You won't find a West Capitol Street, but you can imagine it running due west from the Capitol down the center of the National Mall. These streets define the boundaries of the quadrants. All of Washington's numbered streets run north–south, counting from the Capitol. 1st Street NE is the first street east of North Capitol Street. 1st Street NW is the first street west of North Capitol Street. 1st Street SE is the first street east of South Capitol Street. Just to confuse things, here and there you encounter a Half Street, which is closer to Capitol Steet than a portion of 1st Street. Washington's east–west-running streets all have names that—in most cases—work through the alphabet as they get farther north and south of East Capitol Street and the middle of the National Mall. The streets closest to East Capitol and the middle of the Mall are named for letters—E Street, F Street, and so on. As you continue north and south and the alphabet

by getting rid of your motor vehicle. But sometimes you need a car—to go to the grocery store, for instance, or to visit a friend whose house is not reached easily by train or bus. That's where Zipcar comes is. As with SmartBike, you get a Zipcar card that unlocks motor vehicles that are parked all around town. Unlike SmartBike, Zipcar requires you to make a reservation by phone or online. And you have to return the car to the place you picked it up. You can join for a $25 application fee and an annual fee as low as $50. Renting a car costs $7 an hour, $69 a weekday, and $77 a weekend day. You also can rent a truck, SUV, station wagon, minivan, or convertible at a higher rate. Cars come with gas, insurance, and 180 free miles. Additional miles start at 45¢ each. Once you join, you can rent cars in about 50 cities

is exhausted, you run into streets with two-syllable names—Adams, Bryant, Channing, and so forth. Then you hit three-syllable names (Allison, Buchanan). Unfortunately, you find numerous exceptions to these rules. For some reason—or perhaps for no reason at all—no J, X, Y, or Z street exists. Independence and Constitution avenues take the place of B streets in much of the city. There are no A or B streets on the Mall. Some streets break the alphabet and syllable rules. And the roadways that aren't streets—avenues, roads, drives, places—do whatever they feel like doing. If you understand the basic street grid, however, you can find almost any address and figure out where you are most of the time. If you're looking for 450 H St. NW, you know it's in the Northwest quadrant of the city, eight streets north of the middle of National Mall, between 4th and 5th streets. If you're looking for 850 4th St. NE, you know it's in the Northeast quadrant, between H and I streets. Since there's no J Street, however, K Street becomes the 10th street from the middle of the Mall, and the 1000 block of numbered streets lie between K and L. The absence of X, Y, and Z streets throws the calculation further out of whack. The farther you get away from the Mall, the more this calculation becomes an approximation, but you still can get a pretty good idea of where you are or where you want to go.

in North America. FINE PRINT To join Zipcar, you must be at least 21 years old and have had a driver's license for at least a year. You can have had no more than two moving violations or crashes in the previous 3 years and no more than one in the previous 18 months. You can't have had an alcohol violation in 7 years or a "major" violation (such as speeding 20 miles over the limit) in 3 years.

☎ **866/494-7227.** www.zipcar.com. Washington area locations www.zipcar.com/dc/find-cars.

BY BIKE

★ **SmartBike DC** Clear Channel Outdoor (an outdoor advertising company) has teamed with the DC Transportation Department to

Key Bike Info

You can download bicycle route maps online here: www.ddot.dc. gov/ddot/cwp/view,a,1245,q,629 849,ddotNav,|32399|.asp.

The proliferation of public bike racks makes it easier to use your bicycle for part of a trip. You can take your bike onto Metrorail trains at all times except Monday–Friday rush hour from 7 to 10am and 4 to 7pm. To take your bike on a Metrobus at any time, look for buses with bike racks on the front.

make bicycles available in central Washington for an annual fee of $40. Bikes are locked in special computerized racks at 10 locations in Logan Circle, Dupont Circle, the U Street Corridor (two spots), Foggy Bottom, Farragut Square, Metro Center, Judiciary Square, and McPherson Square. The annual fee buys you a card that opens the locks. Your retrieval of a bike is recorded, as is your return to any rack with free space. SmartBike's website has an interactive map that shows rack locations as well has how many bikes are available and how many rack slots are free.

Contact: ✆ **800/899-4449.** www.smartbikedc.com; rack locations. www.smartbikedc.com/smartbike_locations.asp.

Washington Area Bicyclist Association   This organization of bike enthusiasts advocates for cyclists' needs, organizes cycling events, and publishes a great deal of information that's useful to cyclists. The website contains links to helpful maps.

✆ **202/518-0524.** www.waba.org; maps www.waba.org/areabiking/maps.php.

3 More DC Resources

Disability Services   With some notable exceptions, Washington is a highly accessible city for visitors with disabilities. Metrorail trains and Metrobuses accommodate wheelchairs. All Metrorail Stations have elevators with brail labels beside the control buttons. In the stations, fare-card vending machines, entrance gates, and telephones were built to accommodate wheelchairs. Signs and flashing lights alert the hearing impaired to the approach of Metrorail trains. Metrorail drivers announce arrivals at stations. Passengers with disabilities can get discounts on train and bus fares. (See p. 284 for details.)

A bumpy surface has been installed along platform edges to help the vision-impaired locate the edge. All Metrobuses kneel for easier access, and almost all have a ramp or lift. The TTY number for Metro information is © **202/638-3780.** Unfortunately, Metrorail's elevators are notorious for breaking down—a minor inconvenience for most passengers but a major problem for anyone with a mobility challenge. You can ask which elevators are out of service by phoning © **202/962-1212** (TTY 202/638-3780), or you can check online at **www.wmata. com/rider_tools/metro_service_status/elevator_escalator.cfm.** When entering a Metrorail station, ask the attendant whether elevators are working at your destination. You can also call © **202/962-1212** for information on elevator outages. When elevators are out, Metro provides shuttle buses to serve those stations. Ask the attendant where to catch them.

The Smithsonian Institution's museums, as well as most other DC museums, monuments, and government buildings, are accessible to individuals with disabilities. Get Smithsonian information at www.si. edu/visit/visitors_with_disabilities.htm, © **202/633-2921,** or TTY 202/ 633-4353. Films shown in Smithsonian theaters offer narrated audiotapes for the vision-impaired. Many live theaters have infrared headsets for the vision- and hearing-impaired. Live productions often feature at least one signed performance during the run. Call the theater for specifics. Service animals and power scooters are permitted in all Smithsonian facilities. Most Smithsonian videos are captioned or have scripts available. You can get scripts for audio tours. Manual wheelchairs can be borrowed for free on a first-come, first-served basis at Smithsonian information desks.

The Capitol and congressional office buildings are accessible and offer services to people with disabilities, such as wheelchair loans and interpreters for the deaf or hard of hearing during public tours (© **202/ 224-4048,** TTY 202/224-4049; www.aoc.gov/cc/visit/accessibility.cfm).

The Kennedy Center offers large-print and Braille playbills, audio descriptions during performances (www.kennedy-center.org/ accessibility/schedule.html#audio_described), assistive listening devices, signed performances (www.kennedy-center.org/accessibility/ schedule.html#sign_interpreted), captioned performances (www. kennedy-center.org/accessibility/schedule.html#captioned) , accessible tours, and loaned wheelchairs (© **202/416-8340**). For further information, contact the center's **Office for Accessibility** at © **202/ 416-8727,** TTY 202/416-8728, www.kennedy-center.org/accessibility.

Most major DC hotels and restaurants are accessible; ask when you make a reservation. The DC government serves residents with disabilities through the **Department on Disability Services** (1125 15th St. NW, Washington, DC 20005; ✆ **202/730-1700;** 202/730-1700). FINE PRINT Old buildings and small bed-and-breakfasts may not be easily accessible. Ask when you make a reservation. In chapter 2, we tell whether the lodging places we recommend have elevators.

GLBT Resources The website of **Destination DC**—the organization that promotes tourism, conventions, and special events in the city—contains an enormous amount of information for GLBT residents and visitors (**www.washington.org/visiting/experience-dc/pride-in-dc/glbt-home**). Topics include festivals and other special events, nightlife, arts, culture, a GLBT traveler's guide, a history of gays in DC, and links to other GLBT resources online. The site also publishes descriptions of DC neighborhoods, with attention to gay-friendly locales.

One of the city's most important gay resources, the *Washington Blade* newspaper, went out of business in 2009. Most of the staff immediately started an online publication, called **DCAgenda** (www. dcagenda.com), which is attempting to carry on the *Blade*'s tradition of news, arts, and entertainment reporting. Washington also has a gay news magazine, *Metro Weekly,* which is distributed free at various locations around town and also is available online at (www. metroweekly.com).

The **Human Rights Campaign**—America's largest GLBT civil rights organization—is headquartered in Washington and operates an action center and store here (1633 Connecticut Ave. NW, north of Q St.; ✆ **202/232-8621**).

The Metro DC Gay, Lesbian, Bisexual, and Transgender Community Center, commonly called "The Center," moved into new temporary digs in the U Street Corridor neighborhood at the beginning of 2010. There, the organization hosts a wide variety of programs that range from entertainment to self-help to education to community activism. Subjects include career development, aging gays, arts, marriage, domestic violence, and drug abuse. The center serves as a venue for concerts and other entertainment, including an annual Oscars party. It also coordinates a speakers bureau whose members can address 30 topics of importance to the GLBT community in five languages. (1804–1810 14th St. NW, btw. S and Swann sts.; ✆ **202/ 682-2245.** www.thedccenter.org.)

Whitman-Walker Clinic has expanded to offer comprehensive medical care to all medically underserved communities. But it remains focused on GLBT and HIV services (p. 208).

Hotlines For information about any Washington city government service, phone the **Mayor's Call Center,** © **311.** The **DC Mental Health Department** staffs a 24-hour **hotline** at © **888/793-4657.** You can reach the **House of Ruth Domestic Violence Support Center** at © **202/667-7001,** ext. 515. Rape victims can call the **DC Rape Crisis Center** at © **202/333-7273.** The poison hotline is © **800/222-1222.** The Washington Metropolitan Police Department operates a **Hate Crimes Hotline,** © **202/727-0500.**

Legal Aid The **Legal Aid Society of the District of Columbia** provides a variety of legal services in civil (not criminal) matters to DC residents who can't afford to hire a lawyer. Services range from education and advice to representation in court or before an administrative agency. The organization's priorities are preventing evictions and homelessness, preserving affordable housing, preserving home ownership, ensuring a safe and decent place to live, protecting families against domestic violence, promoting family stability through child support and custody arrangements, preserving automobile ownership, and securing access to healthcare, nutrition, and public benefits. © **202/628-1161.**

Liquor Laws You must be at least 21 years old to drink alcoholic beverages in Washington. You need a government-issued photo ID to prove your age. Because of strict enforcement, DC establishments tend to card patrons more frequently than their counterparts in many other cities. Bars and restaurants can sell alcoholic beverages from 8am till 2am Monday through Thursday, 8am to 3am Friday through Saturday, and 10am till 2am Sunday. Bars and restaurants can sell alcohol until 3am the day before a federal holiday and until 4am on New Year's Eve. Retailers with the appropriate licenses can sell for off-premises consumption from 9am till 10pm daily. Many choose to close on Sunday. You can take away a partially consumed bottle of wine if it is resealed and placed in a tamper-proof container with a dated receipt attached. You cannot carry an open container away from the bar or restaurant where you purchased it. Single-serving containers of beer, malt liquor, or ale cannot be sold in wards 2, 4, 6, 7, and 8. For personal use, you can bring into DC one case of beer or wine or 1 quart of spirits without obtaining a permit.

Lost & Found   If you leave something in a DC taxi, contact the **DC Taxicab Commission** at ℂ **202/645-6020,** fax 202/889-3604, or e-mail dctclf@dc.gov. Leave your name, daytime telephone number, brief description of the item, and the date it was lost. If you lose a cellphone, tell the model, serial number, and cellular phone number. If you have a cab receipt or know the cabby's ID number and/or the vehicle's license plate number, leave that information as well.

If you lose something on a **Metrobus** or within the **Metrorail** system, call ℂ **202/962-1195,** or fill out the online lost-and-found form at www.wmata.com/about_metro/lost_found/what.cfm.

If you lost something in public, you can try calling the **Mayor's Call Center,** ℂ **311,** or the police department's **Property Division,** ℂ **202/645-0131.** But don't expect a miracle.

Newspapers & Magazines   DC's local newspaper, *The Washington Post,* also happens to be one of the world's best. Cutbacks implemented throughout the newspaper industry in recent years have left The *Post* weaker than it used to be. But it's still the best place for Washingtonians to turn for local, national, and international news, as well as for useful information about entertainment and living day-to-day in the Washington area—both in print and online at **www.washingtonpost.com**. The *Post* also distributes a free weekday tabloid newspaper called *Express.*

Washingtonian, Washington's city magazine, also is one of the best around. In addition to interesting feature stories, each issue is packed with various guides to all things DC—dining, entertainment, shopping, best doctors, good places to work, and what have you. These guides are accessible—and searchable—at **www.washingtonian.com**, although you need a magazine subscription or to pay an online fee to view everything.

For local, local news, DC residents turn to one of the four weekly *Current* newspapers—*The Northwest Current, The Georgetown Current, The Foggy Bottom Current,* and *The Dupont Current*—or to the monthly *Capitol Hill Current/Voice of the Hill.* Each covers the neighborhoods you would expect from its name. The Capitol Hill paper publishes an online edition at **www.voiceofthehill.com**. The others archive PDF files of their issues at **www.currentnewspapers.com/archive.php**. *Washington City Paper,* DC's main alternative weekly, covers the news and the local arts and entertainment scenes. You can find it free in public places around the area and online at **www. washingtoncitypaper.com.**

Pharmacies Need a prescription at 3am? Lucky for you, the ubiquitous **CVS** pharmacy chain operates four 24-hour stores in Washington: 6 Dupont Circle NW (at P St. on the circle's west side), ℰ **202/785-1466;** 4555 Wisconsin Ave. NW (btw. Albemarle and Brandywine sts.) in Upper Northwest, ℰ **202/537-1587;** 320 40th St. NE (btw. Benning Rd. and Clay Place) in Northeast Washington, ℰ **202-396-2331;** and 6514 Georgia Ave. NW (btw. Underwood and Van Buren sts.) in Northwest Washington, ℰ **202/829-5234.**

Post Offices For the nearest Post Office, ask at your hotel's front desk, click on "Locate a Post Office" at www.usps.com, or phone ℰ **800/275-8777.** For zip code information, call the same number or click "Find a Zip Code" at the same website.

Radio Stations Some of Washington's more popular FM radio stations are WAMU, 88.5, public radio/news/talk; WASH, 97.1, adult contemporary; WBIG, 100.3, classic rock; WCSP, 90.1, C-SPAN; WETA, 90.9, public radio/classical; WHUR, music-news-discussions aimed at African Americans; WITH, 99.5, contemporary hits; WKYS, 93.9, hip hop/R&B; WMZQ, 98.7, country; WPFW, 89.3, Pacifica/jazz/Third World music/news/ public affairs; WPGC, 95.5, hip hop/R&B; WRQX, 107.3, popular mix; WTOP, 103.5, Washington's top breaking-news station, with traffic and weather "on the 8s" (8 after the hour, 18 after the hour, and so forth); WWDC, 101.1, modern rock. Popular AM stations include WAVA, 780, Christian/conservative; WFED, 1500, news of interest to government employees; WMAL, 630, news and (mostly conservative) talk; WOL, 1450, news/talk aimed at African Americans; WTEM, 930, sports; WWRC, 1260, business/finance; WYCB, 1340, gospel/religious.

Smoking Washington law bans smoking in most public places, including restaurants and bars. Smoking is allowed in tobacco shops, tobacco bars, sidewalk cafes, and hotel guest rooms. Proprietors may impose stricter restrictions, and hotels often designate smoking and no-smoking rooms. Other restricted facilities include banks, educational facilities, health-care facilities, laundromats, public transportation facilities, reception areas, retail and service establishments, shopping malls, sports arenas, and theaters.

Tipping   Tipping, of course, is optional. But most hospitality workers depend on tips for their livelihood. It's customary to tip 15% to 20% of restaurant and bar bills, not counting taxes. Taxi drivers should get 15% of the fare.

Toilets   You're seldom far from clean, safe, and free restrooms when you frequent Washington's tourist areas. You'll find them in all **government buildings,** all **Smithsonian facilities,** major **monuments,** larger **food courts,** and most other **museums, historical buildings,** and **tourist attractions.** It's easy to wander into the lobby of a large **hotel** and find the restrooms. Ditto **fast-food chains, coffee shops, department stores,** and **shopping malls.** One place you won't find them easily is inside the Metrorail system. In a truly extreme emergency, ask a **Metrorail** station attendant to let you use the station facility. Most stations have restrooms that are supposed to be available to the public on request, but Metrorail resists wide use.

INDEX

ACCOMMODATIONS